DANIEL GRAY is the author of the Saltire Award-nominated *Homage to Caledonia: Scotland and the Spanish Civil War*. Since its publication, the book has been turned into a television series and Edinburgh Fringe show. Daniel's previous book, co-authored with David Walker, was the *Historical Dictionary of Marxism*, for which they have still to sell the film rights. He has regurgitated the same jokes in the fanzine of his Middlesbrough FC, 'Fly Me to the Moon', for the worst part cade. Daniel also reviews books for, among others, *History* d, writes a column in *The Leither* magazine and has worked as scripts curator and television researcher. He lives in Leith with Marisa.

llent book about the country's smaller teams... [Stramash]
c the vague romance that still clings to these 'smaller' Scottish
c will make a must-read for every non-Old Firm football fan –
a many Rangers and Celtic supporters too.
I CORD

ve been previous attempts by authors to explore the off-the-
l paths of the Scottish football landscape, but Daniel Gray's
t e is in another league.
SCOTSMAN

he es in a match at each stopping-off point, Gray presents little
rt of small Scottish towns, relating histories of declining industry,
rad politics and the connection between a team and its community.
It' brilliant way to rediscover Scotland.
T HERALD

A great read, because Gray doesn't write about just football, he uses football as an excuse to explore t   *Scotland.*
THE SKINNY

Stramash
Tackling Scotland's Towns and Teams

DANIEL GRAY

Luath Press Limited

EDINBURGH

www.luath.co.uk

First published 2010
Reprinted 2011
Reprinted 2012
Reprinted 2013
Reprinted 2015

ISBN: 978-1-906817-66-4

The paper used in this book is recyclable. It is made
from low chlorine pulps produced in a low energy, low emissions
manner from renewable forests

Printed and bound by
Bell & Bain Ltd., Glasgow

Typeset in 11 point Sabon
by 3btype.com

Map © John McNaught

*To those that push the turnstiles in search
of a more splendid life.*

Contents

WHAT WOULD SATURDAY be without the match? It is a glorious opportunity to blow off steam that has been gathering for a week. 'Oucha dirty!' 'Pitimaff!' 'Dig a hole, Ref!' And all the other choice expressions heard where the big ball is being banged.

Then a new world the next week. The man you dubbed a puddin' is now the cat's whiskers. His antics tickle you no end. 'Give him the works' – 'that's the stuff! – 'shoot!' – 'Goa... hard lines, ower the baur.'

What an atmosphere. Every move charged with electricity. Some of the players charged with dynamite, at least that's what it seems like to the poor fellow who gathers himself up from a sea of mud and politely asks the referee: 'is this Sauchiehall Street or Tuesday?'

But it's all in the game. The blokes in the work talk about it for weeks to come. You haven't the slightest idea. I know a couple of the lads in one of the Clyde Shipyards who got into an argument one day. They were so engrossed, and at times so heated, that it was only when the watchman tapped them on the shoulders and asked them why they weren't away for the Fair Holidays like everybody else they discovered they had been at it for the whole weekend.

Yes, that's FOOTBALL!

Alloa Football Club: Official Handbook and Fixtures, 1947/48

Acknowledgements

I AM INDEBTED to the work of local and football club historians down the years. Without them, much social and footballing history would have been lost, and my hope is that readers of *Stramash* will support their work in future. Interviewees Bernie Slaven, Dick Clark, Duncan Carmichael, Ian Rankin, Jake Arnott, Jim Banks, John Wright, Karen Fleming, Robin Marwick and Vincent Gillen were helpful and fascinating, each in their own way as befits the diversity of their subjects and roles. John Simpson (Alloa), John Litster (Raith Rovers), Forbes Inglis (Montrose), Crawford (Clyde) and Giancarlo Rinaldi (Queen of the South) gave valuable advice on their own clubs' chapters.

Michael Reilly of the Coatbridge Irish Genealogy Project was extremely supportive too. The vast majority of images in this book were provided by Mark I'Anson, artist supreme and a keeper of this nation's football heritage. Aside from that, Mark's advice and anecdotes were treasured, his insistence on feeding me broccoli less so. At Luath Press, enormous thanks must go to Gavin MacDougall for having faith in me again, my editor Leila Cruickshank for her patience and meticulousness, and Tom Bee for the cover. That cover features one of my all-time favourite pictures of anything, never mind football; I am grateful to Stuart Clarke. On a personal level, thanks to The Gaffer for forcing me into a second trip to Greenock, Paddy Dillon (www.thenetherregions.co.uk) for reminding me football could be funny ('who do you werk for?') and Robert Nichols at 'Fly Me To the Moon' for first publishing my piffle nearly a decade ago. My mum's encouragement is as strong as ever, and hopefully a book about football makes sacrifices such as driving me to Chesterfield for a League Cup tie 'to test out your new car' (my words) worthwhile. This football gubbins really started with my dad at Ayresome Park in 1988; a million Midget Gems later and he's still this Danny's champion. Marisa's love and support continues to be boundless and inspiring; one day I'll get a real job so you can finally write your *A History of the Babbity People*.

www.stramashthebook.com
twitter.com/stramashthebook

Introduction

WHEN I MOVED TO Scotland from north-east England in 2004, I was amazed by how few people supported their local football teams. This was not the case in small towns alone, but in Edinburgh too. There, Rangers and Celtic tops were ubiquitous, and both clubs had retail outlets in the city.

I hadn't even watched them play and already I was sick of the Old Firm. Their domination was similar to that of the chain supermarkets and cafés which had made visiting different high streets the equivalent of having a girl in every port who looked and sounded exactly the same. What had happened to those curious names of my youth like Partick Thistle and Queen of the South? These were team names, town names and names that didn't appear on a map which had taken on an air of wonder and exoticism when I was growing up. There had been an otherness about those farthest reaches of the results on *Sports Report* as they were whispered from my dad's car radio. When labelling these places 'pools coupon towns', writer Jonathan Meades defined what so many of us in England felt.

Scottish football was a mystery to me in my youth, and little changed in my first five years here. I didn't help my own cause by failing to engage with it. At least twice a month, I'd make my way to Teesside to watch Middlesbrough, and that by choice. On spare Saturdays, I'd catch up with real life when really I should've adopted a second team here.

Gradually, I fell out of love with these Saturday and Sunday jaunts. On a match day, I remained happy with everything leading up to 3pm: the train journey down the striking east coast; the same old faces in the pre-match pub; the walk to the ground instilled with that feeling that anything might happen. Then, beyond the turnstile, I'd realise I had just contributed to the wages of Mido, a rotund centre-forward with the kind of hateable arrogance that made Liam Gallagher look like *Little Voice* (there are similes referencing events after the 1990s in this book, just not many). From 3pm my team, like so many others, would cagily set about surviving in the Premier League with all its 'Sky money', that catch-all excuse for boring football and the media career of Jamie

Redknapp. This was existence for the sake of moneyed existence, and I wanted out, or at least to see if I could recapture my love of football elsewhere before realising I couldn't and then returning sheepishly to the Riverside Stadium with a bunch of flowers and some chocolates. From August 2009, I would couple childhood intrigue with dwindling interest on a voyage of rediscovery.

This would not be about football alone. While researching my first book, *Homage to Caledonia: Scotland and the Spanish Civil War*, I'd briefly visited a number of small towns across Scotland, each of which had left me curious. Contrary to the parochial warnings of friends in the capital, these had been places of character and intrigue, and now I wanted to see more of them. From a social historian's point of view – and I am partial to a leather elbow patch – if men and women from those towns had been internationalist enough to fight in the Spanish Civil War, then surely other events on a world scale lay beneath. As with the football teams I knew nothing of, what had been the roles of those towns? What part had they played in the making of Scotland and the world? Just as football here always seemed to be about the Old Firm (who, inevitably, pop up throughout *Stramash*, and are enjoyably beaten once or twice), history appeared to be forever linked to Edinburgh or Glasgow and kings or castles. This book is an attempt to pluck the likes of Cowdenbeath and Coatbridge from the footnotes and place them in the main text. In those pages which delve backwards to reach parts of football club histories untouched by mainstream accounts of the game, it is a reminder that their pasts are rich and worth losing ourselves in.

The football and town elements are by no means disconnected. The clubs were release valves for oppressed miners (Cowdenbeath); they were the result of philanthropic acts by Victorians in posh hats (Morton); and they were, glamorously, critically affected by the whims of the 1945 New Towns Committee report (Clyde). All were impacted upon by the World Wars.

There are modern trends which confirm the persistence of society's influence on the game. As small town populations fall, so do small team attendances, and as people shun the diverse high street in pursuit of the homogenous out-of-town shopping mall, so too do they ignore their local teams and follow the giants of the globalised world, whether Rangers and Celtic, or Manchester United and Barcelona. I wanted to see how all of this had made the towns and teams of modern Scotland look, and see how exactly they had managed to survive in a world where big had generally defeated small. And, I wanted an excuse to drink in some different pubs.

Stramash is by no means a comprehensive history of any of those towns and clubs. Dumfries features without mention of Burns, and Ally MacLeod makes only a brief appearance in the Ayr United chapter. Indeed, much of the football history is confined to the pre-World War Two period, so short on highlights have the subsequent lives of the teams been. Rather than seeming irrelevant, I hope those pasts can provide mental refuge and imagined nostalgia for those that don't even remember them; they certainly did for me.

At a time when the Scottish club game is drifting towards its lowest ebb once more, *Stramash* singularly fails to wring its hands and address the state of the game, preferring instead to focus on Bobby Mann's waist-line. Similarly, no attempt whatsoever is made to tackle these towns' social problems, but every attempt to see the good.

There is no 'challenge' element to my travels, just the remit of visiting towns and teams with the intention of sketching their place in the world then and now. My only rule was to stay within the confines of the Scottish Football League, sadly leaving no room for, say, Junior football or the Highland League. My choices of town and team were often governed by Scotrail routes, fixture postponements and whether or not I could convince my wife that I really should miss another of her friend's weddings to visit Cumbernauld (the answer was no, I shouldn't, hence the midweek Clyde fixture). In a cynical world choked with sneering attitudes to admittedly imperfect places and players, *Stramash* is unashamedly positive about its subjects, and a wordy love-letter to local Scotland.

A Note on Terms Used

SCOTTISH FOOTBALL IS OFTEN maligned for being behind the times. In one department this is simply not so: that of pointless renaming and rejigging. Years before consultants charged £400 an hour to rebrand bin men as waste disposal officers, the game's bosses were at it. Keeping up with the names of divisions is incredibly difficult, especially for the reader (for the writer, this just presents another chance for procrastinating instead of typing chapters; my 'Development of the Divisions' colour wallchart is beautiful). As such, I've used 'Division One' and 'Division Two' up until the 1975 shift (so, for example, post-war Divisions A and B are absent). After that, it's Premier League (top tier), Division One (second tier) and Division Two (third tier), and from 1998 the current system of Premier League (top tier), Division One (second tier), Division Two (third tier) and Division Three (fourth tier). Still not clear? Well, it doesn't really matter – by the time the book is published, it'll be The Dobbies Garden Centre Caledonian Sector A.

CHAPTER ONE

Ayr

Ayr United 1 v 1 Partick Thistle, 8 August 2009

'A...A...AH...A-CHOO.' The gangly teenager behind the counter in WH Smith sneezed as if auditioning for a Lemsip advert. At the till, a mother dived in front of her child's pushchair to cover him from snot shrapnel, while behind me three pensioners took shelter among the Women's Lifestyle shelves. In the summer of Swine Flu, everyone lived on edge. Glasgow Central Station was awash with germs, mutual suspicion and Spanish tourists trying to work out the difference between Apex, peak and off-peak tickets.

By the ticket machines, an elderly couple in bright fleece jackets competed to see who could take the most time to make a purchase. 'This,' snarled the young bloke behind me, 'is exactly why old people shouldn't be allowed to use technology. They two are like my maw pointing the TV remote at the kettle.'

On the train for Ayr, Partick Thistle fans mixed with holidaymakers bound for Prestwick International, the former dreaming of promotion, the latter of accurately-named Ryanair airports. Above the hubbub, a woman gave her personal details over a mobile phone, speaking loudly and clearly as if regally proud of her mother's maiden name. It's a good job I'm no fraudster, or Sarah McKenna of 42 Binnie Street, Gourock, sort code 80-12-76, account 84615523, childhood pet's name Twinkle, would be in deep trouble.

The train limped into Ayrshire and after Irvine the landscape became spotty with dunes. This was the rugged terrain in which Alfred Nobel experimented with explosives, and the Ardeer plant churned out munitions which were to alter the course of World War Two. Out of the window, Tenerife-tanned men hid all-inclusive holiday paunches in tank tops on a continuous strip of golf courses. Past them, Arran lurked majestically, a brooding presence set in glinting sea. Shortly after passing through Prestwick Airport, soon to be celebrating 50 years since Elvis

Presley didn't actually – shhhh – turn up on the tarmac there, we crawled into Ayr.

From the station, I crossed the road and paused to look at the Burns statue. Behind me, a painted sign advertised the 'Bodystyle Adult Themeshop' and 'Budds: the wee bar with the big heart?', the question mark implying that it was up to customers to decide. Continuing toward the sea, narrow streets flowed into the grandest of open spaces at Wellington Square. Surrounded on two sides by Georgian villas, the Square boasts the kind of bowling green lawn I am always desperate to perform a slide tackle on. Having won the ball, I'd then test the goal-keeper (a statue of the 13th Earl of Eglinton) with a daisy-cutter from 25 yards. Should the Earl fail to make a save, the ball would crash into the County Buildings.

Instead of sounding like a 1960s DSS tower block, the County Build-ings deserve a more prestigious name. Their columned façade is nothing short of palatial. This stately appearance is more ambassador's reception than council tax administration, though there is something admirably democratic about a building fit for kings being used to take planning decisions over bungalow extensions.

In front of the sea-facing end of the County Buildings sits the Steven Fountain, bright white, intricate and frilly. There, Victorian tourists would perch within envious view of inmates in the nearby prison, demolished in 1930. Peering from behind their iron bars, prisoners could look out to the ocean and listen to merry holidaymakers. Their agony was summed up by the jail's bittersweet nickname; 'The Cottage by the Sea'.

If, in their splendour, Wellington Square and the County Buildings sit uneasily with the traditional profile of British seaside resorts, The Pavilion across the road redresses the balance. Built in 1911 and quickly labelled 'The White Elephant by the Sea', 'The Piv' hosted dancing, roller-skating, boxing and variety shows for much of the 20th century. Its many guises have reflected the ebb and flow of British entertainment culture, from dancing troupes through to the rave scene, and now Pirate Pete's, a (shudder) 'Family Entertainment Centre'.

Ayr's Esplanade spreads over two miles from the harbour to the mouth of the River Doon. It runs parallel to a landscape of sands equally hand-some and haggard, and a sea of dark blues and islands beyond. From Pier Point, a clear day can bring into view Ailsa Craig to the south-west,

Arran to the west, the Cumbraes and Bute to the north-west, and even the peak of Ben Lomond. Unfortunately, it was foggy and overcast when I went, so all I could see was a lady in a pink coat shovelling dog emissions into an Asda carrier bag. Poor weather or not, the situation of Ayr is undeniably dramatic, as an entry in *Groome's Ordnance Gazetteer of Scotland* for 1885 concurred:

> The entire place sits so grandly on the front of the great amphitheatre, with the firth sweeping round it in a great crescent blocked on the further side by the peaks of Arran, as to look like the proud metropolis of an extensive and highly attractive region.

This is an epic place, and even my no-nonsense Victorian *Penny Guide to Ayr* allowed time for contemplation, kindly offering to 'leave you there to your own devices till you saturate your tissues with the ozone of the western ocean.' Unfortunately, owing to a well-aimed shot of white backside paint from a devious seagull, sea spray was not all I saturated my tissues with.

The Esplanade's vast expanse includes the Low Green, a giant communal field gifted to Ayr by William the Lion in 1205. In the 16th century, the town council enshrined in law Ayr residents' right to use the land for games and recreation. It became a popular venue for football, with one of the area's first teams, Ayr Thistle, playing here, and for years at Ayr United's Somerset Park ground, the standard heckle for a clumsy player was 'ye couldnae turn on the Low Green'. It was used, too, by the Royal Flying Corps as a landing strip in World War One, as a concert venue and as pasture for grazing animals, hopefully all at the same time.

With Low Green, Wellington Square and its outlook, Ayr oozes class and has none of the shabbiness that blights so many British seaside towns. Its qualities were well recognised in the Victorian era when it emerged as a prime holiday destination following the arrival in 1840 of a direct rail link with Glasgow. As the *Ayr Observer* reported at the time, 'It is impossible to foresee the full extent of the revolution which this new facility for transit is destined to produce.'

Thirty years later, the *Ayrshire Express* published a booklet entitled *Ayr as a Summer Residence* to proudly extol the town's virtues. Appealing to 'those denizens of Glasgow who live under its cloud of smoke', the booklet boasted of how the locality's

> air of quiet contrasts pleasantly with the continuous rattle of city thoroughfares, and a stranger misses the noisome din of loaded lorries and carts, and crowded omnibuses and cabs, in constant procession.

Under a chapter entitled 'Sanitary Aspects', a headline sadly missing from modern holiday brochures, the author wrote of local health benefits:

> It cannot be surpassed for pure air. Situated close upon the coast, at a moderate elevation above the sea, it is peculiarly exposed to the west winds, as purified by contact with its surface, and full of the elements of life, they sweep in from the ocean.

Having convinced the reader of the 'lusty health' available, a further chapter celebrated Ayr's 'Commercial Attractions', claiming that 'the freshness of the principal articles of diet is in itself a luxury to which residents in large cities are strangers.' It's amazing how romantic the Victorians could be about candyfloss and crabsticks. Never ones to eschew gender stereotyping, those same Victorians neatly broke down the entertainments on offer:

> Ladies may enjoy the pleasure of shopping. Fancy warehouses and extensive drapery establishments provide the numerous essentials for the employment of nimble fingers in wet days and in evening hours, in knitting, sewing, tatting, &c., &c. Gentlemen who, from long-indulged custom, may deem it essential to their happiness that they should have an opportunity of 'taking a look at the papers' can have their habit gratified by becoming temporary subscribers to the Ayr Reading Room.

Mothers and *Scotsman* readers alike were probably not reassured to learn that for children playing on the beach 'accidental death by drowning' was 'almost impossible.'

The chance of death – always an important criterion when choosing a holiday destination – was reduced further from 1881 when Ayr Council undertook improvement works which included the building of a sea wall, toilets and bathing machines. For the first time they sanctioned donkey rides, presumably bringing an end to the dangerous and illegal leisure mule trade.

Ayr remained a hugely popular holiday destination well into the 20th century, its paddle steamer excursions a rite of passage for generations of Glaswegians. Many stayed in Billy Butlin's sprawling Heads of Ayr Holiday Camp, utilised in World War Two as a naval training camp named HMS Scotia. Such was the confusion caused by this nautical prefix, during the conflict Nazi propagandists professed to have sunk 'her'.

Through the summer months, Glaswegians and those from further afield descended on Ayr in their thousands. Sunshine, alcohol and the release of tensions built up in the white-hot heat of Clydeside meant that holiday life was not always blissful. The *Ayrshire Post* for the third week of 1932 brimmed with typical examples of mischief. As the Glasgow Fair holiday period began on 18 July, Ayr teemed with tourists. All-day drinking destroyed their inhibitions and frustrations from home spilled into rioting on local streets. The *Post* detailed how a party from Coatbridge destroyed their bus from within, and then turned it into a boxing ring on wheels. In the Trades Hotel, a mob stormed a card table and robbed those playing of their winnings. On St John Street, the owner of a billiards hall had his hat pulled over his eyes and was beaten for asking four men to conclude their game. When the police arrived, an armed battle with cue-wielding players erupted. At the Esplanade, two men were arrested for brawling. In their defence, they contended the fight had been waged in a friendly spirit. In all, that day Bailie Ross of the magistrates' court presided over 13 different cases. It was a long way from nimble fingers and the Ayr Reading Room.

Short of a violent brawl to enjoy, I headed back through Wellington Square and past the end of Fort Street, site of the horrific 1876 Templeton fire. This almighty blaze started when a threading machine caught light, and was accelerated as the 'extincteur' failed and doused the factory's wooden floors in flammable oil. The inferno burst through the windows and roared up a spiral staircase, cutting off the 28 female carpet weavers, aged between 11 and 21, who worked in the building's attic. Factory foreman David Copperauld tried to rescue the women by placing a ladder where the staircase had been. However, as the *Ayr Advertiser* recorded,

None of them would venture to cross the awful gulf. Terror-stricken and bewildered, they would see equal danger in any alternative, and preferred to remain where they were till the few moments passed away when escape was any longer possible. Copperauld held the ladder till it caught fire; his hands were burnt holding it, and as the flames began to leap higher, the girls closed the attic door, as if to keep them out, and were seen no more. The spectators who had gathered below saw the awful spectacle of girls' arms waving up through the attic windows, and heard shrieks, many of them by very youthful voices, of the most heartrending description.

After 10 minutes, the waving and shrieking came to an end, an eerie calm providing evidence that the smoke had taken the attic girls' lives before the fire could.

From Fort Street, I crossed Sandgate and headed along Boswell Park. Opposite a classically grim Royal Mail sorting office was the scuffed exterior of Mecca Bingo, formerly Green's Playhouse where in 1953 a troubled Frank Sinatra played two sparsely attended shows. In the High Street, Saturday afternoon shopping couples argued outside chain shops and empty outlets, while William Wallace surveyed the scene from his tower and wondered if it had all been worthwhile. I slipped down the orderly cobbles of Newmarket Street and out onto Sandgate, a wide and varied boulevard containing the pale crooked beauty of Lady Cathcart's House and a dedicated lawn bowling emporium. The impressive Town Hall was midway through hosting its 'Organist Entertains' season, 126 years after the keyboards played Oscar Wilde onto the stage there.

Wilde's 1883 appearance in Ayr invited extensive media coverage. With the writer's fame at a peak on both sides of the Atlantic, the Town Hall was packed to capacity for a lecture on 'The House Beautiful'. Both the *Ayr Observer* and the *Ayr Advertiser* described his image at length. 'With regard to the lecturer's personal appearance,' noted the *Observer*,

> it may be stated that it is rendered somewhat remarkable from a mass of dark, well-curled hair surrounding a somewhat effeminate face of a sallow complexion. With one or two exceptions

in matters of detail, the lecturer was attired very much like ordinary mortals.

The *Advertiser*, meanwhile, carried a subtly critical, even sarcastic tone:

His somewhat heavy, though well-chiselled, features have been made familiar by engravings and caricatures; but his hair, instead of hanging down upon his shoulders, as it was wont to do, is in a frowsy brown mass coming down upon the brow, somewhat after the style adopted by some 'girls of the period'. He was in evening dress coat of the cut that was in vogue half a century ago.

Wilde preached to the people of Ayr on the philosophy of decorating a room, and offered practical tips in creating a perfect home. As has often been said, he was truly the Carol Smillie of his day.

Taking in the elegant arches of the Old Bridge from the vantage of the New, I headed towards Somerset Park via Wallacetown. Just over a century ago, crossing the River Ayr meant crossing into a very different place. Far away from the prosperity of the West End and its gentrified visitors, Wallacetown was a district of intense deprivation in which Irish immigrants were abandoned to live in squalor. Dr HJ Littlejohn, a medical officer with the Board of Supervision, reported in 1878 how the area was

inhabited by a low class of the population... the houses were of poor description... this at one time outlying country district still maintains the characteristics of a dirty village... The cottages have manure in all directions in their back courts, ill-kept piggeries abound, and privy accommodation is either totally awanting or of the most offensive description. Ayr itself is one of our cleanest Scotch towns and such adjuncts as Wallacetown must be made to conform to the usages.

This was hidden Ayr, a town where, as Dr Littlejohn wrote, 'all attractions can be seen and enjoyed without the poverty and wretchedness of many of its poorer inhabitants being obtruded upon the visitor.' Wallacetown today is a centrally-planned area of low-rise flats, architecturally bland but spacious, neat and tidy enough to suggest the double life of Ayr is not as pronounced as it once was.

Behind Wallacetown, the rusty floodlight pylons of Somerset Park beckoned me. It was August, time for real life to begin again.

* * *

Crossing the railway bridge from Wallacetown, the mossy canopies of Somerset Park come into view. The authenticity of the ground is immediately obvious. For over one hundred years, people have trekked over this bridge to stand under Somerset's corrugated roofs in pursuit of diversion and the chance to shout at grown men.

The origins of football in Ayr go further than Somerset Park and back to the Low Green. While Ayr Thistle were the first to play organised matches there, it had long played host to mass kickabouts of the flat caps for goalposts variety. From the 1860s, this raw interest in the game prompted the formation of several local clubs, most notably Ayr FC and Ayr Parkhouse. It was an era in which, so the legend goes, pigeons carried half-time scores from football grounds to nearby towns, and one of team names that appear to have been dreamt up by the Romantic Poets; other local sides included Glenbuck Cherrypickers, The Early Risers of Troon, Dailly Pan Rattlers, Trabboch Heroes, Ayr Bonnie Doon and Mossblown Strollers.

As if trying to prove their masculinity in the face of such decadence, players and fans indulged in regular bouts of violence. In 1890, Hearts travelled west to face Ayr FC in a Scottish Cup tie. Keeping goal for the home side that day was Fullarton Steel, an eccentric prone to entertaining the crowd by making saves with his feet alone. After Steel made one such stop, opposition forward Davie Russell thrust a boot into his chest. A scrap broke out between the two sides, and home fans jumped the rope around the side of the pitch to launch an attack on Russell. Pursued by this mob, the petrified forward sprinted for the safety of the main stand and jumped in. He then borrowed a coat and hat, and watched the rest of the match incognito as a petrified spectator.

The intensity with which Ayr FC fans followed their team did not falter down the years. Another Scottish Cup game, this time away at Peebles in 1909, saw them flock south by special train in considerable numbers. The *Ayr Observer* set the scene:

> The good people of Peebles must have thought their ancient town invaded as they saw the force, three hundred strong, making its way under a banner, which, by its torn appearance, might have done duty at Flodden, up the station road and across the bridge over the Tweed into the town.

Though the fervency of football fans in Ayr was undoubted, their numbers remained modest. It soon became clear that the town was simply not large enough to support two Scottish League sides; if local football was to prosper, Ayr FC and Parkhouse would have to merge. After talks between directors of the two clubs during the spring of the Peebles match ended in gentle mud-slinging ('the members feel very annoyed,' wrote Ayr FC secretary H Murray in the local press), hopes of an amalgamation dwindled. Only a mediocre 1909/10 season for both pushed Ayr's footballing bureaucrats back around the negotiating table, and in May 1910 they announced the creation of Ayr United Football Club.

The new club found rapid success, winning the second tier title two years after their establishment, only to be denied promotion in a brazen act of protectionism by the Scottish League. Unperturbed, they cantered to the championship again the following term, 1912/13, and were accepted for promotion to Division One. Along the way, 'The Honest Men' played their biggest game to date, another cup tie, this time against Airdrieonians. A record crowd of 9,000 clustered at Somerset Park to see the home side defeated 2–0, and the obligingly partisan *Ayr Advertiser* claimed that 'No unbiased spectator could deny that a fair result of the game would have been a 2–1 victory for Ayr. It was the fastest and most exciting all through that has been witnessed for years.' More negatively, The *Advertiser*'s reporter bemoaned working conditions, writing how

> The pressmen were shunted from under cover to the top of the open stand, which possibly enabled the directors to harvest a few more shillings but which would have rendered the position of the pencillers untenable had the threatened rain put in an appearance. As it was, the breeze played many pranks with 'copy'.

At the start of 1914, Ayr were becoming a fixture in Division One. By the end of it, troops had marched across their pitch under a banner that read 'A Hearty Welcome To Men From Ayrshire Who Join Us'. An inspection of Ayr shareholders' annual report for 1915 captures the conflict's impact:

> The continuance of the war has had its effect on the finances of the club. The withdrawal of so many of the club's ardent and enthusiastic followers, away at their country's call, reducing the size of the gates and depleting our income. The playing strength of the team has been well maintained and in spite of the financial strain, a credit balance is the result of the year's workings.
>
> Killed on active service were three United players – J Bellringer, R Copperauld and S Herbertson.

In peacetime, the spectre of horrors past understandably lingered. Where desired, release through football was limited by the conflict's lasting reach. With a post-war shortage of trains, improvisation became key to following one's team. When Ayr played Kilmarnock in December 1918, fans took a tram to Prestwick, walked 13 miles to Riccarton and caught further transport to Rugby Park. Appealing to popular memories of the Great War, the *Ayrshire Post* colourfully illustrated the irritation this journey brought:

The Kaiser has always been famous for the quality of the language he uses when in his high falutin moods, but the floe of 'flowery' composition which was heard in the vicinity of Tam's Brig on Saturday about one o'clock surpasses anything the deposed Hun head was ever father of. The cause of the fiery outburst was the non-materialisation of a certain means of transport to Kilmarnock, which had been promised to a coterie of rabid football enthusiasts.

This devotion to reaching the match is recognisable to supporters today. Similarly, there is something familiar about the Brake Clubs that terrorised towns in the early decades of the last century. The Brake Clubs were, essentially, supporters' clubs with an eye for brawling. Setting out in horse-drawn wagonettes, and later charabancs, gang members followed their instinct for trouble across Scotland, rioting inside and outside of football grounds. In December 1920, members of the Rangers Brake Club stood among a 12,000-strong crowd at a buoyant Somerset Park. Leading 1–0, all was well with the Gers. In the away end, bugles sounded, rattles clicked and banners were proudly unfurled. Ayr, though, had the temerity to score an equalising goal, and shortly afterwards, when a Rangers player was fouled in front of the away end, and in full view of the Brakes, an air of hostility grew. As the *Ayr Advertiser* related under the headline 'Rowdyism Rampant',

> A section, just immediately behind the Ayr goal, did not relish the idea of their favourites losing a point. Stones, bottles and other missiles, it was alleged, were thrown at some of the Ayr players and the referee had to stop the game and appeal to the police to try and restore order at this particular point.

Ayr keeper George Nisbet was struck by stones and Brake Club members attempted to invade the pitch, although, The *Advertiser* continued, 'the police had by this time been reinforced and managed to keep the mob

George Nisbet proves that you can wear a turtleneck jumper and still look hard.

in check.' In the town centre after the game, the Brakes proceeded to go on the rampage. The following Monday in court, burgh prosecutor LC Boyd's charge sheet reflected their early evening spree. On Fort Street, one John Somerville had turned a car straight into a building. Boyd found him guilty of drink driving. Others were charged with using Rangers flagpoles to attack police officers on the High Street. Over the following days, Boyd dispensed numerous sentences for breaches of the peace ranging from swearing to assault. For Rangers' next visit, the Brake Club were re-routed to avoid residential areas.

Ayr were to play Rangers frequently in the inter-war years, only spending two seasons outside the top division in that time. Their 1928 Division Two title was inspired by the exploits of the extraordinary Jimmy Smith. A native of Old Kilpatrick village, Smith had arrived at Somerset Park via Dumbarton Harp, Clydebank and the Gers. From the start of the 1927/28 season, the goals flowed – early on, he scored five against Albion, and then two hat-tricks in a fortnight. By Hogmanay, Smith had plundered 35 league goals. In total that season, he scored 66 times, eclipsing the exploits of Dixie Dean and earning himself a place in *The Guinness Book of Records*. That summer, Ayr travelled to Scandinavia where they defeated Sweden 3–1. Smith scored two of the goals, and was branded 'The British Champion'. Ayr had found its golden boy.

It was proving to be something of a halcyon era for mavericks at Somerset Park, yet the next to come along, Hyam Dimmer, is far less well remembered than Smith. Often the tallest man on the pitch, from 1935 inside forward Dimmer used his wiry frame to Ayr's advantage. He was renowned for gyroscopic contortions, a human magic box of tricks, flicks and pirouettes who revelled in creating laughter on the terraces and bemusement among opponents. As encyclopaedic club historian Duncan Carmichael told me,

> The odd thing about Hyam Dimmer was his complexity of motions. He was more interested in entertaining the crowd and making goals for others than in scoring himself. There was a home match coinciding with Students' Day. Students were dressed up, running about with their collection tins. Dimmer was trying to match them. He had a sense of devilment about him. Not only did he have the temperament to humiliate opposing players, he had the ability to do it.

Dimmer was an enigmatic maestro, as quietly approachable off the field as he was devastatingly extravagant on it. His unusual handle added to the mystique, as Carmichael continued:

> 'Hyam' is something that I don't understand. The name Hyam is synonymous with showmanship. He was brought up in Scotstoun, which was a rough shipbuilding area, and he's got a name like Hyam! You can only think his life must have been a misery at school with a name like Hyam. It was his name, it wasn't an adopted name, it wasn't a nickname. Such a flamboyant name for a player with a flamboyant style.

Contemporary match reports from the *Ayr Advertiser* and *Ayrshire Post* detail that flamboyance. In a September 1936 thrashing of Forfar, 'though keeping a solemn poker face, he had the crowd in a good humour with his football wizardry and cheeky capers.' Three months later on Boxing Day, Dimmer confirmed himself as 'football's number one entertainer' in an 8–1 mauling of Montrose. That season, he scored 25 goals and conjured up many more for others as Ayr took the title. From the next term's opening, a 6–2 victory over Queen's Park, Dimmer proved his majesty at a higher level. That day, 'he had the defence running in circles and the crowd laughing.' Predictably, his devilish artistry invited robust treatment from defenders; against St Mirren, 'Dimmer tried some of his surrealist stuff on an opposition which did not appreciate art.' His style could also arouse frustration among teammates and even supporters, goading report card-like opprobrium in the local press:

Hyam Dimmer, knobbly-kneed magician.

> Hyam started off not too well and created a bad impression by dillydallying in a way which aroused the alternate delight and ire of the spectators. Dimmer is a born footballer but he has a habit of using his feet more than his head – which on occasion has made him more annoying than useful.

At the outbreak of World War Two Dimmer remained, aged just 22, far from footballing maturity. Military service robbed him of his prime: the Scottish Football Association's announcement on 4 September 1939 that 'in view of the government order closing all places of entertainment and outdoor sport, football players' contracts are automatically cancelled' ended Dimmer's top flight career with Ayr. Though his time passed too quickly, this gangly magician had charmed football, his on-field excesses tolerated and even celebrated as a mesmeric trapping of genius.

* * *

When the Scottish League recommenced at the end of World War Two, Ayr United were controversially placed in Division Two and did not win promotion again until 1956. Four years later the club marked its Silver Jubilee optimistically, with an officially-produced booklet entitled *The Ayr United Story* concluding:

> The future? If we knew the future it would be uninteresting. The end? No, rather the beginning. For Ayr will surely be United in the effort to keep the 'Auld Town' on the soccer map. Who knows, perhaps at the end of another 50 years United may have won all the honours that have eluded them. There's that first Scottish Cup win for example.

1960 represented a watershed as Ayr looked to move from the romantic ages of Smith and Dimmer and into the future. That future did bring glory – the reigns of Ally MacLeod; early 21st century cup runs – and yet one of the club's greatest achievements half a century on is just how much it retains a vintage air. Whether their paymasters like it or not (a recent proposed stadium move was abandoned due to wrangling with the local council) nothing speaks of this more than Somerset Park.

From a nearby railway bridge, it's possible to see just how tradition-ally situated the ground is. By 'traditionally situated', I mean it is nes-tled close to a vast railway junction and an area of disused factories, both ghosts of a bustling and choking past. Beyond the begonias and endless rule lists of a local bowling club, the Railway End comes into view. Here during the 1930s stood football's only gender-divided fans, with male and female supporters segregated into their own respective areas by signs and fences.

In the club car park, men of a certain age milled with expertise, most eventually committing to a trip into the Club Shop or Lottery Office. A smart old moustachioed local read the team sheet, shook his head and walked away disgruntled, the season written off in one withering look. Partick fans, upbeat and numerous, swarmed past the Main Stand's ornate stained glass windows, philistines marching by high art in pursuit of a Scotch pie. Turnstiles clacked busily, mucky brown iron gates promising riches aplenty.

The scene inside Somerset Park was similarly evocative, its three terraces and wooden-seated area encasing a lush green pitch and misfiring footballers rocketing warm-up shots into the crowd. And then, as if imploring me to snap out of sickly reverie, my eyes met with an advertising hoarding asking me to 'Watch Out, Chlamydia's About'. It's what Jeremy Beadle would've wanted.

In mild August rain, the Ayr players entered the pitch. Their centenary black and white hooped shirts combined with the hundred-year-old din of the Somerset Road End to give a feeling that nothing would ever really change. The public address system remained silent, leaving supporters' chants happily audible, a welcome departure from the choreographed preamble I'd been used to in the English Premier League. In the unisex away enclosure, Partick fans ushered the season in with a dose of Celtic-bashing.

The grass burst glorious Lincoln Green. Alabaster by-lines and penalty areas lay freshly painted. The players lined up in their vivid and ancient colours. Summer's hiatus was over and hope sprung for the long season ahead. The stage was set. And then Partick booted the ball straight out of play from kick-off. It was not a minute past three o'clock on the first day of the season, and already groans were audible.

The season kicks off. In celebration, Partick's number 11 does an impression of a skier.

Quickly, the gear shifted from

ridiculous back to sublime. Thistle goalkeeper Jonny Tuffey sauntered out of his area, controlled the ball and passed it neatly down the line, only to find Ayr forward Mark Roberts ready to intercept. Disregarding a name more Futures Investor than footballing genie, Roberts nonchalantly curled the ball into the net from 45 yards as if possessed by the spirit of Hyam Dimmer.

To my right hand side, a husband and wife, both with more ears than teeth, took it in turns to tag-team the linesman with abuse. 'Barry Manilow bastard.' 'You cannae see past yer nose, ye big prick.' 'We'll help ye linesman, ye Stevie Wonder prick.' In benevolent response, Thistle fans passed around an inflatable shark, which was either a Situationist statement I failed to understand or a cry for help.

On the pitch, towering Ayr defender Kevin James coped admirably with the dual threat of Prestwick-bound aircraft and Partick cross-field balls. In front of him, Ryan Stevenson tore around like Wolf from *Gladiators* doing an impression of a Tasmanian devil. His tattoos alone could be found guilty of GBH.

As seagulls circled ahead of a half-time raid on dropped pie fillings, a slalom dribble and cut-back from Partick's Mark Corcoran provided a cheap equaliser. The Ayr keeper dived late, backwards and almost sarcastically, a dad letting his son win in the park.

After half-time, Ayr stirred groggily and hit a post, provoking the first cherished crowd 'yeeeeeeeaaaaaaaaawwwwwwwww' of my season. Then, substitute Kevin Cawley was sent clear through on goal but instead of shooting elected to file his tax return and paint the wings on an Airfix Messerschmitt Bf109F.

His hesitance prodded Partick into action, but only of the half-arsed, Sunday afternoon soap omnibus variety, and before long the game petered out into a subconsciously negotiated one–all settlement. As I left the ground, a rare bit of noise over the public address system relayed news that the 'Ayr United official match sponsor 163 Chinese Takeaway Man of the Match is number 7...' 'Prawn toast!' interjected the male half of the tag-team abusers. It was going to be a long season.

CHAPTER TWO

Alloa

Alloa Athletic 1 v 0 Stirling Albion, 12 September 2009

'IT'S NOT THE Old Firm that's failed football. It's me and the other clubs who don't get enough local fans that have failed Scottish football.' In his office, Alloa Athletic owner Mike Mulraney is holding forth. 'My job is to make the local fans want to watch Alloa. It's my job to make sure they get the right kind of service when they get here, and to have an enjoyable day, and at the end of it to feel they got value for money, not to say don't go and watch Celtic and Rangers just because you live in Alloa.'

His is an unusual attitude, free of the victim status so many officials of smaller clubs maintain. Mulraney refuses to bemoan this Scotland of powerless small town clubs, Old Firm day-trippers and B-roads clogged by Highland Hoops. He recognises Scotland's familiar, attendance-sapping Saturday morning backdrop of blue and green coaches leading an exodus in search of Glasgow glory, but does not blame those travelling. Instead, Mulraney insists that smaller clubs should change their own business models and base themselves around the one thing the Glaswegian titans lack: homespun community spirit.

It's unlikely that were I to enter his Ibrox office, the Rangers chairman would offer me a can of Diet Irn-Bru as Mulraney did. At first, I presumed this to be a tactic aimed at diverting my thoughts from awkward questioning; power-play, Clackmannanshire-style. As it turned out, Mulraney could barely have been more friendly and forthcoming, and in any case my questions were far more Partridge than Paxman (for some reason, being behind the scenes at a football club does this to me. During a tour of Somerset Park, even the sight of a Board Room bar towel had me nervously bleating at length. I'd be far from intimidated if meeting the Queen, but show me a tea lady called Agnes who's served Gordon Dalziel his Bovril and I go to pieces).

The Mulraney Group has a portfolio of property, engineering and leisure interests throughout Alloa, and owns 90 per cent of the football club. If all that sounds a bit Biff Tannen in *Back to the Future II,* it shouldn't: Mulraney talks repeatedly of community and of the club as a 'social asset.' The sporting arm of his group is named 'Wasp Leisure', after Alloa's nickname, and the team's gold and black home colours are plastered all over its branding and website. As he explains, 'ours is a well known local company, we're fans of football, we're fans of Alloa Athletic and we believe we can implement the best business practices we use elsewhere into the club.' His ultimate aim is to create 'a true community club: supported by its community and supportive of its community. We don't think a team like Alloa can survive in the long run if it doesn't become integrated.' Posters bearing the words 'Your Club Needs You' are scattered throughout the town and Alloa run child development schemes as well as offering schoolchildren free match tickets. It's an operation that runs deep, one in which Alloa Athletic are at the centre of something wider than match days at Recreation Park (known as 'The Recs'). As Mulraney continues, 'It's critical that the community recognises themselves through their team and the team recognises its worth for the community.' Every year, 100,000 locals use Alloa's all-weather pitch, allowing him to justifiably claim 'we've got more users coming through the doors than many SPL teams.'

Since the Mulraney Group took the reins at Alloa, they have invested vast sums on ground improvements and continue to do so. A former bus depot adjacent to Recreation Park has been purchased and converted into a community sports centre. Mulraney's determination to make the club live within its means and invest in infrastructure rather than player transfer fees has led to some fan criticism: how will new toilets in the away end help bring about promotion? As a lifelong supporter himself, Mulraney is open about the difficulties embodied in letting head rule heart. 'It's hugely difficult, the most difficult call. Yes, we [the Alloa board] too will sometimes say that we should go out and buy players. But if we fund it out of an unsustainable source...when you make that decision to the detriment of the football club you are controlling then it's time for you to stop and get out.' The ghost of Gretna still stalks heavily, if usefully.

The football club also has a further role, that of keeping the town of Alloa in the national consciousness, albeit through the voices of Jeff Stelling or James Alexander Gordon. As Mulraney admits, 'The club is a branding opportunity for a town like Alloa. If you live in London, the only way you're going to hear about Alloa is watching results on Sky Sports. How would you have heard of the town if it wasn't for the football team?' It is the same story across post-industrial Scotland. Cowdenbeath is known not for its coal but for the Blue Brazil. Greenock is Greenock Morton, not a shipbuilding powerhouse. Only the football teams keep the memory of the places alive nationally. The town is now an adjunct of the football club and it sometimes feels as though the former was named after the latter.

The variety of industry that once existed in Alloa makes its almost complete collapse profound. What was once an engine room is now a dormitory town, its inhabitants travelling to Edinburgh and Glasgow for work as well as football.

* * *

The train curved around the rock bearing the National Wallace Monument, its engine slowing to a hissing noise of contempt; 15 years on, even Diesel Multiple Units remain critical of Mel Gibson's *Braveheart*. Rich green against autumn sun, the Ochil Hills towered in the background, and the route took on the feel of a heritage railway. This sedate atmosphere was not helped by a complete lack of away fan patter on board, unless you count the three-year-old in front of me's 'car bah bike' as a tactical insight (and let's face it, Steve Claridge has uttered less profound sentences).

Entering Alloa, the chimneys of the United Glass plant cough and splutter down by the River Forth, a lone statement of the town's industrial past. The factory's silhouette of robotic arms and giant concrete conveyor belts is poignant in its solitude. For hundreds of years, the Clackmannanshire skyline

The Alloa glassworks boy band pose ahead of a forthcoming *X-Factor* audition.

was cluttered with the trappings of industry and trade which used the harbour to transport goods from Alloa to the world. Disregarding its self-effacing nickname, the 'Wee County' defied its size to become one of Scotland's most important economic arteries. Other than United Glass, the legacy of this history is local pride in what went before, fervently demonstrated by Jim Banks and Dick Clark of the Clackmannan Society. Having served a signifigant part of their working lives in Alloa, in retirement both are now committed to telling its history, and making sure the town's lineage does not slip from view. 'Everything was happening in Alloa by the early part of the 20th century,' Jim enthuses. 'We had the breweries and the biggest distillery complex in the world. This was surrounded by the coal industry. We had the wool industry, and of course the big one was the glassworks, which was a massive industry.' Dick chips in, 'then there was the British Electrical Products/Harland, producing pumping machinery which went all over the world. And shipbuilding; there were limitations, it wasn't quite Clydeside, but it was very significant. In the textiles industry, Paton and Baldwin had in excess of 3,000 employees and buses that came in every day from a 20-mile radius, working 24-hour shifts.'

The town benefitted from its geographical location. As an early local guide specified, 'a thirty-miles circle, with Alloa at its centre, would have in its circumference Edinburgh, Glasgow and Perth.' Further afield, the port offered access to the Low Countries and Baltics, spurring 1791's *Statistical Account of Scotland* to label Alloa's glassworks 'the most conveniently situated of any in Britain.' Economic growth stemmed from Clackmannanshire coal, king unless you happened to be a woman or child doing the dragging and carrying. To that end, Robert Bald, an enlightened engineer and colliery manager, banned the employment of women and girls well before the government did, although as he admitted 'they had no other work so there was a great deal of hardship.' 'As well as being an engineer,' local history enthusiast Jim told me, 'he was a man of the people in a way, a wee bit like Robert Owen.'

Bald worked for the Mar family, long-time owners of mines and much of the county. Until his exile in 1715 for leading the Jacobite rebellion, the 6th Earl of Mar had been something of a visionary, designing a system of 'lades' to purloin water from damper neighbouring burghs and transport it to Alloa to mechanise his pits. Mar oversaw the construction of Scotland's biggest man-made dam to store the water, and that water in turn served Alloa's people, and serviced the evolution of distilling, milling and even snuff production. Company employees built a system of wagonways to transport coal from the outskirts of town to the port.

From those tracks and the Mar coal lade, Alloa shot to prominence, leading Dick to comment, with tongue not entirely in cheek, 'I always maintain that the Industrial Revolution started in Clackmannanshire before in some respects even in the Midlands. That's maybe stretching it a wee bit, but it was so big.'

Workers from Buicks take an instruction to bring everything including the kitchen sink along for a photograph session a little too literally.

Providing resources and inspiring the growth of the port, the visions of the Mar dynasty and Bald also led to the birth of Alloa's most famous export: beer. In 1645, a local Parish Council minute used a hybrid of Middle English and modern txtspk to report:

> Pnt. Minister and elders, ye browster compeirit, and confessate selling of drink in tyme of sermon. Acted ye sd. day that qt. somever person sall be found to sell drink in tyme of sermon hereafter sall pay 40p., and make public repentance.

Three years later, one Margaret Mitchell of Tron Well ignored the threat of a 40p fine to start her own home brewery. Alcohol was clearly, in every sense, in the blood, and so when Mar's work began to pay dividends, aided by a supply of pure water from the Ochil Hills and quality local barley, large breweries added their chimneys to the industrial skyline. In 1762, George Younger built his Meadow Brewery. The Alloa Brewery, Meiklejohn's, Townhead and others soon followed, and by the middle of the next century, this small town had eight ale factories turning out their wares for customers in Britain, the United States and the West Indies. The 'Burton-on-Trent of Scotland' flourished. Possibly over a pint or two of heavy, patriotic poet John Imlah used verse to celebrate Alloa's beery heritage:

Awa' wi black brandy, red rum and blue whisky
An' bring me the liquor as brown as a nut
O! Alloa Ale ye can mak a chiel frisky
Brisk, faeming a'fresh frae the bottle or butt.

An awa wi' your wines – they are dull as moss water
Wi' blude colour'd blushes, or purple, or pale;
Guid folks gif ye wish to get fairer and fatter.
Then aye weet your weasans wi' Alloa Ale!

Gif ye wish healthie habits an' wad be lang livers,
Then spirituous drinks ye s'oud never fash wi';
But Alloa Ale ye may drink it in rivers,
An' the deeper ye drink, aye the better ye'll be.

Concerned that too many were taking Imlah's advice to quaff by the river-load, Reverend Peter Brotherston, Minister of the Parish of Alloa, was less enthusiastic:

In the town of Alloa, there are five hotels and inns, 27 taverns, and 30 grocers where spirituous liquors are sold. There are also eleven taverns or public houses in the villages, making a total of no less than 72, which are more than the necessities people require.

The economic benefits of Alloa's breweries could not be denied by even Reverend Brotherston. By 1890, Younger's alone had its own railway siding and glassworks, directly employing 150 men. In his 1890 work *Noted Breweries of Great Britain and Ireland*, visiting the 'sylvan' surroundings of Alloa, Alfred Barnard described the poetry in their work:

It is an interesting sight to walk along, look down upon the busy workers, and watch their rapid movements. The fillers sit in front of what looks like a key-board, and the deft way in which they manipulate the bottles, so that none of the precious liquor is wasted, the rapidity with which they pass them on to the corkers is wonderful to behold.

When World War Two began, Alloa still had eight breweries. The rot, however, had set in, and brewing historian Charlie McMaster's account of the Mills Brewery is indicative of the downward spiral:

By 1941, the brewery was in a very decrepit and ramshackle state, having for a number of years previously been run as a virtual one-man operation, with casual labour being employed at weekends for such duties as cask-washing. Apparently, as the story goes, the owner, Old Man Henderson, used to go down to the local bus station when he needed some casual labour, and round up some reprobates, and employ them for the afternoon for a couple of half-crowns and all they could drink!

At the same time, Grange Brewery housed Polish prisoners of war and employed them in malting at Younger's. Brewing was losing its importance, and when the markets of the British Empire began to close following the war, Alloa's industry went into terminal decline. In the 1950s, local favourite Graham's Golden Lager became Skol, and four breweries remained. Now, there is one, and Skol is only remembered through bored YouTube trawls for old television commercials featuring vindaloo-chomping Vikings.

The near extinction of the breweries was part of the slow death of industrial Alloa. For 300 years, the town by the Forth had adapted and evolved with every twist of time and fate. Its strength lay in the slog it had to offer, and the way its people created good from bad and turned their hand to coal or cloth, shipbuilding or Skol. Together, they built Scotland's Infant Hercules. By the 1980s, they didn't even have a railway station.

* * *

Leaving Alloa's station, rebuilt, reopened and looking like a smart request stop in a German village, an impressive, wiry sculpture greets travellers. It depicts a man in overalls and flat cap, representing the industrial past, supporting a child, personification of a rosy future. Behind the sculpture, an Asda has landed on the site of the former Alloa Brewery. If the art whispers the message quietly at you, the supermarket bellows patronisingly like a British holidaymaker talking slowly to a foreigner. The future is here: where once we brewed, now we sell. And, John Imlah's rivers are now only 24 cans for a tenner away.

New and old again screamed from beside the leafy path that leads to Alloa Tower: on one side, a Tesco Extra, on the other the ornate front of the Kilncraigs Woollen Mill, now masking an adjoining steel and glass block housing the Centre for Creative Industries. Peeking cheekily from behind a fluffy army of trees is Alloa Tower, built by the Mar family (well, built by some poor buggers they got to put up the thing) in the 15th century. Suitably imposing and grand, the tower boasts 11-foot-thick walls. The flagstones leading up to the Tower are subtly engraved with dates in Scotland's past and an advert for 'Reversing Safety Products'. Content with the directional mobility of my lifejackets and helmets, I proceeded on to the Tower which I realised, rather than the climax of an entire castle, was just that. A fire ravaged through the rest in 1800, leaving 89 magnificent feet of folly.

The Tower sits in a meadow, once a part of the Earl of Mar's expensive and expansive planned garden, portrayed by Daniel Defoe as, 'by much the finest in Scotland and not outdone by many in England. There is everything that nature and art can do, brought to perfection.' Dewy-eyed through a mixture of emotion at suddenly encountering this leafy heaven and hayfever, I walked on by the Old Kirk, its ruined wings resembling the close-to-chest arms of a shivering child, and towards Broad Street. Here, Alfred Barnard was charmed by what locals refer to as Lime Tree Walk, writing of:

> A thoroughfare 80 feet wide, leading down to the harbour, with a magnificent avenue of lime trees, affording an agreeable shade in the summer, which rejoiced in a wealth of verdant beauty.

The social classes mix on Lime Tree Walk.

Now, newly planted limes have replaced those donated by Dutch sailors many moons ago. The sailors had become stranded in Alloa and offered the trees as gratitude for the hospitality shown to them, albeit records do not indicate just how far the local welcome went. Pausing for thought no longer, I continued over cobbles to the town centre, passing a bunch of tall blond children wearing clogs on my way. On Bank Street, I lazed on the steps of the ornate council building, defying its stone-carved old school Protestant motto of 'Work to-day, play to-morrow'. With the uncommonly hot sun streaming onto old stone, I recognised for a moment the Alloa that Barnard described:

> We found Alloa dressed in a wealth of foliage and blossom; the brilliant sunshine tinged its churches and old tower with beauty, and every object upon which the eye could rest was illuminated by its glorious sheen.

Looking up and spotting shimmering, well-garnished buildings, I was with him, only with the whir and revving of a boy racer's Peugeot sound-tracking the moment. Along the road, a large painted red cross marked the spot where in Alloa's heyday thousands of green-overalled factory girls amassed during shift changes. There, a policeman would stand on a large crate, forlornly attempting to bring about order. Recounted over time in a thousand bad accents, a local story tells of an American visitor asking, 'Gee officer, who are all these folks?' 'That's the mill yins', replied the officer. 'Gee, the millions!?' came the disbelieving reaction. On those corners now are The Sun Studio (a tanning salon rather than a page three photography centre), a Semichem, the Treetops Bar and First, an outlet for all your porcelain doll, AM/FM clock radio and bong needs. Suddenly, while eyeing up a particularly appealing Fine China King of Pop Mug, I found myself jumping onto the road to evade a speeding pensioner in an electric mobility scooter. As I looked at her riding into the sunset, from beneath swirling dust I made out a registration plate marked 'Turbo Gran' on the back of the vehicle. This was Alloa does Wild West. If only I'd purchased the Air Sport Gun, just £3.99 at First.

In her reckless actions, Turbo Gran was paying homage: the incident took place on Mill Street where 'Gutty' McKenzie used to perform his cycling tricks. Through the 1940s, Gutty – named after the type of shoe he wore – would weave closely in between crowds and queues on his bike, often using it as a monocycle or bucking bronco. Unfortunately, Gutty was rather a large chap, and after a number of collisions, his act was banned by magistrates.

My ruffled post-Turbo Gran state was not helped by a shop window advert which disturbingly read: 'Beautiful Boys and Girls. Gorgeous Colours. £40. Wormed and Litter Trained', at which point I realised the postcard above for Arlene Allison photographers had slipped and obscured the word 'Kittens'. In search of respite, I stumbled into The Thistle Bar and settled down with a pint of imported lager in tribute to Alloa's brewing heritage. In the *Wee County News*, Clackmannanshire Listeners were advertising a meeting in which people could 'learn more about listening over a cuppa.' This would be especially useful, I noted, as Stirling and Falkirk Ramblers were holding their AGM the following night. Unfortunately, my smug chuckle at spotting this revelation attracted attention, and, coupled with newbie status, acted as a green light from this particular pub's resident Accoster. The Accoster wore a polo-neck t-shirt tucked into chinos and a moustache that had seen better days. He opened our discussion with an observation dressed as a question.

'Reading the paper, then?'

Resisting all obvious sarcasm, I replied along the lines of:

'Yes.'

To an Accoster in small town Scotland, my accent was encouragement enough for a whole new line of questioning, and a perch next to me.

'Oh you're English. Whereabouts are you from?'

After a few more of these, and then a 15-minute Accoster soliloquy with some breathtaking changes of subject (my favourite was 'yes, I've never been to Middlesbrough. I've just bought one of those 2 Litre Audis'), I was finally asked what exactly I was doing in Alloa.

'What you going to watch *them* for? Rather you than me. Who's gonna read *that* anyway?'

My heart suitably filled with pointlessness, I headed for the door while he was in the Gents, possibly telling the condom machine about his static home in Dunbar. The sight of black and gold Alloa shirts swarming towards Recreation Park soon lifted my spirits. I walked past the end of Whins Road and along Clackmannan Road beside august Victorian houses. At The Recs, supporters loitered beside Mike Mulraney's new walls before entering the neat and fresh confines of the ground. Unchangeable, the sun-hit Ochils glistened behind the away end, shadowing the ground impressively as they long had.

* * *

Alloa Athletic was born in 1883 and moved in at The Recs aged 12. Prior to that, in 1891, Jock Hepburn became the only Alloa player ever to win a Scotland cap, a fact that points to a history mooching between the lower leagues. The high times have been short-lived but, fans who were there would argue if they weren't all dead, spectacular.

The first of those peaks surrounded the footballing intellect of one man. 'Wee' Willie Crilley was born in Cowcaddens in 1903. Standing just over five feet tall, he matched deft footwork with prolific goalscoring, the minute master with a clinical eye. Crilley lived to play football, turning out on Sundays for a Glasgow Meat Market side named Pale Ale. Wasps folklore holds that Wee Willie once ran after the ball through the legs of an opponent centre-half, took it around the goalkeeper, and then asked the supporters in which part of the net they wished to see him score. In his second season after signing from Cambuslang, Crilley's exploits

Willie Crilley ahead of the club's annual cartoon prisoner fancy dress party.

saw one journalist proclaim him 'the wonder man of modern football.'

That season was 1921/22, Alloa's first in the new Division Two. From the off, Crilley sparkled, his virtuosity providing escape for the watching band of brewers, miners and millers. Against King's Park, a Stirling side later bombed out of existence by the Luftwaffe, he scored five goals in an 8–1 victory. The *Alloa Circular* newspaper reported how:

> Crilley appeared to be in his element, and wriggled like an eel through the mire. He was as elusive as a 'Scarlet Pimpernel' and popped up when least expected.

Press accolades went beyond the local. The *Glasgow Citizen* enthused:

> Much of the history that is being made in the Second League these days must be written around the wonder goal getting boy, Crilley, who has several times taken Alloa round a nasty corner. Already his name has travelled far beyond the Ochil Hills, and Alloa are contemplating handing out copies of the commandment which forbids coveting to all strangers who strike the town.

Surprisingly, even rival town and team newspapers joined in, the *Stirling Observer* offering that 'Crilley is a wonderful player, not far removed from being the best centre in Scotland', and a sore *Stirling Sentinel* masking its praise behind an industrial jibe: 'Regarding Crilley, he is the idol of Alloa. I don't blame the bottle-blowers.' Wee Willie's haul at King's Park upped his running total to 23 in 16 matches. By the season's end, he had scored 49 league goals, inspiring Alloa to an emphatic title win. In the town, Crilley was hero-worshipped, with songs ringing from terrace and barroom alike:

> Come away wee Willie Crilley, we like to see you play,
> For your size you're a big surprise, you're the marvel o' the day,
> Long may you wear the black and gold you treat us to a tee,
> Oh tricky Willie Crilley of Alloa AFC.

That particular number was written by Willie McKenzie, father of Gutty and a devoted Wasps fan. Even he would have recognised that Crilley was no longer Alloa's secret wee genius and that his star was rising, as an article in *Sports Magazine* demonstrated:

> [Crilley is] the wonder man of modern football, and the wonder does not lie in the fact he has scored over 50 [league and cup] goals, but that he should be such a successful centre-forward although he stands only five feet two in his socks.

Following the final game of the term, Celtic signed Crilley for £800. Yet after just three appearances at Parkhead, he returned to The Recs, the Boy

Alloa's title-winning side of 1921/22 and some men in magnificent hats.

Wonder coming home. Plagued by injury, Crilley only occasionally flashed brightly in a Wasps team easily relegated from Division One, before leaving for a new life in the United States in the summer of 1923. Wee Willie died in Brooklyn, aged 51, far away from the glass-blowers whose Saturday afternoons he had illuminated.

Fifteen years on from Crilley's departure, an Alloa promotion side emerged again built on one man's brilliance, this time that of manager Jimmy McStay. Over the 1938/39 season, he crafted a multi-talented side remembered by the *Alloa Advertiser*'s chief reporter, Willie McLaren:

> The immaculate works of Hugh McFarlane at centre-half, the impeccable precision of McDonnell's passes, the heart-warming running of Moore, the drive and power of Gallagher and Gillespie, the subtleties of wee Smith, and the touchline trickery and shooting by Fitzsimmons were all part and parcel of an Alloa side which was labelled 'Entertainment'.

As well as winning a place in Division One, McStay's team of engineers and coopers gave The Wasps one of their greatest ever Scottish Cup runs. As in the days of Crilley, townsfolk rallied to support the team. A crowd of 13,000 saw a 3–2 victory at home to Dunfermline, with the *Alloa Advertiser* reporting 'All industry had been brought to a standstill and the terracing was thronged with mill girls, shop girls and shop keepers. Everybody was there.' That result meant a tie against the mighty Hibernian in Edinburgh, and a surfeit of stories since filed under 'romance of the cup'. It was an afternoon fondly recalled in an *Official Commemorative Handbook* some years later:

> Alloa station had never seen such a throng. Men and boys dominated but there was enough feminine colour to complement the black and gold favours worn by almost everyone. The time was just after noon, Saturday 4th March 1939 and the folk, in happy holiday mood, awaited the first of the three special trains to whisk them to Waverley Station in Edinburgh. Not only trains were being filled; service buses were triplicated and special buses were hired; private cars were filled and on the move.

The ever Alloa-mad Willie McKenzie cycled to Edinburgh, hopefully without the aid of riding tips from his son. In total, 6,000 fans made their way south-east and saw their team tear into Hibs, taking a 1–0 lead. 'They got the shock of their lives,' continued the *Handbook*, 'Alloa took over and with Moore unstoppable on the right and Gillespie worrying the life out of Miller, Hibs' defence was flying distress signals.' The embattled home side reacted with panache, scoring two quick goals, before the moment which, the report continued, turned Alloa's afternoon:

> A swinging bit of play left Fitzie on his own on the left in a splendid position. His left-footer beat [Hibernian goalkeeper] Kerr, hit the underside of the bar and the ball was at least a yard over the line: [referee] Mr Carruthers again said 'No'.

The Wasps' 'goal' would have pegged the match at 2–2. Instead, Hibs claimed a decisive third. The *Daily Express* agreed that the home side were 'definitely lucky to be in the semi-finals. Alloa had their First Division opponents tucked underneath their arms and it remains a mystery why they did not spank them soundly.' Moving seamlessly from one cliché to another, McStay's team could now forget about the romance of the cup and concentrate on the league.

In the final match of the season, Alloa needed to equal or better the result of promotion rivals East Fife. Their opponents at The Recs were Brechin City and once again, wrote Willie McLaren, the football club became the focal point of the town:

> The Alloa folk had again tasted football at its best. Black and gold were to be seen everywhere. Players were greeted in the streets on training nights and escorted from the station to The Recs on Saturdays. [Vice-chairman] Willie Stanton's grocer's shop window was surrounded by fans on a Thursday night – Saturday's team was posted there after the weekly meeting. And fitba' was the talk of the home, factory and town.

At The Recs, locals were horrified to see an aggressive Brechin side take the lead. From there on, the *Alloa Advertiser* relayed, 'City defenders mowed into the Alloa forwards like a scythe through foliage.' Bruised, The Wasps scrambled an equaliser that would potentially be enough for promotion. Brechin's tactics hardened from the cynical to the brutal, with one late tackle provoking a pitch invasion by a number of irate home supporters. Alloa would not be deterred and, overcoming the loss to injury of two players, emerged victorious. For some home supporters celebrations could wait, as the *Advertiser* continued:

> Spectators swarmed on to the field en masse. The intentions of most of them was to settle their differences with the Brechin players. Many of the latter were kicked or interfered with.

With the stooshie cleared, manager Jimmy McStay was hoisted aloft by a public blissfully unaware that war was about to rob them of their day in the sun. While the 1939/40 Division One season proceeded, as the *Alloa Circular* detected in its report of a match at Partick Thistle, priorities had shifted:

> A staunch contingent of Alloa supporters, determined to cast off for a spell the gloom engendered by the international situation, accompanied their favourites to Firhill Park on Saturday. Summer-like conditions favoured the game but the prevailing sense of uncertainty restricted the attendance to around the 5,000 mark.

When league action recommenced in 1945, Alloa were placed in the same Division Two as Ayr United. They have not returned to Scottish football's highest division.

* * *

At the peaceful, peacetime Recs in September 2009, the ambience was one of a village fête. Cadet soldiers shook buckets and people walked by, not through complete stinginess but in fear of pulling out a £2 coin from a pocket of change. Staunchly white arms and legs offset bright red faces that had fallen asleep in the beer garden. Outside the club shop, a man in golfing casuals held a foam cup of Irn-Bru in one hand and a hot dog in the other. He gazed frequently and guiltily from side to side, as if waiting for his wife to return from the tombola stall to berate him. When the teams were announced it felt like an uncouth interruption to the bucolic calm, but even these were enunciated in the flat tones of a lost child announcement.

In the ground's sunny open areas, spectators clustered to lean over the hoardings and achieve that perfect back of neck tan. I moved behind

Alloa's defensive wall melts into insignificance beneath The Ochils.

the goal to the Clackmannan Road end for one of the finest views from a football stadium, that of The Ochils. Illuminated under a holiday-blue sky, the hills curved and pointed dramatically and distractingly. I found myself thinking of the countless fans who had stared bleakly at them through home defeats down the years. This was also the place behind which Gutty McKenzie plied his trade as a bottle collector, with fans hurling their empties over for him to collect.

The division's top two teams sprinted onto a pitch luminous with the combination of plastic and dazzling sunshine. Along one side, the functional Main Stand quickly filled, while opposite 500 Stirling followers raised their hands to their foreheads as pointless visors. The surface lured both sides into copious passing and reduced the threat of thunderous derby tackling to zero, the spirit of Brechin 1939 exorcised by the plastic priest.

With a quarter of an hour gone, unable to join in with the delicate tip-tapping upfield, the Alloa goalkeeper, David Crawford, hoofed a clearance forward. Doing an impression of Riverdancing table football players, the Stirling defence advanced as one, allowing Alloa's Andy Scott to run between them and towards the goal, a protestor breaching non-contact riot police. Scott paused, awaited the bounce and kindly assisted the ball over the keeper and finally into the net. The goal roused only a reserved, cricket-like reaction from the Alloa faithful. Some were clearly shocked, others wary of any sudden movements stinging their lobster skins.

Behind the goal, the slight commotion woke Alloa's youthful Ultras, a teenage collective dressed in Hawaiian shirts and shorts. They were soon working through a fine array of homophobic chants as only 13-year-old boys dressed in pink can. Indeed, it was from them I learnt to the tune of 'Seven Nation Army' that 'all of Stirling are gay.' Come on lads, if you're going to indulge in prepubescent bigotry, at least get the grammar right.

The fixture meandered to half-time with more polite passing and well-mannered tackling. Though the football was pleasing on the eye, it made me realise just how important to the game the bursting noise of a 50/50 challenge or the crowd's ire following a rash tackle is. This was like the feeling of arriving to see your favourite band and hearing the lead singer announce 'we're just gonna play stuff from the new concept album tonight.'

During the break substitutes repeatedly hammered shots into the stand, and a woman beside me sheltered her pie as if it were a child facing the firing squad. When play resumed, the away side charged forward impressively and became addicted to winning and misusing corners. In goal for Alloa, David Crawford parried, caught and punched, and in front of him centre-half Scott Buist was on an heroic mission to block the ball with every area of his body. This pleased me: while reading The Wee County News in the pub, I had been concerned about the impact upon morale of Biscuitgate, described therein by captain Scott Walker:

The guys have a shooting competition every Thursday night at training – the loser buys the biscuits. Buist lost a few weeks back and decided to crunch up all the biscuits and put them in Crawford's bag and all over his clothes. Crawford did get his own back, though, when he mashed up a banana and put it in big Buist's pocket.

The days of Deep Heat in jockstraps are clearly over, with the focus now on baking and fruit. I blame that Arsene Wenger. When Buist did miss Stirling crosses (that mulched banana can take ages to get out of your fingernails), they generally rolled out for goalkicks. Tired and increasingly clueless, the away side began to resemble horses kicking a medicine ball around in treacle. The whistle, a shot putting them out of their misery, finally sounded and at last The Recs roared. The derby had been won, the Wasps were top of the league and all was good in old Alloa. The town that had been enchanted by Crilley and carried McStay on its shoulders once again saluted its community club and, like the child in the station statue, looked forward.

CHAPTER THREE

Cowdenbeath

Cowdenbeath 5 v 0 Peterhead,
10 October 2009

WITH ITS INSIDES mined hollow, Cowdenbeath High Street is drooping. Over the last century, subsidence has created a hill out of a steady rise. Where once the entire street could be seen from end to end, now the railway bridge acts as a barrier between the gentler southern and steeper northern halves. Close to the station at Christie's Bargain Store, the geographical uncertainty of life had bred a gung-ho attitude: judging by paint mark scars, its proprietors had recently removed the number in their 'Original 99p Shop' sign as if pondering a price increase to £1.

Further down the street, a slightly hirsute woman stood outside Big Impressions 'Ladies Plus Size Fashion' apparently making an obscene hand gesture, but on closer inspection cradling and shaking some mint imperials. On a nearby corner sat Gordon Brown's constituency office, standard issue red curtains covering every inch of window. A lone sign advertised opening hours, and scrawled among its print in red felt-tip pen were the words 'Knock on window and I will let you in.' I stood, imagining the now ex-prime minister himself had scribbled the invitation and hoping there was a similar one at 10 Downing Street. Brown's office is only a short walk from the old Miners' Welfare Institute building on Broad Street, a large and slightly daunting, school-like mansion. There, during the 1984 strike, the corridors and rooms were the hub of local action, its soup kitchens brimming with talk of solidarity and Scargill. Latterly, it housed Bar 39, possibly the only place in town to offer paper receipts with your pint.

Back on the High Street, there was no trace of the old tollbooth that had been the epicentre of this former hamlet, later a barber's shop and finally a howff. It was through there that Queen Victoria passed, pithily noting in her journal 'We changed horses at Cowdenbeath', which back then passed for a celebrity endorsement. The wind blew a tinny version of Oasis' 'Don't Look Back in Anger' across from Cowdenbeath's Central Park ground, offering a rueful theme tune for Saturday shoppers lingering in Farmfoods' doorway. In Budgie's Hardware, a man called Malk advertised of 'Work wanted to hang curtin poles and curtins etc.' His advert was one of many offering poorly spelt services and sales, and it occurred to me that it was not the recession that left so many High Street shops unoccupied, but a secondary, underground economy. In one final strike at capitalism, the citizens of this historically radical town were operating outside the market. That, or Malk just liked writing on postcards.

Back under the railway bridge and uphill, Vendetta Tattoos was heaving, word of their 'Get your hit list on an arm – five names for the price of three' offer having spread. I crossed Stenhouse Street, formerly home to the school of Jennie Lee, Scottish socialism's First Lady, and James Whyte Black, a Nobel Prize winner who invented the beta blocker, before being pulled over the road by the magnetic force of a veterinary shop noticeboard. There, numerous flyers gave notice of missing pets: 'Have you seen this cat? He answers to the name of Clarence' (I always wish 'answers to the name of...' was followed by 'it's not his real name. I don't know where he got it from.'); 'Missing. African Grey Parrot. Grey with a red tail. From Sinclair Drive. 30/09/09'; 'Dog missing. King Charles Spaniel. Female. Neutered, 10 years old. Black/white. Missing from Kelty. She is deaf. Answers to the name of Fido.'

Next door on the town hall's 'Information' board there were no such notices from which the pain of others could be ridiculed, chiefly because there was no actual board to display Information on. Peering through its empty iron frame, I wondered if this was a political statement from an authority that once ran the Red Flag from its pole. It was a question I'd never get the answer to, there being nowhere to check.

The town hall is a dignified building, its modest clocktower squatting above dusky red stone. It is civic but restrained, reflecting local democratic traditions. A flagstone records service and civilian losses in World War Two, the latter category including three Bairds and two Hunters, killed by a bomb on Stenhouse Street. Beneath, a lamentably fresh engraving marks the death of local soldier PTE Jamie Kerr in Iraq. Just 20, Kerr fell in Basra in the same week his MP became Prime

Minister, two very different lives linked by one High Street and a far away war.

I continued upwards beyond the burnt-out carcass of the Crown Hotel, a recent fire leaving nothing but its splendid limestone shell. Outside here a century ago John Slora perched one of Cowdenbeath's portable picture theatres and showed silent movies. From beside the stage, Slora provided his own sound effects, meaning that an entire generation of children grew up thinking that galloping horses in America made the noise of toffee tins being banged together.

Doing my own entirely accurate impression of a seriously unfit man, among a row of stylish villas I mounted the steps at the far north end of the High Street and spluttered my way up to the town's main war memorial and its finest view. From there, Cowdenbeath bustles along silently in the foreground while Fife unfurls as if a child's car mat, its implausible mix of rolling green hills and hazy industry suddenly comprehensible. Not for the first time in Fife, I was reminded of Teesside, where the Cleveland Hills are a backdrop to the towers of silver and smoke which inspired the look of Ridley Scott's *Bladerunner*. Taking in Cowdenbeath and thinking through what I'd seen earlier, I couldn't help but admire its resilience. By rights, the town should be dead and buried: mining, its reason for existence, ceased long ago and very few people earn or spend money here today. Yet it doesn't feel like a victim, nor look too shabby. Far from it.

Here, resilience is in the blood. From the war memorial can be seen Mossmorran, once devastated by one of many local mining disasters. In 1901, 16 miners were deep below the dense surface of the Donibristle pit when an avalanche of peat and water crashed in. The colliers quickly became trapped; the people of Cowdenbeath reacted by darting to their rescue. Shortly afterwards, the events were outlined in a book, *Character Studies of the Miners of West Fife*:

> A very praiseworthy feature is the willingness with which a miner will risk his life in the hope of saving the life of a fellow-workman. In such unfortunate disasters as Donibristle there was no need to call for volunteers to risk their lives.
>
> Notwithstanding the fact that experience taught them the great risk, volunteers vied with each other to make a last effort to rescue the imprisoned men. And when all was over and the

roll was called, who was found missing? Four of the original party of volunteers. This action portrays the true miner. Who in their class would not have done likewise?

Eight men died that day, with the last body lying undiscovered for 14 weeks. Airing wider concerns about the mining industry, Jimmy Murray, a poet-barber whose shop occupied the old tollbooth, wrote:

Was it an accident, or was it neglect?
Well perhaps it is hard now to say
But we all know the men lost their lives
While toiling for five bob a day.
Was that all their poor lives were worth
Was it enough to keep want from the door?
Well our masters they don't give a snuff
They swear they can't pay any more.

Mining was both Cowdenbeath's tormentor and its maker. Until the late 19th century, 'Cowdenbeath' had been only a small cluster of farms. When machine technology advanced, companies began to exploit a landscape long suspected of blanketing bounteous supplies of coal. Migrants converged on Fife from across Scotland and later Ireland to earn a living eking 'black diamonds' from the earth. In the 1870s, Cowdenbeath's population rose from a farming handful to 1,500, and by 1890 that figure had doubled. As the number of inhabitants rose, working and living conditions fell in this dirty new town. In his 1941 *History of Cowdenbeath*, Robert Holman described the visit of local MP Augustine Birrell:

He came in a cab, and in High Street he asked his agent what place they were in. On being told it was Cowdenbeath, he remarked that if he stayed in a place like that he would get drunk every night.

The town Birrell visited was a dark, unrefined one where the comfort of locals came a poor second to the financial greed of mine owners. As Holman continued:

There were two seasons in the year, one when there was mud and the other when there was 'stoor'. It was not a rare thing to see a foot passenger leave behind him or her a shoe on the sidewalk and have to hop back to retrieve it or wait until some kindly disposed person retrieved it.

Reacting, the town's decision-making organ, the Beath Parochial Board, met in the backroom of a butcher's shop to formulate a plan for independent burgh status and with it the power to create an infrastructure. With that granted, elections were held and nine councillors returned. It was far from the most competitive of races. Candidate Archibald Hodge made only one speech, recorded as 'Well, if ye pit me in I'll be pleased, but if ye dinna want me and dinna pit me I'll be better pleased.' Unperturbed by apathy, the new council formally settled on the name Cowdenbeath, installed gas-powered street lighting and laid pavements, which rapidly became a tourist attraction. It was at this point that councillor James Laing announced excitedly 'Without doubt Cowdenbeath is the Chicago of Fife', which was either a piece of admirable optimism or the result of an all-expenses fact-finding junket to look at Illinoisan sidewalks. Laing carried on, announcing that the High Street 'would soon resemble Princes Street in Edinburgh', a not entirely incorrect prediction – both now contain shops flogging porcelain pipers for a quid. It was a time of speculation, a coal rush from which a town sprouted.

In the early 20th century, Cowdenbeath's population reached 14,000, three quarters of whom were employed by the Fife Coal Company, Britain's largest mining enterprise. Despite pavements and lampposts, living locally remained unpleasant. Miners lived primitively and pokily in hovels swiftly erected by pit owners beneath the shadow of the bing, sharing in the constant threat of death and disaster. Yet their exploitation did not breed submission, but a sense of togetherness.

The solidarity felt between miners and their families found voice in left-wing politics, a constant in the town's history. It was here in 1875 that one of Britain's largest Co-operative Societies was founded, and here a century later that William Sharp was elected as Britain's first ever Communist Provost, his beat including a street named Gagarin Way in tribute to the Soviet space hero. In between, French activist Lawrence Storian chose to launch a branch of the Anarchist Communist League in Cowdenbeath, and Willie Gallacher, the first Communist to reach the Commons, became the local MP. Perhaps unsurprisingly, it was in

Cowdenbeath that the British government at one time perceived the threat of Bolshevik revolution.

In the spring of 1921, local miners were locked out of their pits after refusing a 25 per cent wage cut. On 4 April, they held a rally in the Empire Theatre and marched through town accompanied by the Beath Pipe Band. The marchers were astonished to see a chimney smoking at the Dalbeath Pit, given that among their number were those who fired its furnaces. As one, the crowd made for the mine's boiler room where they found colliery officials working to keep machinery running. A number scarpered but one, William Spalding, was unable to elude the baying mob and found himself seized and carried away. After parading their human spoils through town the miners settled on Union Street and, rejecting calls for more violent action, attempted to stage a meeting with Spalding. They were soon interrupted by a robust police charge. Batons of the law met with the miners' pebble missiles, and Spalding was bundled onto a tram away from the ruckus. With the area rapidly cleared, a temporary calm descended upon Cowdenbeath.

The following morning, newspapers carried stories claiming that the miners were plotting a revolution with Cowdenbeath as its epicentre. This rumour-mongering was taken seriously enough for concerns to be raised at Cabinet level that a Soviet-style uprising was in the offing, and foster a feeling that government authority would have to be reasserted. Nine days after the battle of Union Street, a convoy of buses arrived in Cowdenbeath before sunrise. On board were a crew of soldiers and marines, instructed to place the town under martial law. As the *Dunfermline Press* reported, 'rate payers woke up to find that the burgh had been converted into what was virtually an armed camp.' Soldiers were instructed to guard pit heads and assist the police in arresting alleged insurrectionists. Eight men were detained and transferred to Dunfermline, the strains of 'The Red Flag' reverberating as they were thrown into cells. All were found guilty of various disturbances, with three imprisoned for a year. Though the mines slowly returned to action, Cowdenbeath's rebellious spirit could not be quashed. In 1926, upon hearing that striking miners were planning a raid on local armouries, Communist Party leader Harry Pollitt rushed north to persuade Fifers that the rest of Britain was not yet ready for revolution. Chicago was doing a good impression of St Petersburg.

* * *

Thoughts of mining and politics as two of the intertwined ingredients that held Cowdenbeath together led me to thoughts of another: beer. Back on the High Street, I went in search of The New Goth, a perfect watering hole for those who like a dose of history with their pint. Disappointingly for some, the pub is not named after a Goth version of the 'New Man' (perhaps a New Goth would smile a bit and be in touch with his masculine side). The pub's name comes, in fact, from its former life as an establishment run under the Gothenburg System.

When a Cowdenbeath miner's shift was complete and the underground hell in which he sweated left behind for another day, his relief was often channelled through the bottle. Augustine Birrell had not been far from the mark. Alcohol provided a release and, sensing the growth of a droothy town, publicans swarmed in. At the same time, a local Temperance Movement emerged to ward miners off the demon drink. Perched somewhere in between the two were advocates of the Gothenburg System, newly exported to Scotland from the Swedish city. Believers in Gothenburg principles accepted that alcohol consumption was inevitable and argued that a majority of pub profits should be put to social use, turning bad into good. In the mining communities of Kelty, Newtongrange and East Whitburn, Gothenburg pubs were created and each run on the principle of profit redistribution. To discourage session drinking, the pubs were characterless inside – think Slug and Lettuce with a social conscience – and the sale of spirits limited. Cowdenbeath's Gothenburg opened in 1901 and adhered to those same principles. In its *Rules of the Cowdenbeath Public House Society Limited*, shareholders pledged to take a dividend of no greater than five per cent, with 'surplus profits applied to such purposes of public or *quasi* public utility in the Burgh of Cowdenbeath or neighbourhood.' The Goth's 'Bevvy for Benefit' principles funded a number of local improvements including the town's public park, opened in 1911 and used by 20,000 miners for a mass rally during their 1926 strike, another aspect of Cowdenbeath's interlinked nature. It must have provided a fantastic excuse for the quaffing of that seventh pint – 'if I don't have this, there'll be no new climbing frame for the kiddies.'

Today, the proprietors of the Goth have certainly adhered to one founding principle, that of an unwelcoming appearance. Outside, the paintwork is modelled on the skin of a chain smoking 97-year-old rhinoceros and a weed the size of a Christmas tree sprouts from the side door. A white 'Menu' board in the window is blank, another victim of the High Street information thief. At the bar, in an ideological shift as seismic as Labour's dropping of Clause IV, there is fiscal encouragement to drink spirits, a single shot leaving change from £1. I sat with my disconcertingly vague pint of bitter and tried to picture the scene here a century ago, a feat made easier by the film of coal-like dust peppering the room's edges. Here, filthy miners would cram to gulp and laugh away their life beneath the town, with political discussion in this characteristically socialistic pub always likely. When Saturday came, many of them would find further release across the road at Central Park. Supping up, I continued in their footsteps.

With pits, politics and pubs, football was one of the four entwined graces that dominated life here. It was miners that made up most of the crowd once they had won themselves free Saturday afternoons and spilled out of hostelries into the ground. On the pitch, the starting XI was often staffed entirely by their colleagues from the pit, and the team rapidly assumed 'The Miners' as their nickname.

To learn more of the interconnectedness of local life, I spoke to Ian Rankin, a man more associated with Edinburgh but, like his most famous literary creation, resolutely a Fifer, and one schooled in Cowdenbeath at that:

> There was that sense of solidarity. My Dad was not a miner but every one of his brothers was and he had five of them. Both his sisters had married miners. It was very much in the blood. The miners provided for the towns; they paid for the swimming pool – I remember when Cardenden got a swimming pool in the late '60s. That was paid for by miner subscription, and I'm pretty sure the snooker hall was the same thing. There'd be trips to take kids to the seaside. There was a real sense of community about the place.
>
> There was no doubt the football went hand in hand with this working class community. There was a sense that the miners put a lot into the towns, and the football club put a lot into the town and the town put a lot into the football club, and there was that

pride that a lot of the players were born locally. Mining, solidarity, football, it all seemed to be linked. Willie Hamilton was our MP, and he was very anti-monarchy. We had councillors who were hardline old Communists. A lot of working class solidarity, a lot of left-wing politics, but also a place that had a real pride if you did well. If our footballers did well and went off to play for English teams: great. We were really proud of them. There wasn't that thing you get in some areas of British culture where if you do well then you're beyond the pale. We were very proud of people that did well especially if they were self-motivated, which of course footballers are. There is that thing in Scotland about the democratic intellect and the self-made man. We're supposed to like it when people do well through hard work and plugging away – if you don't get it handed to you on a plate and you deserve what you get when you succeed.

Until its closure in 1960, the winding gear of Cowdenbeath's Number 7 pit soared over Central Park's Main Stand, a symbol of just how much the fortunes of the football club rested on those of the collieries. When lean times engulfed underground Fife, attendances fell. They dropped too after the nationalisation of mines in 1947, following which pitmen earned enough money to travel further afield for their football, and to Glasgow. Cowdenbeath's average crowd for the 1947/48 season was 5,600. Five years later it had fallen to 2,800.

At around the same time as that second figure, the *Official Guide to Cowdenbeath* boasted:

> Through the medium of its football club the name of Cowdenbeath has been brought before the sporting public of Britain with consistency for over half a century.

Though much of this notoriety was attained by events on the pitch, headlines were regularly courted off it as the club lurched between crises. In 1909, four years after joining the Scottish Football League, members of the board were eventually defeated in their bid to close the indebted company down. From 1932 to 1935, crippling debts left Cowdenbeath permanently on the brink, with only the generosity of locals saving them from the abyss. It was a similar story at the end of World War Two as the Supporters' Club oversaw a public appeal to meet £2,000 worth of liabilities, and from 1956 when a new Cowdenbeath Football Supporters' Association donated £26,000 over five years. This pattern continued through the second half of the last century and into this. As costs continued to far outweigh income, Central Park was used for pony trotting, speedway and finally stock car racing. Money-spinning plans to move the football club out of the town, mirroring the reviled 'franchise' relocations of Meadowbank Thistle and Wimbledon, surfaced, with transfers first to Glenrothes, then Dublin and most recently the Edinburgh home of junior league Spartans FC mooted and vehemently resisted by fans.

Supporters' organisations have long played a key role at Cowdenbeath and continue to do so. Those that throw themselves into fundraising and campaigning now have a proud sense of their club's history. With the pits gone, the politics softened and the pubs closing, Central Park is a relic that binds. If its pensionable walls could speak, they would talk of 1920s glory days and mention first the team of miners that won promotion in 1924 and the following season finished fifth in Division One. That year, 1924/25, was arguably the greatest in their history and began amid restless anticipation in West Fife, as the *Cowdenbeath and Lochgelly Times* reported on the eve of the new term:

> The Cowdenbeath supporters are now anxious to see the baptism of their team to First Division football, and to judge for themselves the team's prospects in their new sphere.

The squad of pitmen they turned out to see was a slight, skilful one, with average height no greater than five foot nine. It was crammed with talented footballers: goalkeeper John Falconer, who once saved three penalties in one match; James 'Hooky' Leonard, a crowd-delighting genius, rated by Robert Holman as having a 'hectic but brilliant career', his fondness for Friday nights in Cowdenbeath's pubs matched only by his fondness for tormenting opponents; and Willie Devlin, a goalscoring colossus who ended the season on 33, Division One's highest.

With their attacking panache came a defensive vulnerability and fine wins were often followed by heavy defeats. As the *Cowdenbeath and Lochgelly Times* put it following a 4–0 drubbing at Ayr, 'There is no half-way with Cowdenbeath. They either mak' a spoon or spill a horn.' The next weekend, league leaders Airdrie visited Central Park and were defeated, as, a few weeks on, were Celtic, by 3–0. The Miners soon secured enough points for their outstanding final position. 'The season has been remarkable for Cowdenbeath,' wrote the local paper, 'Who would have thought in their first year of membership they would take fifth place in the First Division?'

Much of the team's success was founded on a sense of solidarity carried out of the pit and onto the pitch. In a diary of the club's 1928 German tour published by the *Dunfermline Journal*, captain Willie Rankin disclosed details of the squad's train journey from Edinburgh:

Willie Stewart, from the late 1920s a tricky Miners winger who was eventually transferred to Manchester United. Never has Fife seen such a magnificent quiff since.

> Stories and singing whiled away the time until bedtime, and then the spirit of socialism set in strong so that the players did not see why the directors should have pillows and they should have none. So a raid took place, and the players were triumphant as they bore off the spoils of the campaign in the form of pillows.

In the Hungry Thirties, with finances strained, European tours seemed a tender and unlikely memory even given the efforts of the outrageously gifted inside-forward Alex Venters. After he departed for Rangers, the team slipped and by the start of the 1934/35 season were back in Division Two. By 1938/39, The Miners had rebuilt sufficiently to once again win promotion as champions ahead of Jimmy McStay's Alloa. Their hero that season was Rab Walls, a *Roy of the Rovers* character waiting to happen. He scored 54 goals in 33 games, a total only ever bettered by Ayr's Jimmy Smith. Cowdenbeath won the title by 12 points and in the summer of 1939 locals eagerly awaited the return of top drawer football. Joy reigned in their world, especially in August when local MP W Watson told a Cowdenbeath Old Age Pensioners meeting that there would be no war, as the *Cowdenbeath Advertiser* related:

He said he had always believed they would not be engaged in war. He did not see any reason for an outbreak in hostilities. He thought there was sufficient common sense left in the world yet to see that any differences that existed were settled on common-sense lines.

In the week Watson made his speech, Central Park hosted Celtic, the same newspaper commenting of the away side's 2–1 victory, 'Cowdenbeath collected the honours and the sympathy. Celtic took the points and very little credit.' Within days of the game, led by right-back George Jordan, who had previously refused a move to Arsenal, several of the home line-up enlisted in the armed services, depleting Cowdenbeath's squad to the extent that they were soon unable to field a team. Staggeringly, the Scottish League fined The Miners £500 (take that, Hitler!), a sum that hastened their wartime closure. When football recommenced in 1945, Cowdenbeath were another club incensed to find themselves placed in Division Two. One man forever absent was Jordan, killed at Normandy aged just 27 years old.

The team were third bottom in that same second tier in 1949 when the League Cup quarter-final draw paired them with Rangers. Belying their position and a miserable lack of form, Cowdenbeath, led by talisman Alex Menzies, astonished the home side with a 3–2 victory at Ibrox in the first leg, making them the first lower division team ever to win there. Over the following week, talk of the second leg gripped the town. Even the Citizens' Advice Bureau got on board, dropping their normal role of helping consumers obtain refunds for faulty mangles to flog tickets. At kick-off, nigh on 26,000 people had convened at Central Park, a figure unimaginable ever since. On 89 minutes and 46 seconds, the score was 4–3 on aggregate. Cowdenbeath were going though. In the *Cowdenbeath Advertiser*, 'Old Stager' painted the scene:

> The atmosphere was tense as the minutes passed into seconds. Surely Wellington never longed more for Bloucher than did the crowd for the whistle to go. Then the blow fell. Rutherford glided in and gave Moodie no chance.

Rangers had equalised with 13 seconds remaining, forcing extra time. 'Old Stager' continued:

The shades of night were falling fast as the teams lined up for another strenuous half hour. Only then did the optimism of the crowd begin to falter. At the back of their mind was the fact that Rangers would be trained to the inch; full-time professional players, training and coached every day, as against the necessarily spasmodic opportunities for training of the part-time professionals of the home side. And so indeed it proved.

The away side scored a third goal, handing them a 5–4 overall lead at the tie's end. As the *Advertiser* suggested, Cowdenbeath had come 'within half a minute of registering the football sensation of the century.' The result gave fans hope that a return to better times was imminent. 'Old Stager' sounded a typically triumphant note:

> Cowden are definitely back on the map of Scottish football. Since the war, they have seen lean years, but undismayed, and not withstanding being the target for many bricks from their own friends, the directors and officials have never faltered to regain for the club some of its ancient glories.

It was a false dawn equalled 21 years later when The Miners spent a season, their last ever, in the top flight. For the next two decades, the club loitered, often without intent, at the league's lowest level. Then in the 1991/92 season, the recently-dubbed 'Blue Brazil' clubbed together and clawed themselves back into Division One, now the second level of Scottish football.

The class of 1992 is still lauded in Cowdenbeath, its memory kept alive in Ron Ferguson's superlative *Black Diamonds and the Blue Brazil*. As well as being a pleasing side to watch, the squad brought to an end 20 years for which the word 'underachievement' is a term of hyperbole. Another 20 years on, that season's right-sided midfielder John Wright warmly reminisces as he sits in his Kirkcaldy home. Although a childhood Raith Rovers fan and later player, it's the Blue Brazil that retain a hold over him:

> I seem to have an affection for Cowdenbeath. I dinna ken what it is. Just a wee feel. I went to watch them a few weeks ago and all the crowd were saluting. That '92 team gets treated like gods.

As he drifts back elsewhere – to the Central Park dressing room or floating in a cross – Wright speaks of 'the best team I played in, for everything: camaraderie, workrate, the lot. We played for the jersey.' As ever at Cowdenbeath, nothing ran completely smoothly. In April, as the promotion race approached its denouement, a fire broke out and destroyed the Main Stand outside and in:

> I picked the paper up the following day and saw it. The boys were gutted, and there was a lot of history in the stand lost. The next thing you know we're changing in Portakabins. Just a disaster, a nightmare time. You couldn't swing a cat. A wee scrawny shower. It put a downer on the club.

Wright and his teammates persevered with their charge and travelled to Alloa on the final day of the season with promotion only a draw away. Notwithstanding home crowds of between 300 and 400, several thousand away supporters accompanied them to Clackmannanshire, some overtaking the team bus ('Basically just a big potato bus. It turned everybody's heads on the motorways'). They saw their side cling on to a point and at long last become upwardly mobile. Sensing it would be rude not to in the circumstances, fans triumphantly invaded the pitch, and as Wright remembers 'it was bedlam. Fans on the pitch, trying to pull your boots off you, your jersey.' Supporters and players alike guzzled champagne deep into the Cowdenbeath night. With the post-Thatcher landscape leaving 3,000 of 11,000 inhabitants unemployed, it was an uncommon few hours of cheer. The team had once again provided the town with a release from its trying existence.

It was to be a brief respite as events that shocked the local public and surprised even the players unfolded over subsequent weeks. On 21 May, promotion-winning manager John Brownlie left the club, having been offered what he felt to be a derisory new contract. Cowdenbeath supporters were astonished that the man who had steered them to long-craved glory was gone. They were not alone, as John Wright attests:

> We all reported back for signing on terms on the Monday and still didn't have a clue what was happening. It wasn't until the end of the following week we found out, totally out of the blue. I found out in the paper.

On the eve of their return to the higher echelons of the Scottish game, Cowdenbeath were without a manager and a main stand. Further, a number of players threatened strike action over the departure of Brownlie and their own terms and conditions. Both inside and outside of the club, there was a feeling that chairman Gordon McDougall cared far more for Central Park as a motor sport venue than a football one. As Brownlie commented in *Black Diamonds*, 'perhaps if I drove a stock car I would have kept my job.' A disastrous year loomed. The team failed to win at home all season and accumulated just 13 points in total. On its mention, Wright still looks traumatised, and after a period of silence offers only 'That season was a disaster, and I took all the defeats home with me.'

The team were unable to suffer in dignified silence, their record-smashing run of bad form pricking the British media's voyeuristic conscience. Over three seasons, they failed to win at home for 101 weeks. Infamy breached even the parochial walls of my Yorkshire school playground, each miss-kicked sodden tennis ball being greeted with a derisory 'aaaaggghhhh, Cowdenbeath', bewildering on-looking dinner-ladies. Seventeen years on from those playground days, it was finally time for me to visit what John Wright wistfully called 'that special place.'

* * *

Beside Central Park, two Peterhead fans perused the meal deal board on the maroon pebbledash walls of the Shimla Palace Indian restaurant. Breaking with local tradition, the signs were packed with information, and the £7.95 Executive Lunch enticed this pair of north-eastern yuppies in. With no £7.95 Curious English Visitor meal on offer I went straight for the turnstiles, located in an off-white and blue wall resembling an abandoned cottage, only more charming and with a sign prohibiting cans, bottles and cartons (Cartons! Those Ribena-hurling yobs must've been back). I asked the teenage girl behind the Confession-like mesh if the supporters' bar was open. Far from knowing the answer, the perplexed girl didn't even appear aware she worked at a football ground, as if she'd been drugged and told this was the counter at Miss Selfridge.

In the sizeable space between the turnstile and the pitch, scattered vehicle parts suggested a cluttered farmyard rather than a football ground and acted as a reminder that other tenants dwell here. Stock car racing has taken place at Central Park since the early 1990s, the pounds of petrol-heads often swelling the football club's coffers for rare reasons other than malnutrition. Above the doors hang dual signs translating for each sport, but being an intrepid traveller I battled on through the language barricades and found the bar. There, 15 of us peered through rectangular windows onto the pitch as the players warmed up in front. It made me realise for the first time, and I had often wondered, what it would be like to watch a match played inside a giant fish tank. In a congenial but suppressed atmosphere similar to that of a wedding reception before anyone is drunk enough to dance, I sipped ale and read the fantastically-detailed programme. After 15 years of Premiership 'match magazines', I was genuinely shocked to find within its pages articles worth reading. It contained a number of winning puns too, such as a breezy column entitled 'That's Fife'. Mind, I was a little concerned that an advert for the National Strategy and Action Plan to Prevent Suicide might point to a less than entertaining playing style.

Inside the goldfish bowl, I sat in the smaller of the two conjoined main stands in front of the Peterhead contingent, less a travelling army and more a gang of curry-sated middle-aged blokes. The gang's vitriolic haranguing of Peterhead's players was incongruous given their liltingly

Life in the goldfish bowl.

pleasant accents, like hearing your granny swear. From the off, they
had much to gently bemoan as Cowdenbeath, pursuing their first promotion to Division One since John Wright's favourite year, eased to a
2–0 lead. For the away side, Bobby Mann continued to play the ball
out of defence with aplomb, a waddling elder statesman with more
Bargain Bucket banquets than ambassadorial receptions behind, or rather
in front of him. With feet full of talent and a stomach full to bursting,
the club captain's actions screamed the words 'cult hero'. Responding to
the scoreline, Peterhead threw on Scotland's most well-travelled player, A
Trialist. The gawky forward looked more likely to try out for a job as
an IT helpdesk officer than a footballer, and didn't help his cause by
later asking a prone injured teammate to switch himself off and on
again. On the Cowdenbeath bench, manager Danny Lennon achieved
the incredible feat of looking measured and authoritative while sat in
front of 23 used tyres on a folding chair from Argos's 1987 office range.
His team thrived, and in defence athletic centre-back Joe Mbu showed
little interest in letting any opposition player touch the ball. The only
blot was provided by the referee, who appeared jealous of the attention
lavished on the players and reminded all of his presence with a series
of elongated toots on his whistle.

At half-time, I hiked to the terracing on the opposite side of the
ground and leaned on a bright blue crush bar. From there, the pitch
was a fair distance away, undoubtedly a boon during lean times. Where
Somerset Park was daintily authentic, these brutal and exiled slabs of
concrete were industrial heritage, and for that every bit as worth pre-
serving as Ayr's home. At the pie hatch a hungry teenage lad muttered
to his friend about how long he'd been waiting for chips. From a side
room the woman serving them picked up his griping with sonar effi-
ciency and invisibly barked 'I'VE ONLY JUST PUT THE BLOODY
THINGS ON, SON.' When the match recommenced, I was pleased to
find the crowd on this side had an irrational hatred of the referee. Each
abuser took his turn as if singing in a round, and on the odd occasion
two volleys of calumny collided, an awkward, first date silence was
palpable between them. It had the feeling of a polite medieval market
square at stocks time. Occasionally taking a break from their bile, the
Cowdenbeath fans had much to cheer as their side fired in a further
three goals, finishing 5–0 winners. This team of scaffolders, postmen

and neoclassical ballet dancers (Brian Fairbairn, according to the official website) were playing football Falconer, Leonard and Devlin would have recognised. The only shame was the presence of just 271 spectators, a number as unfamiliar to the team of miners as neoclassical ballet (to a man they preferred Ballet Blanc). As the game wound down revving engines could be heard in the car park, and at the whistle's final protracted blow, stock cars rolled in and goal nets were removed with a number of footballers still to leave their pitch. The vehicles' rasping exhausts replaced the bellowing fans and petrol's whiff overcame that of chip fat.

Risking over-analysis of why I found Cowdenbeath, the team and the town, so strangely likeable, I turned to that man Ian Rankin for his own pithy take on the place:

Cowdenbeath was like a lot of Scottish towns, there was one main street you drove through. There was a beginning and an end and you were out again. And it had pubs that would serve you in your school uniform, so it was a delightful place as far as I was concerned.

Yet another use for Central Park is signalled on a terrace wall.

CHAPTER FOUR

Coatbridge

Albion Rovers o v o Annan Athletic, 21 November 2009

IN THE MIDDLE of the 19th century, George Coleman of County Tyrone took his cows to market. Once sold, they were ushered onto a boat bound for Scotland. As the crew prepared the vessel for sea, George leapt aboard. This impulsive act landed him first in Glasgow and then in the filthy industrial hive of Coatbridge. His story was one among thousands as the sons and daughters of Erin left Ireland's famine behind to toil in Lanarkshire, a belching, fizzing county of steel and coal. When George sailed, 1,000 Irish were arriving at the Broomielaw every week, many then traipsing en masse out of Glasgow in search of work. The *Glasgow Free Press* labelled Airdrie and Coatbridge 'the nearest thing possible to two Irish colonies'. By 1869, over a third of the Coatbridge population was Irish-born.

In the ever-present spirit of immigration to Great Britain, Irish arrivals undertook jobs often spurned by the indigenous population. They worked hard where the danger was greatest and played hard to find solace. Contemporary author Andrew Miller wrote of Irishmen labouring at the furnace jaw:

> Blast furnace men have always been easily distinguished from the rest of the community by the peculiar red and scorched appearance of their faces, caused by the intense heat to which they are exposed, a heat which creates in them a great thirst, and often a desire to quench it in something stronger than water. Many of them thus acquire habits of intemperance, and with all their good wages, they are generally, as a class, comparatively poorer than many of the labouring classes with scarcely half their incomes.

The migrants lived in hurriedly built single-end homes whose rapid abundance spawned distinct areas such as the imaginatively titled duo of Irish Land and Paddy's Land. Notorious among these was the 'Slap-Up', a cheek-by-jowl community of 2,000 people sited to the west of town. Above the law or undeserving in its eyes of protection, the Slap-Up was a lively enclave of booze, bets and brawls in which life ticked over with stoic jollity, much of it provided by unintentional street entertainers like Jobby (quiet at the back) McPeat, a chronic gambler with a lifetime of betting slips under his bunnet. It was an area fiercely protective of its identity, upheld in part by the fighting exploits across town of Poodle Porteus, the hardest man ever to be named after a Crufts winner.

Carving out a lasting template, Slap-Up residents ignored Albion Rovers in favour of Celtic, with coaches transporting fans to Parkhead every fortnight. Coatbridge then as now was also home to a large collection of Rangers fans, and when their paths crossed with the Bhoys of the Slap-Up, a friendly exchange of rosettes was never likely. On one occasion, Gers fans returning from a victory at Dundee rode home through the Slap-Up. There, locals waited by the canal armed with boat hooks. As the travellers passed, they were picked off one by one, hoisted into the air and suspended above the water. Never had sectarian tensions had such slapstick results.

Uglier aspects of Slap-Up life were cushioned by the feelings of collectivism, compassion and humour coursing through its animated streets and lanes. During the Depression, the Sheriff's officers took furniture as compensation for late rent, passing chairs and tables through front windows and onto the street. In the Slap-Up, those same items swiftly arose as if by magic and were forced back inside the house by neighbours as officials left via the front door.

The Slap-Up lived on until the early 1960s when its dilapidated, century-old 'temporary' housing stock was finally razed to the ground. A big part of Little Ireland disappeared, and the Coatbridge Irish, now second and third generation, melted into the general population. Indeed, they soon *were* the general population and remain so: a 2006 survey in *The Times* found Coatbridge to be the 'least Scottish' town in the country, and a third of the current population can still count relatives in Ireland. The mix has not always been harmonious, with the politics of Belfast frequently, and sometimes bloodily, replicated.

The Irish chose Coatbridge in the mid-Victorian era because there and then Scottish industry bloomed. They were complemented in various waves by migrants from Lithuania, Italy and the Highlands. The town and wider county of Lanarkshire offered bounteous raw materials, its coal and ironstone feeding voracious Britain and her Empire. Coatbridge mushroomed from a set of hamlets into the 'Iron Burgh', Scotland's colossal blast furnace and its eighth largest town. Iron-smelting dominated, though other industries grew in accompaniment, such as brickworks, boilermakers and a prolific confectionery sector that was to give the world Tunnock's tea cakes. The town's motto became 'To labour is to pray', and 'blind poetess' Janet Hamilton captured its urgent work ethic in 'Oor Location':

> A hunner funnels bleezin', reekin',
> Coal an' ironstone, charrin', smeekin';
> Navvies, miners, keepers, fillers;
> Puddlers, rollers, iron millers;
> Reestit, reekit, raggit laddies,
> Firemen, enginemen, an' Paddies.

Even the most ardent advocate of the dignity of labour could not romanticise when it came to the town's 'bleezin', reekin'" appearance. It may have been a heartland but its arteries were fatally clogged. One writer described Coatbridge as 'hell with the lid off', while commentator Robert Baird went further:

> There is no worse place out of hell than that neighbourhood. At night the groups of blast furnaces on all sides might be imagined to be blazing volcanoes at most of which smelting is continued on Sundays and weekdays, day and night, without intermission. From the town comes a continual row of heavy machinery: this and the pounding of many steam hammers seemed to make even the very ground vibrate under one's feet. Fire, smoke and soot with the roar and rattle of machinery are its leading characteristics; the flames of its furnaces cast on the midnight sky a glow as if of some vast conflagration. Dense clouds of black smoke roll over it incessantly and impart to all buildings a peculiarly dingy aspect. A coat of black dust overlies everything.

It was an otherworldly, at times surreal place in which 'anywhere in the streets at night one could easily read a newspaper by the light of the furnace tops.' When in 1885 Coatbridge gained burgh status, it should have been subject to the pollution-curbing measures of the Public Health Act. However, iron magnates pushed for and won an exemption, their factories' profitability placed above the health of those that lived in their shadows. As 1953's *Coatbridge Official Guide* concurred, 'if action were taken against the iron-masters because of the smoke-nuisance, the result would be a mortal blow to the main industry of the township.' Well into the 20th century it was observed that locals moved around with scarves or hankies across their faces, as if fresh from dental appointments.

There was little relief from the oppression indoors. Until burgh status was assured, no authority had responsibility for housing, meaning workers were forced to live in houses 'tied' to their jobs. As such, the sack meant eviction and the only way out of these 'cubicles of consumption'. The houses provided were barely worthy of the name, a truth that still held in 1914 when the Royal Commission reported on Rosehall Rows, an image of which illustrated George Orwell's *The Road to Wigan Pier*:

> They consist of four long parallel rows of single storey hovels. Most of them have no rones to carry the rainwater from the roof. Rainfall simply runs down the roof and then runs down the walls or falls down by chance as the wind decides. Coals are kept below the beds. The closet accommodation is hideous. A number of these hovels are built back to back. The closets outside are not used by the women. In some of the rows seven or eight people occupy a single room. The sanitary conveniences were in a state of revolting filth.

A few hundred yards from Rosehall loomed Gartsherrie House, its eight bedrooms outshone only by its plush tennis lawns. Dwelling there in Coatbridge's dirtiest boom years were the Bairds, a wealthy dynasty of iron masters. Such was their influence, the area became something of a company town, earning the nickname 'Bairdsville'. The family built their subordinates a theatre and even gifted them the land that became Cliftonhill, Albion Rovers' home. These philanthropic acts masked a ruthlessly exploitative operation that invested significantly more in country estates than municipal facilities. Every inch the tacky *nouveau riche* yearning to become part of the royal family by joining a polo club, the Bairds ploughed £1 million into country estates in the 1850s alone. Forty years later, Abingdon Baird threw £3 million of iron profits into women and horse racing, squandering the rest of his wealth. He died leaving 86 horses in his will, one for every swearword invented by iron workers to describe him.

With inequality so visible, protest and revolt was frequent. In 1820, an uprising was violently put down by the Lanarkshire Yeomanry. An unrelated Baird, John, was hanged and beheaded for his role in the rebellion, though the warning symbolised in that act could not curtail the area's radicalism. Armed forces charged a subsequent miners' strike, which served only to provoke further, lasting action that spanned the birth of the trade union movement through to the campaign to keep Ravenscraig steelworks open at the end of the 20th century. As in the Slap-Up, a brutal life was often made bearable and hopeful by social action and interaction. The people of Coatbridge, Irish and otherwise, would let nothing beat them.

* * *

In 1967, long before the eventual closure of Ravenscraig, Coatbridge's remaining furnace was mothballed. The air cleared, vast ex-industrial spaces gaped and the sci-fi world of bright white nights seemed like a dystopian dream. In keeping with the times, all that remains of the past is tourism, in the shape of Summerlee Museum of Industrial Life. I'm often concerned that sparkling attractions like this undermine the experiences of a miner or steelworker in Victorian Britain. There's something not quite right about being able to buy a feta and rocket panini next to an exhibit about the Mossmorran disaster. This feeling was encapsulated by the exclamation marks in a leaflet for Inveraray Jail museum I recently picked up:

> For minor offences the punishment could be thumbscrews, being branded with a hot iron or having your ear nailed to a post!

> Try out the punishments – the Whipping Table and the Crank Wheel!

Thankfully, those fears were soon allayed. I'd like to pretend it was the gravitas-drenched slogans chiselled into the iron gates of Summerlee –

The tram outside Summerlee. Orange in real life, honest.

'In memory of all those who lost their lives at work' and 'The past we inherit the future we build' – that did it. In reality, my affection was clinched by the thought 'OH WOW, A SHINY ORANGE TRAM'. Summerlee is so comprehensive, gripping, nonchalantly attractive and, well, ace that as you walk from coal mine to tram depot to canal basin you can't quite believe it costs nothing to get in. Indeed, the only downer was the nagging feeling that any minute I'd hear a security guard go 'there he is, he thinks he can just waltz in for free, the wee chancer'. In reality, I heard only a woman with the relentlessly hostile voice of a furious pneumatic drill. Even the offer to her child of a Fruit Shoot sounded like a threat, and I particularly enjoyed the additions of 'so I am' and 'so it is' at the end of her sentences. I presumed these words were spoken in sarcastic homage to *Coronation Street*'s Jim McDonald, but on reading up it seems to be a commonplace linguistic legacy of Little Ireland. I like the idea of words and ticks subconsciously keeping alive George Coleman *et al.* That's the greatest exhibition possible.

Eluding the security guard in my head for one final time, I left Summerlee for the town centre. At the museum gates an elderly lady pouring tea from a flask nudged her husband and said 'That's the rain on', a Scottish phrase pleasingly full of calm acceptance and lacking in complaint. As whoever is in charge of turning the rain on and off cranked it up a notch to 'pelting', I walked under a dingy maroon bridge carrying two of Coatbridge's many railway lines. At one time, the town had so many of these lines that it was impossible to come from the wrong side of the tracks. I splashed past the Airdrie Savings Bank, former location of the Royal Hotel where local doctors met in 1848 to discuss remedies for Coatbridge's cholera outbreaks over tea and cakes. In the end, houses were fumigated and whitewashed, and tar decanted onto the roads and set alight to purify the tainted air. Opposite rested the Whitelaw Fountain, shabby yet elegant, lamb dressed as mutton by smog. It was built in 1875 as a monument to the ending of congestion by the tram age, but soon moved as it got in the way of traffic.

With the rain now tumbling in shards, I stumbled upon the gentle hill of Academy Street. There the pink sandstone town library did its best in difficult circumstances to look dignified, while the Baird family's stately Gartsherrie Academy had been transformed, inevitably, into flats. By-passing a café/bar (make up your bloody mind) named The Mint, I opted for the Day-Glo bright lights of a greasy spoon next door in tribute to old Coatbridge and its newspapers by night. Inside, the ageing orchestra played a symphony of chinking cutlery on plates, and I settled down to a pot of tea and the *Airdrie and Coatbridge Advertiser*. The headlines therein were absurd when read among the warm sound of pensioners recounting tales told a thousand times before: Murder Leads To Knife Blitz; £100,000 bill after thugs start blaze; Boozed-up son shouted and swore at father; In court for hurling abuse at ex-girlfriend; Toilet tantrum led to wife assault; OAP in court after firing drunken volley of abuse at his wife. In the *Advertiser*, Britain was broken. From the rim of my tea cup, it looked in pukka shape. The true Coatbridge was probably somewhere in between, but what a boring newspaper that would make.

I trickled back down to the Main Street, a sad and familiar stretch of discount chains and empty shops. Still though, people smiled behind the raindrops and talked on corners, and the owner of Truly Scrumptious cafe left her outside furniture defiantly intact. St Patrick's Church punctu-ated the scenery of drab commerce pleasingly, its stained-glass windows enriching the street. The spire-strewn skyline in Coatbridge speaks of a town in which religion has long been a significant feature. A century ago, the Catholic Church watched over its flock, often benevolently, some-times imposingly. Through the 1890s, Father Hughes of St Augustine's in the Slap-Up took his campaign against the evil of parishioner-drinking to extreme levels, stalking and dragging men out of the pub, and smash-ing bottles of liquor with his cane. Hughes' confrontational demeanour split opinion: to the hardworking man who wished to drink away the oppression of the furnace, he was a menace; to others, a guardian amidst immoral squalor. Meanwhile, the *Coatbridge Express* depicted him as 'a priest of the most pre-possessing character. Handsome, witty, and full of zeal', and I'm sure that as he scythed through a bottle of Jamieson's landlords were thinking: 'my, what a good-looking chap.'

I walked on, past the sallow breeze-blocks of the Quadrant Shopping Centre, the front of which resembles a Russian oligarch's garish super yacht. It was this building that in 2007 sealed Coatbridge's receipt of a Carbuncle Award, the title of Plook on the Plinth, *Prospect Magazine*'s ever-so-helpful way of calling the town Scotland's ugliest. In their citation, *Prospect* claimed:

> The Quadrant shopping centre looks like it was lifted directly from the set of *Camberwick Green*. A new clock tower, which looks as if it was designed on the back of a beer mat, marks the town centre, a throwaway gesture compounded by the addition of some appalling public art-cum-street furniture.

Gimmicks like this may fuel a good old guffaw among those with job titles like 'media architect' (strictly all lower case, and perhaps even one word), but for ex-industrial towns they are the equivalent of kicking a man when he is down and then returning half an hour later with a steamroller to finish off the job (and in any case, Motherwell is much worse). As the town's reassuringly 'old' Labour MSP Elaine Smith said at the time, 'I think these awards are particularly unhelpful for towns like Coatbridge that have risen from the ashes of their industrial past and really improved themselves.'

Even Smith must admit that regional authorities, architects and planners have made mistakes; from all angles, the centre of Coatbridge is dominated by three elephantine tower blocks built in 1997. Continuing a gradual ascent to Cliftonhill, I watched as the third Chuckle Brother, estranged and overweight, rubbed his hands together in excitement before entering the Atlantic Fast Food Takeaway, soon to be named UK fish and chip shop of the year. While that was an award to be celebrated, Coatbridge would later 'win' another to be rued, the not-entirely-coincidental title of fattest town in Britain.

* * *

On the road to Cliftonhill, supporters shoehorned into buses wearing and waving their club colours. Unfortunately, those colours were the blue, white and red of Rangers stretching across the sated bellies of Ibrox-bound locals. I thought back to how busy Coatbridge's Celtic Shop had been earlier and felt a familiar strain of emptiness. It was almost as if the Wee Rovers a few hundred metres up the road didn't even exist.

The club was cut and pasted onto the league tables in 1882 when Albion and Rovers merged. They joined Division Two 20 years later, and were elected to the top flight in 1919. As one-time chairman Robin Marwick wrote in his affectionately colourful history of the club, *The Boys From the Brig*, 'joy was unbounded and when the news reached Coatbridge, the town was in a tizzy of excitement.' Albion faced competition attracting fans not only in Glasgow but from a crowded regional scene too, as the *Coatbridge Express* opined on the dawn of Rovers' first season in Division One:

> With four First Division organisations operating within half a dozen miles of one another, Lanarkshire enthusiasts should find themselves well regaled with league football. It is now up to the Rovers to prove themselves. They must have a team of worth in the first place, and in the second they must have an adequate home to receive the football elite next season. There will have to be no sleeping Rover from now on, since the old dog has got the chance of its life to make good and bring Coatbridge into the light of first-class football.

From the off, Albion's existence was a string of financial struggles very occasionally interrupted by the distraction of on-field success. After World War One they launched an appeal to raise funds from a hard-up general public existing on the government's Local Victory Loan scheme. When Cliftonhill opened on Christmas Day 1919 it was some way from completion as the board scratched around for money. With Coatbridge grit they carried on regardless, 8,000 fans rushing their turkey and missing *Eastenders* to excitedly attend a game with St Mirren. It mattered not to them that the players were forced to change and bathe in temporary huts. As the *Coatbridge Express* concluded, 'The Rovers' new ground is yet a long way from perfection, but all things in good time, and the managers must not be harassed into scamping what is necessary for a fine home.' That home benefitted in its early years from the dramatic presence behind the goal of Cliftonhill House, a Scottish baronial mansion which in its half-demolished state was suggestive of a ruined castle.

That same season, a fine Scottish Cup campaign distracted fans even further from Cliftonhill's work-in-progress appearance. Albion eased into the second round with victory against Shotts club Dykehead, in what the *Coatbridge Express* called 'a regular country Cup tie – a battle in the mud.' They were then granted a bye as macho-sounding Huntingtower FC chickened out of a tie, before dismissing St Bernard's of Edinburgh in round three, presumably distracting the opposition goalkeeper with a tin of Pedigree Chum. In the quarter-final, 13,000 supporters crammed into Cliftonhill to witness a 2–1 triumph over Aberdeen. The *Coatbridge Express* kept up the animal theme in its match report:

> The whole game was something akin to a batch of blood horses v a batch of Clydesdales. The Rovers were nippy, fast, and went straight at the hurdles. The Dons were willing but slow and cumbrous in their movements.

For a place in their first ever Scottish Cup Final, bottom of the league Albion faced Rangers, seven points clear at the league's summit. With a moniker destined for cup heroics, Billy Ribchester equalised for the underdogs to force a replay. As so often in a narrow failure to beat one of the Glasgow big yins, the local paper claimed Albion had won 'a moral victory'. The two could still not agree upon a decisive result, drawing 0–0 and necessitating a second replay. As the word 'plucky' groaned tiredly through overuse, Scotland expected Rangers to finally get their way with a handsome win. The Wee Rovers were having none of it: Willie Hillhouse wound his way through the Gers defence and made it 1–0. Guy Watson repeated the act, and Albion prepared for a Hampden tryst with Kilmarnock.

Coatbridge once again reached 'tizzy' status. Poems appeared in the press from eager supporters including this from an author who, perhaps tellingly, signed his or her name only as 'HH':

> On Rovers, on; one final test:
> Coatbridge from you expects the best;
> One final effort, staunch, together.
> And limbs bred on the Monkland heather
> Shall win the day.

Young fans procured a gigantic metal plate from a steelworks, named it the 'Coatbridge Gong' and painted 'The Death Knell' on its front. At Hampden, they banged it among 96,500 people, the highest ever attendance for a non-international match. That total stunned football 'Because,' the *Express* explained, 'two country cousins were the contestants the powers calculated on a 50,000 crowd.' The Hampden masses enjoyed a seesaw encounter, with Rovers' lead soon equalised and then eclipsed. When Willie Hillhouse levelled at 2–2, 'The outburst of cheering might have been heard at Coatbridge and Hillhouse himself was so overjoyed he danced a few steps of a hornpipe.' Being fundamentalist breakdancers, Killie were unimpressed by his moves and shortly afterwards blasted in a winner. As was customary, they were presented with the trophy in the Reading Room of the Queen's Park Pavilion to the sound of polite applause and notes of thanks, the 1920s version of fireworks, ticker-tape and a trophy-hoisting skipper screaming 'GET IN THERE YOU FUCKING BEAUTY!' Albion commemorated their run to the final by finishing bottom of the league.

For their entire history, Albion have rapidly switched from high to low. In 1922, Jock White became the first and last Rovers player to win a Scotland cap. The following season, the club were relegated. For a decade they toiled to reach the heady heights of mediocrity before securing promotion in 1934, their last title for 55 years. Even that achievement was tempered by the awareness that Cliftonhill remained ill-prepared for Division One football. That summer, the community intervened. Day and night volunteers built terraces and painted the ground,

Albion's 1923 relegation squad, including, front row second left, the most frightened footballer ever.

with many giving up their Fair Holidays to take part. These scenes were repeated two years on as local tradesmen built further terracing and a car park ahead of a cup match with Rangers. Though the Gers won 3–1, as the *Express* noted the match would be long remembered,

First because of the inspiring sight of 27,500 souls on the stands and enclosure and secondly because at one period in the early stages Rovers looked likely winners. The Coatbridge club did not get one smile from Dame Fortune. High falutin' football was almost impossible. On a frost-bound pitch football was almost out of the question. The footing was too uncertain and the ball light, bouncing, and extremely difficult to control. But what we got was strong meat – lusty booting, daring, dashing and rapid raiding.

A week later for a league game with Hibs, just 1,000 people were in attendance.

Albion's addiction to implosion continued down the years. After a triumphant elevation back to Division One in 1948, Coatbridge's finest took eight points from 30 matches, exited the cup with a 5–1 loss at Larbert, faced vitriolic and repeated barracking from their fans for lack of effort and saw the board disband following an emphatic vote of no confidence.

In 1961, the club's board launched a New Deal, changing Rovers' colours from blue and white to the now familiar primrose and red and

Laughing at a football during a Rovers training session in the 1940s.
Topless is a young Jock Stein.

appointing Dunky McGill as a player-manager with the resources to build his own squad. Albion finished 18th. Pre-season in 1964 saw them beat former player Jock Stein's Celtic 2–1 in the Glasgow Corporation five-a-side tournament, and 2–1 in a game with the full-strength European champions in 1967. In the first of those years, Albion had been threatened with expulsion from the league, and their place handed to bitter rivals Airdrie ('Oh! The disgrace for a club whose chequered career had seen service at the highest level but whose present form left much to be desired!' wrote Robin Marwick); previous to the second victory, they had scavenged a lawnmower, nets, corner flags and a sideboard from recently-deceased Third Lanark.

Supporting Albion has seldom been easy. As Marwick put it, 'lady luck has never had a peg in the Coatbridge dressing room.' Pleasures have to be taken where they can: in the 1970s, they came from the appetising, horrifyingly pun-able thought that the Rovers team included players named Curry, Sage and Rice; in the 1980s, from the dizzying talents and off-field shenanigans of Victor Kasule.

From 1982 until 1986, he plied his maverick trade at Cliftonhill and partied hard in the long hours between training and games. Born in Glasgow to Ugandan parents, Kasule was usually the only black footballer on the pitch. He made his Rovers debut in a tough era: when I spoke to him, John Wright had been being appalled at the racial abuse meted out to Kasule by his fellow professionals. Off the pitch, things were little better, with his first, scoring, game for the club coming weeks after a brutal riot during a cup tie with Airdrie. It was the cunning, elusive Kasule's talent, rather than his colour, that most Rovers fans noticed, as Marwick told me nearly three decades on, his eyes gleaming in reminiscence:

> Vic was a character and an amazing football player. The manager must have gone wild with him. He just did his own thing. He wasn't a team player. Didn't do as he was told. I've no doubt managers would just have to tell players to get the ball to him and let him do his thing. I saw him run half the pitch with the ball, beating half a dozen men, and he could score goals.

Kasule's charisma, recalled Marwick, meant 'He was ever so popular with the lassies. I've heard of him being chased down the road by parents'.

As intelligent as he was silver-tongued, this son of a zoologist and a teacher 'was a clever boy. He had already been to college and things before he came here. Aye, a likeable character.' Using the excuse of his prolific stint at Cliftonhill in the same team as Kasule, I spoke to Bernie Slaven, my own hero as a Middlesbrough supporter in the 1980s and '90s. On a crackling line from deepest Teesside, Slaven remembered:

> Vic, aye, the only black player in Scotland at the time, he was a skilful sort of winger. He could be lazy, he could be exciting. I remember we went to the Player of the Year Awards at a hotel. I'd been awarded Second Division player of the year, and somebody had bought a bottle of champagne for the table. He took the reins and he ordered about two dozen bottles of this champagne, and we're thinking: 'who's paying for this?' He was signing the bill with somebody else's name. As we left he was collared by the owner.

Encouragingly, if with a hint of after-dinner anecdotage, Slaven was unable to 'recall him receiving racial abuse, certainly not in the dressing room, and there weren't enough fans in that division to give anybody abuse, let alone racial abuse!' By the time Kasule left for Meadowbank Thistle in 1986, Slaven had given up his gardening job in Castlemilk and signed for Boro. The two met again when Kasule joined Shrewsbury Town, where his footballing comedy and outrageous, Hyam Dimmer-like dexterity won him idolatry. There, Kasule's on-field reputation began to overtake his off-field infamy, with *The Guardian* describing him as 'an armoured car of a winger with a cannon for a shot.'

Still, for every great goal there was an incident like the crashing of John McGinlay's car in a trip to the off licence after training, the singing of a George Benson song to a referee ('It was Give Me The Night,' he later said in an interview with *Goal* magazine. 'I couldn't believe that we were beating Palace, who had Wright and Bright playing. The ref said I was time-wasting. I told him to chill. He said, "One more of those and you're booked." So off I went with the song.') or the stealing of a packet of crisps from an alarmed child standing by the corner flag.

At the end of the 1990s, Kasule returned to Scotland and Hamilton Academicals, a signing protracted after the player left his registration papers in Shropshire. Accies secretary David Morrison told the *Hamilton Advertiser*:

I've signed whole teams faster than Victor Kasule. He is now
our player, unless he disappears between Shrewsbury and here,
but we have sent a driver with him to make sure he comes back.
He went home to get some clothes as yesterday he was still
wearing what he stood up in when he arrived here.

In a testament to his charm, skill and cheek, Kasule rapidly became a
figure beloved of locals. Supporters nicknamed him 'Vodka Vic', demonstrating how much he was viewed as one of them, but ignoring the fact
he disliked the spirit. Less amused was his manager, John Lambie, who,
after one misdemeanour too many fined and sacked Kasule, prompting
nomad days for the Glaswegian which took in Ireland, Malta and
Montrose. In 1993, aged 28, Kasule's niggling Achilles tendon problem
forced him to retire, his undoubted potential forever lost. For the few
thousand who were there for the ride, his attitude to the game remains
unforgettable, if unlikely to be replicated in the staid world of 21st century football. 'I didn't really give a shit about managers, directors or
chairmen,' he continued in *Goal*. 'I didn't take football very seriously.
To me it was just fun. As soon as they started paying me, all the fun
went out of it.' His was an outlook part-punk, part-Corinthian ama-
teur. The affection felt by fans for him paved the way for more black
footballers in Scotland, a serious achievement obscured behind the
mythology of Vodka Vic.

The individual brilliance of Slaven and Kasule shone among typically lean times at Cliftonhill. In 1984/85, Slaven scored 31 goals, more
than any player in Scotland that season. To do so, he defied conditions
every bit the caricature of an impoverished small club, as he continued
on the phone:

There was no finance. They were scraping for every penny. A lot
of the lads were getting short-changed. The pitch was poor, the
crowd was disastrous, 200 people there if you were lucky. No
atmosphere, but you plodded away. The ground was like a park
that never got finished. I remember when I was trying to get my
30 goals my mother came to her second game ever. It was windy
and the glass blew in and nearly hit her. That's an indication of
what it was like. Somebody should've set it alight years ago.
Pollock Juniors was like Wembley compared to Cliftonhill.

Smashed windows in the side of old Cliftonhill.

As the unkind '80s passed, decrepit Albion drifted on until, recorded Robin Marwick, in the summer of 1988 the board met

> ...in this atmosphere of despair and gave some thought on how to reverse the depressing trend of four decades. Forty years when the club had virtually stood still, had been the butt of comedians and had lost the goodwill of generations of Coatbridge supporters who had long ago given them up as no-users, non-triers and unambitious in the extreme.

The playing staff was overhauled, and Cliftonhill saw its first lick of paint in many a year. Rovers' squad, as profiled in Marwick's *Champion Albion*, included physiotherapist Jim Maitland, a trained hypnotist, and John Bishop, a 'Fast raiding winger who lives with his parents in East Kilbride.' After 42 years of nothingness, Albion defeated Dumbarton and finally achieved lift-off. Marwick presented the scene:

> When Referee Valentine blew for full-time the elated fans flooded onto the pitch to greet their heroes. Players were divested of their jerseys, hoisted on shoulder tops and Drew Sim of JJ Lees plc, the Match Sponsor, was sufficiently caught up in the spirit of

the moment to double the man of the match award to £50. At last the Championship was won, the nightmare of the past forty years was over. The pubs and clubs in Coatbridge were to enjoy a night of unrestrained revelry until the wee small hours.

* * *

In keeping with the plot, Albion came straight back down the following season. Of lasting disappointment to Marwick was the way in which the wider town failed to get behind the team during its first and last high for decades. Only 871 attended that Dumbarton promotion game ('surely we could have got 1,000. Football is a strange thing.'), 365 the one after. It was then, his pained expression confirmed the day we met, that he realised they had lost the long battle to attract Old Firm fans to Cliftonhill. By the time Marwick ascended to the chairmanship, things were so desperate that he proposed a groundshare with Airdrie, a move obstructed by Rovers fans. Fifteen years on Albion Rovers persist, driven by the weighty will of those few striding past the Rangers buses for Cliftonhill on a wet November day. It felt good to be among such rebelliousness.

Unfortunately, I was soon a rebel alone as the yellow-scarved filed into a pub named Innishmohr. After a fair hike in which the Monklands valley sprawled before me, a First World shanty town of flat industrial units where chimneys once raged, I spotted the peculiar sequin-like flood-lights of Cliftonhill. On the back of the Main Stand a hotchpotch of bricks, boards and adverts vied for attention. Weathered yellow and red signs welcomed me, while a giant Reigart Demolition placard offered Rovers 'Good luck', those speech marks offering a hint of sarcasm. I squeezed through the turnstile, behind which a steward attempted to swing around a railing and then had the cheek to look at me in a baffled manner. Similarly puzzled by my appearance was Annan's substitute keeper – unless I'm mistaken, the glance he threw me as he trudged onto the pitch for a warm-up questioned not only my presence but my entire existence. As I peered behind me, it became clear that I was the only person in the ground not bound by employment terms to be there. I was 27 years old, alone in the Cliftonhill rain. It was a satisfying melancholy like the damp glow after a Sunday night childhood bath. Or I was going slightly mad.

Within the stand's constricted bowels were a closed tea hatch and the club shop. There, 'used replica tops' were on sale at £10, although it didn't say by whom they'd been used or for what, and a fiery white-haired woman offered beanie hats at the same price, boasting 'they've nae nits in them'. On the big screen, Jeff Stelling talked about Manchester United. Just before 3pm, I lodged myself in the red wooden seats above and realised the sky had fallen dark (someone should build some kind of open blast furnace to brighten things up). Albion, in high visibility blue and yellow, began the game full of energy, striking the post inside a minute. This was to be a premature ejaculation of effort. For the next 44 minutes, Rovers and Annan traipsed about on a pitch that lurched from quagmire to swamp as time elapsed. The ball was not passed but scooped from the slosh as the players faithfully recreated a 17th century field game between Derbyshire villages, only with more foul play. A luminescent advert for the glamorous Hollywood Bowl on the stand opposite laughed at its own sense of irony.

As the half slogged on, a hush engulfed the seating area and I realised that once again football was making those that had paid to watch it ponder the pointlessness of their existence. More blasé fans sat similarly quiet thinking 'I could do a job at this level.' Breaking the meditation like a janitor interrupting a yoga session, Annan's Derek Townsley, the beanpole's beanpole, thundered into a challenge. For a good few minutes thereafter, perhaps in order to keep warm, the players took turns to kick one another. Half-time was signalled by the referee being unable to complete his three peeps due to an advanced state of blue-lip. I rose from my seat, convinced I'd contracted trench foot, before heroically continuing to the tea hut.

At half-time, the rain bounced off the cinder track and gushed down the empty three sides of the ground. Supporters blew on their teas to cool them and bounced on the balls of their feet to check they were still there. To avoid further medical complications I loitered in the terrace area for the second half, and was kept awake by the stench and sound of a man my mum would have described as 'tiddly'. His favourite habit was the warbling of tracks from Oasis' third album at Annan's Britpop-coiffeured number 11, Lewis Sloan. It was a bizarre but impressive undertaking: each time Sloan received the ball, Tiddly Man picked up at the exact part of 'Stand By Me' he had sung last, verses and all. It was as if he had 'pause' and 'play' buttons on the side of his well-refreshed cheeks. Down the line, five Annan followers leaned against a metal bar and barked with surprising ferocity for middle-aged gentlemen in cagoules. Their anger was directed mainly at a linesman shivering yards in front of them on the touchline, another surely caught in existential musing. 'If I wave ma hand will you gie me offside?' asked one of the Sons of Peter Storm. 'No but I'll fucking break it,' Tiddly pleasingly retorted.

The game ambled on as if trying to provoke the comment 'both sides are lucky to get nil.' Albion's left-back passed a ball straight to Annan's centre-forward. He politely returned the favour, at which point the left-back thumped his spherical gift straight out of play. 'Come on, Rovers,' came a cry. 'Come on, Annan,' followed the reply. 'Come on, *somebody*,' called out a third voice, possibly mine. It was a long way from Vic Kasule, but at least Albion fans knew that bad times could only mean one thing for their club: good ones around the corner.

CHAPTER FIVE

Montrose

Montrose 0 v 1 East Stirlingshire,
23 January 2010

WHEN I STARTED going to watch Middlesbrough, half-time entertainment consisted of a schools' penalty shoot-out. Uncomfortable adolescent lads from across Teesside would queue up to mishit Mitre Deltas into Ayresome Park's Holgate End, a maelstrom of indifference. Over the years things developed or regressed, depending on your point of view. Local girl 'Jet from *Gladiators*' would sometimes turn up and do a few cartwheels to the hearty accompanying tune of 'get yer tits out for the lads' (though admittedly this ceased when the club barred my granddad from attending matches). Then for a time there was a quiz in which rubbernecked men from Redcar would fail to identify Port Vale's home ground, goading strangely enthusiastic jeers from the stands. I can also remember lucky supporters being offered the chance to kick a football through a putt-sized hole with the aim of winning some ridiculously far-fetched prize, like the presidency of Angola.

Coca-Cola once ran an advertisement carrying the slogan 'Half-time is there to remind you what life would be like without football', to which the answer presumably was, 'what? Ace of Base records and a bloke who used to be on local radio trying to get a Mexican Wave going?' Actually, half-time came to remind me of everything I disliked about football.

Only at Montrose did I remember all of the above. In just five Scottish League games, I'd been cured. So far, half-times had meant tinny but barely noticeable Kaiser Chiefs singles at worst, and at best a few nervously-read scores from elsewhere. The rest of the time, supporters were left to moan quietly among themselves. My interval epiphany occurred when the Links Park tannoy rudely burst into action, inducing complete silence and then the request: 'If there's a qualified referee in the ground, please make yourself known.' Having never heard the question 'is there a doctor on the plane?' (do medical professionals travel Ryanair?), I enjoyed this tremendously.

Wearing the kind of smile that tends to put people off men on their own, I climbed down the stand and returned to the Supporters' Club Bar, a place I'd been happily, if confusingly, ushered into for a beer before the match. Steam from the tea urns engulfed frames containing old team photos, and paper plates sagged under the weight of sausage rolls. Taking great care to shelter pastry flakes from the carpet, a dozen Montrosians amiably talked over the previous five months and 45 minutes. Their team had not won all season, and today trailed East Stirling 1–0. In the previous week, *The Sun* columnist Bill Leckie had written a piece outlining their deficiencies. Montrose responded strongly in what was possibly the only incidence of a match programme statistics column being used to ridicule a journalist:

> 1 – number of 'pat on the head columns' written by Bill Leckie in *The Sun* on Monday about 'winless' Montrose. You could see what he was trying to say in his article but it didn't really come across that way when you read it, thanks Bill you patronising hack.

There were reasons to be cheerful approaching today's match. A week earlier, Montrose had led 4–2 at home to Stranraer (they conceded three late goals and lost, but that's not the point) and a trip to Hibernian in the last 16 of the Scottish Cup awaited. All in blue, they entered a Links

A crowded midfield area.

Park plastic pitch sparkling with rainwater in the hope that things were on the turn. After 20 minutes, they were 1–0 down. 'Mon the Mo', came the numerous replies to the goal. Behind the breached goal, four East Stirling fans took turns to wave a skull and crossbones flag, hammering the Montrose goalkeeper Andy McNeil as they did so. Less than three years earlier, he had won a League Cup; now, a bearded bloke carrying a Morrisons plastic bag was calling him a wanker.

In front of McNeil East Stirling were comfortable. In attack, Stephen McGuire and Derek Ure (official website profile verdict: 'his first few appearances were electric and had the scouts keeping tabs on his career. But things tailed off a bit.') ran at such creative angles I wondered whether they were an art installation. They were aided by the midfield guile of Jamie Stevenson, formerly of Alloa and Real Mallorca. His Mallorca spell, which came about after a scout saw him playing 7-a-side with an uncle there, didn't leave much of a mark on the world, except the outstanding BBC *Sport* website picture caption, 'Recreation Park is a far cry from La Liga.'

In the moments before half-time, some people on the pitch decided to fall over. Marek Tomana, Montrose's adroit Slovakian number seven, took delivery of a sodden ball to the head, momentarily glanced around and dramatically collapsed. 'Lie back and think of Bratislava,' the man next to me called out. Twice more the dense pinball took men out, before the referee keeled over holding his calf, possibly in embarrassment. I was happy though, and that's all that counts: through his misery, I'd got my half-times back.

Bolstered by the welcome blubber of flaky stodge, I followed my fellow Supporters' Club members back up to the Main Stand. Immediately, horizontal rain of the type

From the cosy bar to outdoors.
Shame, really.

usually confined to big screen storms at sea battered my smug dry face. For dessert, winds blew in and picked at my skull like the knitting needles of a psychopathic Super Gran. On the stormy plastic, the away side continued to dominate in a casual manner. With this pace and the excess weight on display, the game put me in mind of an all-stars charity fixture, only with fewer people willing Bradley Walsh to gore himself on an errant gatepost. Goateed Montrose manager Steven Tweed attempted to rouse his side through a series of instructions so lengthy that he could easily have been reading from the pages of a classic novel, which would have explained a lot, not least forward Paul Tosh's decision to dress for his role in a Regency frock.

By the whistle's final blow, Montrose had failed to muster a shot on goal. Having passed through the booing stage long ago, the band of home supporters that remained shrugged with hands in pockets and tilted their heads convivially to gesture a return to the bar. I walked by the side of the pitch, its floodlit wet patches resembling discarded bits of silver tinsel on a garish carpet, and out of the ground.

* * *

After bumping into not one but two men with steamed-up glasses, I came to a section of the Links, a ragged grassy area between decorous houses and the sea. It was hereabouts in 1879 that Montrose first played football. The club adopted the nickname of local residents, 'Gable Endies', a reference to their town's unusual housing style. Within 12 years of Montrose's foundation, one of their players, Sandy Keillor, had earned the first of six Scotland caps. As well as a heroic left-sided forward, Keillor was an occasional cricketer and a champion golfer. By the time he won his opening cap in 1891, Montrose had moved to their current home, built on land rented from the nearby Old Kirk.

A year after Keillor's cap, the Gable Endies were on course to become the finest side in the region. They coasted to the final of the Forfarshire Cup, one of many county tournaments across Scotland lost or downgraded in time. Hundreds of Montrosians travelled to the Dundee home of Our Boys for a showdown with East End, only to find their team had been delayed. On arrival, the players leapt off their train, dashed for the ground and ran straight onto the pitch. Once they caught their breath the goals flowed, and Montrose went 4–2 ahead when Keillor 'standing on firm ground outside the scrimmage,' as the *Montrose Standard* recounted, 'sent a swift high shot over the heads of the other players and it entered below the bar in splendid style.'

East End promptly 'entered a protest against the match being continued for the Cup on the grounds of darkness. As it was perfectly light, however, the referee let the game proceed', undoubtedly muttering something about carrots as he jogged away backwards. When Montrose rattled in a fifth, their followers 'cheered and waved their hats in a boisterous manner', a feat sadly impossible with a modern £10 beanie, nits or not. With each goal, a telegram was dispatched home, so that 'Within five minutes after a goal had been scored in Dundee those in Montrose knew of it, so complete were the arrangements for the transmitting of the news.' Complete, that is, unless it was Chris Kamara's turn to pass on the tidings. In the end, they won 5–3 with East End accepting defeat in a manner exposing the myth of Victorian fair play, as the *Standard* went on:

> ... at the close of the game, Brown, the captain of East End, intimated a protest against the Cup being awarded to the Montrose team on account of their being late in arriving and thus having to finish the game in semi-darkness and also on account of the heavy state of the ground. At first the Montrose men could scarcely believe that a protest had been lodged and regarded the whole affair as frivolous.

Their appeal meant that Montrose could not yet receive the trophy. Rightly convinced that a hearing would later correct that anomaly, the team were welcomed home at 9.30pm by a jubilant crowd as 'wildest enthusiasm among old and young spread through the town like wildfire.' They were shuffled onto horse-drawn carriages fronted by the Militia Brass Band and slowly progressed through the human treacle, perhaps passing and kissing an air-trophy in the absence of the real thing.

Trophies, intangible or otherwise, did not bring enough financial reward, and from the start of the 20th century the familiar tale of hand-to-mouth existence applied to Montrose. To raise revenue, Links Park was let to circuses, women footballers and cattle (well, their owners). In 1923, Club Secretary and local historian Bill Coull wrote,

The 1929/30 Montrose team show far too much cleavage.

The directors felt the washing bill for players' kit was too dear. The trainer was notified that the strip must only be washed monthly in future unless in very dirty weather.

For much of the century, Montrose existed to exist; anything else was a bonus. Rarely for a *Stramash* team, their mildly successful era came *after* World War Two, during the 1970s. Under Alex Stewart and then Kenny Cameron, the Gable Endies found money and impetus, awakening for a time the snoozy minnow. In 1973, they progressed to a Scottish Cup quarter-final with 9,000 people, Links Park's record crowd, witnessing a 4–1 reverse against Dundee. Through spiky programme comments similar to those aimed at Bill Leckie, the tie gave the club an opportunity to rail against over-committed rivals ('we are comfortably off and pay our bills every month') and amid national calls for a cull of Scottish League teams protest 'we apologise for our existence and continue to give our thousand or so faithful fans somewhere to go on a Saturday afternoon.' Montrose reached the same stage of the competition in 1976, and went on to trump that with a passage to the semifinal of the League Cup and their highest ever league position, third in Division One, now Scotland's second tier. The almost-good times were brief and, save for a Division Two championship (Montrose's only

Football on the other side of the water at Ferryden, looking across to Montrose.

national silverware) and a couple of promotions and instant relegations, the club gently bedded down and squatted in the league's basement.

* * *

With the days short and so little of Montrose seen, I found a guest house for the night. Among furniture neatly pitched between antique and retro (when a barman later asked me where I was staying I said '1953.' 'Oh,' he replied, 'is that the place on The Mall?') I heaved my way in to strangling reams of bed sheets and read the commanding wall signs. 'Please shower before breakfast'; 'Please do not eat fish and chips, Chinese or Indian food in this room'. Through the night, a cuckoo clock took great pleasure in waking me on the hour. I like to think the sign I scribbled on the back of my pizza box – 'Please shut that bloody clock up' – still hangs on my room's wall.

On Sunday morning, after an aimlessly pleasant walk on sand, grass and pavement, I ended up behind the football ground on Links Avenue. In 1929, Christopher Grieve, more commonly known as Hugh MacDiarmid, burned his letters and papers here. MacDiarmid created his most renowned poem, *A Drunk Man Looks at the Thistle*, in this town, and worked for the *Montrose Review*. As Grieve, he reviewed the poet's works, threatening libel action against anyone who claimed the two were the same man. Grieve/MacDiarmid's Montrose was the home of the Scottish renaissance, with Violet Jacob, Helen B Cruikshank and Edwin and Willa Muir, and artists William Lamb and Edward Baird all frequently gathering to write, paint, sculpt, criticise and argue about whose turn it was to put the kettle on. As MacDiarmid, quoted in the Montrose Society's *Montrose Town Trail*, put it:

> There was something in the atmosphere and layout of Montrose very conducive to creative work and most of the discussions on which these new forward-looking movements were based took place there.

Today, the Links Avenue atmosphere was conducive only to being stared at from twitching net curtains, so I walked on alongside pretty pale red villas towards the lower reaches of the Mid-Links. At the centre of a path in one of the Links' many small gardens lumbered a perkily crimson old monument, the top of which appeared to be a stone version of the TV-am egg and cup. An etching of former Provost George Scott appeared on

The artistically updated likeness of George Scott.

the side, adapted recently by local artists to include a comedy penis in the forehead area, and a fat spliff resting between his bearded lips. In fact, the slapdash artists had not done their homework: there is no evidence of Scott relaxing in this manner, though after all his visionary work and the scant thanks he got, no-one could have blamed him if he'd stuck Portishead on and emptied Chicken Cottage of its spicy wings.

Scott arrived in Montrose as a garden designer of repute. In 1868, he became a Liberal member of the town council, and began working on a masterplan to turn the wild and boggy Mid-Links into a collection of public gardens and lawns. Scott's Improvement Committee convinced the council to put their plans into action, and work began in 1875. In the letter pages of the *Montrose Review*, complaints and rebuttals flowed. Scott was labelled a 'dictator', his work

> a failure – not a single line of beauty is to be seen, nor is it in keeping with the surroundings. The public have been excluded from their own property in a very high-handed way.

It seemed that some locals treasured their right to tramp across unkempt slough. Most of the letters appeared pseudonymously, a fact not lost on Scott in his stormy rebukes:

> [the letters] are exceedingly ill-timed and injudicious, because whether they are true or false they cannot fail to have a prejudicial effect on the success of our Bazaar. I will not fight with unknown foes, least of all with irresponsible anonymous scribblers, whose apparent animus towards myself is only equalled by their gross ignorance. Let me say to your readers – do not be misled by such croakers, do not for one moment believe that such matters represent the general feeling of the people of Montrose on the subject. The people of Montrose have supported these improvements out and out. They desire to see the gardens changed from a STATE OF BARBARISM into a STATE OF CIVILISATION.

A man of will, tenacity and the ability to shout using capital letters way before the invention of Caps Lock, Scott saw most of his project through before dying, in office as Provost, in 1890. His achievements were increasingly appreciated as time ticked by. The prose of a 1947 guide to Montrose, subtitled *The Garden City by the Sea*, was infused with Scott's legacy:

> There is a clean spick-and-span freshness about the whole town which gives the collected impression of town-in-country. At one moment you feel most decidedly that your surroundings are urban

indeed almost city-like. An instant later, you are spirited off by some sudden intimation of leaf and flower, some little trick or illusion of breeze and fragrance, to utter and complete rurality.

As I studied the monument's plinth, further profound words caught my eye. I mean, did you know that 'Ruthana has STIS', as well as an odd name? Or that 'Ruthana loves Thomas', though she is bound to be heartbroken as 'Thomas is gay'? Proud of society, I ambled on to New Wynd. There 200 years ago, somewhere between Argos and Paws & Claws Dog Grooming Service, lived George Beattie, a solicitor poet to rival Cowdenbeath's barber bard. Beattie would eavesdrop on his neighbour John Findlay, a Town Officer, and turn his juiciest tales into verse. Snubbed and ridiculed by his lover Miss William Gibson, Beattie committed suicide, and you just wonder if he frantically tried to loosen the noose when he suddenly thought of the response, 'Yeah, well you've got a boy's name'.

Shunning the improbably named Paradise Computers, I soon reached Montrose's handsome High Street. A wide thoroughfare lined by commanding and varying old town houses, it has the unmistakeable air of a Low Countries market town, if you ignore Fads Decorating and Clinton Cards. Doctor Samuel Johnson found Montrose 'well-built, airy and clean', and he would have been delighted to know that I agree. Every few metres are closes: down some sit opulent houses or orderly gardens; down others lurk locked gates and takeaway detritus. The gaping windows, prim arches and nobbly tower of the dramatic Ballhouse and Steeple watch over a distinctly un-British town square. There looms a bright white statue to Joseph Hume MP, a celebrated radical, and a far smaller, more appealing bronze sculpture by William Lamb of 'Bill the Smith', a New Wynd blacksmith. The High Street, along with the houses by the Mid-Links, bring civic grandeur to Montrose, as that 1947 guide enthused:

The township is by far the most dignified and sightly on the Angus coast. Some of its terraces and streets give the impression that the builders of Edinburgh's great squares and quadrants of the New Town, having completed their labours, over-flowed into the Angus area and continued to erect fine dwelling-houses on a somewhat lesser scale.

While an improvement on the Cowdenbeath intelligence black-out, the square's information bulletin was light on detail, carrying as it did only a couple of adverts for Alcoholics Anonymous. Still, Montrose is a place to look at and not read or pick on spelling, so with head up I set out for the harbour. The centre's rangy buildings soon gave way to the modest coastal homes, garages and stubbornly alive pubs of Ferry Street. I skirted the edges of California Street and America Street, both abandoned 20-metre-long dead ends that said 'kerb-crawling' more than 'Golden State' and 'land of the free'. On Wharf Street, the water finally opened up before me, and opposite the scabby pebbledash of the old Seaman's Hall, I reached my destination: the statue of a dog.

Walking down the lengthy, neglected streets of the harbour area, it became clear that, as so often in these small Scottish towns, the wealth displayed upstream was created downstream. For hundreds of years, the port here bustled with arrivals and departures, Hanseatic products and their sailors shaping much of the town, including its appearance. In its function as Scotland's third largest tobacco importer, the port had its dark side. Ships sailing for Virginia picked up human cargo from West Africa en route, turning them over to the slave trade. A Baltic vessel brought live goods too, in the form of a Russian bear. In the early 20th century it would be paraded around town on a chain, with cloth tied to its paws to control its 'dance' moves. In *Changed Days in Montrose*, one Dorothy Meldrum recalled, 'It had a huge muzzle and it didn't really dance, just lumberingly moved from one foot to another.'

Looking across the waterfront today, it was still, unlike Alloa's, active, with gargantuan container ships queued up. Beyond the bridges that link detached Montrose with what can seem like a different world, the similarly colossal Basin rippled, its status as a nature reserve keeping it lushly wild. In the foreground, my canine focal point stared proudly the other way, and out to sea.

Bamse the Sea Dog arrived in Montrose aboard the Norwegian ship *Thorodd* during World War Two. An industrial-sized St Bernard, he was a registered member of the crew and had a steel helmet to show for it. With Norway occupied by the Nazis, Bamse and his colleagues took to the oceans to perform minesweeping operations from their Montrose base. The dog became more than a mere mascot, fearlessly remaining on deck beside the ship's gunner during aerial attack, 'facing the enemy, with his teeth bared.' On land, Bamse clambered onto his back legs and used his six-foot height to break up fights between drunken sailors. While stationed in Dundee, he even pushed a knife-wielding mugger into the sea.

The people of Montrose were quickly besotted by Bamse. Ignoring rationing, butchers, bakers and grocers kept him well fed, and others supplied him with beer while he waited to shepherd crewmen home from the town's pubs. When he died suddenly in 1944, Montrose entered a period of mourning. The town's malaise was depicted in *Silent Heroes: The Bravery and Devotion of Animals in War*:

> The shock and grief were palpable and sincere. It was, as one person described it, as if the silence that descended upon the little vessel was a special silence. A great emptiness was suddenly there. No member of *Thorodd's* crew was unaffected. Grown men who had stoically endured a cruel war, separation from their families, grave losses and exile from their country, cried openly. This was a very personal bereavement to them. Grief was not confined to the *Thorodd*. It was instantly echoed far and wide, in the naval depots, on visiting ships, on the streets of Dundee and Montrose, in the taverns and on the buses, and in all the local schools. There could not have been a more loving bond between two peoples, the Norwegians and the Scots, than that which Bamse created.

* * *

In the spirit of Bamse, and slightly alarmed that I'd been staring at a bronze dog for all of 20 minutes, I muddled my way towards the beach, at the south end of which his remains are buried. Tripping across brilliant sands (or, as an understating Victorian once described them: 'a beach of pure sand, dipping at so fine a gradient beneath the wave, and affording so smooth a carpeting for the feet as to allure even the most timid to the luxury of sea-bathing') I eventually ended up at Pavilion Amusements. Behind me stretched Links greenery and after that the football ground; in front, the dusty gold and dusky blue of sand and sea. My 1947 guide felt the same instant affection:

League upon league of gold-dust bind and ribbon that sun-drenched coast of Angus in the long intervals between cliff and township, and in no part of this brilliant arc do the colours of light fall more generously than athwart the links and gardens of Montrose. Its solar renown is indeed proverbial, and if I were in the habit of framing local proverbs I should feel moved to write: 'There's naethin' atween bonnie Munross and the sun'.

It was time for some candyfloss in the wind.

CHAPTER SIX

Kirkcaldy

Raith Rovers o v 4 Inverness Caledonian Thistle, 13 February 2010

AS WE CLATTERED over the Forth Rail Bridge on a morning more soggy chip than crisp, a lady in thickset glasses detailed her divorce agreement down the phone. Attempting to turn love lost into an inventory of gains, she excitedly repeated the fact that the solicitor had won her custody of what she kept calling a 'George Formby Grill'.

The list continued as we rounded the curve through Inverkeithing, shunting by a ship waiting to be added to a giant pile of rust, and then the grand old Caldwell papermill, finally closed in 2003 after nigh on a century's churning. Fife's intriguing settlements continued: the jagged outline of Aberdour Castle; Burntisland's mansions, grassy Green and white sands; Kinghorn's ancient sea front. Through the right hand window, the River Forth frothed with waves like cavalry charging one another. Out of the left, Fife's pimples became hills, some masking mines of old. The Kingdom's mix of beauty and graft again became plain.

With the divorcee mourning the sour loss of a Breville sandwich maker, we pulled past Raith Rovers' Stark's Park home and into Kirkcaldy, the 'Lang Toun'. I already liked the place because any locally-produced official guide which puts its subject down in the following way deserves respect:

> We have a notion that we have not received holidaymakers hos-
> pitably, and so they have treated us in like fashion by returning
> again from Raith without knowing or caring to see our town at
> all. Few events of much historical import happened in it or near
> it during what we call ancient or mediaeval history; and in more
> recent times it seems to have escaped prominence.

The words of *Davidson's Illustrated Guide and Handbook to Kirkcaldy* soon appeared unfair. Arriving in Kirkcaldy via the station is an immediately refined episode. A war memorial brings gravity, the museum and library enlightenment, and the gardens they watch over a smattering of forestry, plus further works by artists from Montrose's Ruthanian stable.

The museum is refreshingly old fashioned with not an interactive screen in sight. Objects speak for themselves, and no amount of 'interpretation' could enhance the experience of reading a scribbled banner bearing the words 'Coal not dole. Help my Dad save his job for me'. Its lordly outside appearance should fool no-one; this museum is a monument to working class history every bit as much as Summerlee.

Brief captions evoke folk memories. 'The town quickly became the linoleum-producing capital of the world', reads one, and from the middle of the 19th century, that was indeed the case. Floorcloth maker Michael Nairn switched to linoleum in 1860 and sparked a century of production. His family would later gift the town the museum in which I now stood, being tutted at by a curator for allowing my mobile phone to erupt. The linoleum trade brought with it a stench Langtonians embraced as their own, much to the bemusement of outsiders. A 1948 French guide to Scotland perceptively surmised the mood, reporting 'It's not unpleasant, but it's pervading. If, however, you ask a Kirkcaldy man about the smell, he'll look at you blankly and demand, "what smell?"' Generations of Scots caught the whiff through their carriage windows, an ordeal recorded in poet Mary Campbell Smith's 'The Boy in the Train':

I'll sune be ringin' ma Gran'ma's bell,
She'll cry, 'Come ben, my laddie.'
For I ken mysel' by the queer-like smell
That the next stop's Kirkcaddy!

Though linoleum was king, other industries emerged with salt production, weaving, mining, fishing and shipbuilding employing many. Artisans also set up as, among other things, calenderers, dancing masters, hackle-makers, oil cake and manure merchants and umbrella makers.

Leaving the museum with a handful of leaflets for attractions I'd never visit, I headed downhill by the boarded-up expanse of the former Station Hotel and the Adam Smith Theatre, currently hosting a play called *Journey's End*. In the DV8 nightclub, a window sign requested 'No football colours. No industrial footwear.' I continued by a pale brown

Tesco modelled on a Soviet-era Siberian abattoir and thankfully landed on Kirk Wynd, every bit as dashing as the supermarket was vile. There sat the Parish Church, somehow sheepish *and* imposing, former home to John Philip, a black rights activist stripped of his inheritance when a relative, Robert Philp, took unkindly to him adding an extra 'i' to his name. 'If ma name is na guid enough fa them then neither is ma siller', Philp is alleged to have said. Kirk Wynd also housed a monument to Robert Nairn, a son of Michael, that very few people merit: a Wetherspoon's bearing his name.

As is customary, the High Street was cluttered with the usual outlets, with older buildings retaining their lofty dignity. Though 1950s civil megalomania tore much of Kirkcaldy's old heart away, areas like this have managed to clasp hold of their history. For instance, a plaque identifies the former site of Adam Smith's home. As the world-changing economist worked on *An Enquiry Into the Wealth of Nations*, local legend, that fertile and amusing beast, claims that deep in thought he walked all the way from this location to Dunfermline in his dressing gown without realising. 'But I'm just working out how we can ensure growth in consecutive periods' would have been a fantastic explanation if the 1776 version of men in white coats had picked him up along the way.

In finest day clothes, I carried on until the green murk of the Forth rolled ahead. At the Tourist Information Centre, a helpful but no-nonsense assistant showed little interest in discussing the suitability of *Casualty*'s Clive Mantle for the role of Tommy Cooper impersonator (this wasn't a random opening gambit: a wedge of leaflets advertising said event protruded from the Centre's promotional shelves). With a paper bag tearing under pressure from pamphlet purchases, I ambled down Sailors' Walk towards the Robert Hutchison Flour Mill. Beyond that was Dysart, a suburb which once, according to the Reverend William Muir in his 1855 work *Antiquities*, counted a famous name among its residents:

> There is no doubt that our shore has often been the scene of many a rough encounter with the Danes, but unfortunately for the inhabitants of Dysart, a more formidable enemy took possession of one of their caves – this was the devil. There can be no doubt that they made efforts to eject so dreadful a tenant, and one

who doubtless would make himself very troublesome – but the inhabitants of Dysart were too timid to take effectual measures to eject him, or too weak to succeed.

The Harbour Bar enticed me before Satan could, though I did compensate the red-faced blighter by investing in a pint of Inferno bitter. Comfortable, peaceful and without a nacho in sight, this was pub of the season so far and further validation of one of my few travel rules: never pass by a bar with frosted windows. Whether it's a good boozer like this, 24 eggs for £1 or a black eye, you always leave with a story to tell.

Beginning the long walk to Stark's Park, I set out along the Esplanade. Tankers were dotted on a sea improved by two pints and a sky by the emerging sun. Looking across to Edinburgh, it was a perfect scene. This was an outlook of which one-time resident Thomas Carlyle wrote:

> The beach of Kirkcaldy in summer twilight, a mile of the smoothest sand, with one long wave coming on gently, steadily and breaking into a gradual explosion beautifully sounding and advancing ran from south to the north, a favourite scene, beautiful to me still in the far away.

It is interesting to note that Carlyle penned his tribute in 1830, a time in which whaling ships trailed their bloody catches to shore. According to the logbook of the ship *Caledonia*, quoted in *Whaling* (Kirkcaldy District Museums), their crews also brought 'Esquimaux curiosities and white bears, like collies, chained to the decks,' and on one occasion an Inuit boy named Aukotook Zininnuck.

Long predating and out-lasting the Esplanade's whaling business is its yearly fair, the Links Market. Founded in 1304, the Market remains an annual, much-loved local fixture. Its history has often reflected that of wider society. In 1919, *The Fife Free Press* reported that its shooting galleries

> gave outlet for the prowess of the demobilised soldier who has become a marksman since the last Fair, and who transferred his rifle practice from shooting Huns to breaking bottles.

In its busiest, if unimaginable today, years, monkey-adorned barrel organs entertained, while challengers stepped up to be pummelled in boxing booths by the 'Professor of the Fistic Arts'. There was an appetite for freak shows like The Bearded Lady, The Smallest Woman in the World, The Headless Lady and the World's Tallest Man, actually a coffin filled with a skeleton. Sweetmaker and, you guessed it, poet Jock Mackie painted the picture through a rhyme republished in Carol McNeill's lively history of the Links Market:

> Big moothed men and games o' chance
> Darked-skinned girls in native dance
> Fat ladies, dwarfs and monster rats
> Bows an' arrows, cowboy hats,
> Helter skelter, chair o' planes,
> Roonaboots tae please the weans;
> Bingo stalls, coconut shies
> Great big wheels up tae the skies.
> Young boys in the strip-tease tens –
> Let's hope their mither's never kent.

Moving inland, I walked towards Linktown through Glasswork Street, once home to another Langtonian who changed the world. Though he departed for Canada aged 18, Sandford Fleming and Kirkcaldy remained forever close. In North America, he instigated Canada's Pacific Railroad, pioneered the laying of underground telegraph cables between worlds old and new and came up with the idea of Standard Time. By tea time, he was in dire need of a nice sit down and a cup of tea.

In these narrow streets, I thought of another, quite different character I'd read about, Jimmy 'Boxer' Lyndsay. Operating at the turn of the last century, Boxer was a wiry-bearded cadger who flogged fish hauled across town by his faithful donkey Persimmon. Both would drink beer as they worked, and sleep in the same stable. Persimmon is now sadly forgotten and undoubtedly would have benefitted from signing up with the same publicity agency as Sea Dog Bamse.

All this pondering of days gone by had left me quite frankly lost on my way to Stark's Park. Like Persimmon shuffling behind Boxer, I adopted the age-old tactic of following a group of men, a move that can get one further lost, beaten up or worse, to the match. Sadly, in this case it was the latter. Within minutes and without the men having to stare at me more than 32 times, the angles and gradients of Stark's Park sparkled in the winter sun.

* * *

Like its Fife stable-non-mate Cowdenbeath, Kirkcaldy left me feeling intrigued about the region of Fife. Similar to the Yorkshire I'd grown up in, it seemed to be so many different things, and an area viewed suspiciously if not in open hostility by the rest of the country. I was unaware of any other people in Scotland who identified themselves by their county, as do Fifers, rather than their city or town. It was time to buy Raith Rovers fan Ian Rankin another pint of IPA and ask him, once he'd stopped telling the bar staff about the new and final series of *Big Brother*, whether Fife was 'different'.

In his youth, Rankin was enlivened by the Fife punk scene and now sees in its rampant DIY ethos something that chimed with the county's egalitarian tendencies:

> There was definitely possibility. If you were a young guy, music was a way out. You didn't see it much in Fife, but if you looked hard enough you saw it. Nazareth had been big in the '70s as a rock band, there'd been a few folk who'd come out of Fife and been big, then when the Skids came along, I used to go and see the Skids every bloody week they played at Kirkcaldy in the Station Hotel. It seemed like an egalitarian working-class thing. New York punk came out of the art house, but a lot of punk didn't, a lot of punk came from just kids hanging about and saying 'well I could do that'. Punk was really important then. Punk said: it doesn't matter if you've got the skill, do it, give it a go. So I thought fuck it I'll give it a go, I'll try and write poems, short stories, novels. I tried to put together a wee fanzine I printed off in Home Economics when no-one was looking. There was no-one saying 'don't do it.' 'Do you want to be singer in a band?' 'Yeah, why not?' All you needed was a microphone and you were singer in a band.'

In his case, that band's debut took part in the YMCA centre across the road from Cowdenbeath's Central Park and had some rather unfortunate consequences:

> We played our first gig to some special needs kids who were on a day out. And we were very pleased with the strobe we managed

to borrow from somewhere, but of course all the kids started having epileptic fits. So we'd to switch the strobe off and put the house lights up when we played...

Punk was a continuation of Fife's tendency to look out to the world, as Rankin continued:

Maybe people think it's going to be insular in its mentality, but it isn't. Remember Fife gave Adam Smith and Carnegie to the world; these were outlooking guys. Look at the writers who have come out of Fife, even in the 20th century: Iain Banks, Val McDiarmid, me, John Burnside. Artists like David Mack, musicians like Jackie Leven.

Without wanting to idealise a land he had long since left, he strongly felt the identity and otherness of Fife:

I go all around the world and if people say 'so growing up in Edinburgh...' I say 'I grew up in Fife', I always correct them. It still seems quite tribal. There's that sense it's a nice big welcoming tribe. It was a fantastic place to grow up, because it was all the clichés really; you knew all your neighbours, you could keep your house unlocked when you went out; half your family lived within walking distance. There are certain things about Fife. It was the ancient seat of the kings of Scotland, so we had that sense of being a kingdom. It's Central Scotland, but it's as separate as it can be.

When you meet other folk from Fife, wherever you are in the world, you've immediately got a connection of sorts, and I think it goes back to that sense that they've probably come from the same stock as you. Fife was farmland until mines were discovered. People moved east because of the coal. They went to Fife in the early 20th century. There was this explosion of people, a bit like America. Here's this brand new place and you're all setting up shop. And that drips down, that sense that we're all coming from the same, we're Jock Tamson's bairns. There wasn't a sense that there was middle class, upper class, working class whatever, and I thought that was great. There were still problems: racism, the first Asian shops opening up were a shock to the system for a lot of people in Cardenden. An undercurrent of religious bigotry. It's not an Eldorado, or a promised land.

Rebus was always going to have to be a Fifer. He needed to be an outsider. I felt like an outsider and I'd been in Edinburgh at that time five or six years and I still didn't know the city, what made it tick, I didn't understand the mechanism, so I thought he has to be an outsider as well, someone who doesn't understand it. Why would he want to become an Edinburger? He's proud of his Fife roots.

And so, I couldn't help thinking, despite him not being real, he should be.

* * *

Fife's status as a working-class area built largely on mining meant football was at its core as much as coal. The result is a high concentration of league teams – not to mention Junior clubs – similar to that of Lanarkshire. Choosing who to support could be another tribal issue, or it could come down to practicalities, as in the case of Ian Rankin:

> Your football allegiance could be as bizarre as the amount of buses it would take you to get to a match. So to get to Dunfermline was two buses, you had to change. To get to Cowdenbeath was two buses. To get to Kirkcaldy was one bus, so it was a hell of a lot easier to get there for a game.

When Raith Rovers Football Club was established in 1883, limited travel options meant a reduced chance of watching teams from elsewhere. It was later said that the club came into being when a future secretary, Bob Donaldson, found a football while bird-nesting and took it to be an omen. In the home town of Adam Smith there were, appropriately, a number of competitors vying for their market slice. One such team were Kirkcaldy Union. Raith, named after the Laird of Raith on whose land they first bided, faced Union in an 1897 cup tie. That day, town rivalries exploded, with supporters charging onto the pitch for some of what Danny Dyer would later call 'nightmare'. Angered at having his match day disrupted, Councillor Robert Stark released a bull from the next field which quickly cleared the hordes. The park on which the teams met had been rented from Stark, and from 1891 Rovers moved in permanently.

After 22 years of relative quiet there, Raith vanquished Hibs, St Mirren and Clyde to reach Hampden and the 1913 Scottish Cup Final, where they would face Falkirk. 'Having set ablaze the noble Forth that laves the linoleum centre of Scotland', as a letter in the *Kirkcaldy Times* had it, they were ready to swoop on Glasgow and bring the cup to Fife for the first time.

A crowd of 45,000 collectively rolled their eyes as kick-off was delayed for the unusual reason of forced niceness, as the *Kirkcaldy Mail* reported:

> The rival skippers indulged in a most exceptionally long handshake due to the fact a refractory camera was not working sweetly enough to catch them in the act, so that a repetition was necessary to allow the token of brotherly love being recorded in the 'speshuls'

At half-time, Falkirk led 1–0. Soon after, '[Falkirk] centre-half Logan, going forward to their aid, shot through quite out of McLeod's reach' to double the lead. 'Our spirits went down – not the liquid kind, dear reader,' the *Fife Free Press* journalist continued, protesting a little too much. The match finished, as the *Kirkcaldy Mail* starkly confirmed in spacious print:

> Falkirk – Two goals.
> Raith Rovers – Nothing.

'Despite the carping criticism of Western scribes,' said a comment piece underneath, 'the game was one that upheld the best traditions of Scottish Cup finals.' Although the first Final without a member of the Old Firm in 17 years, Celtic benefitted from 1,000 free tickets in what appeared to the *Mail* 'remarkably like a piece of favouritism.'

In the summer of 1921, Raith took a decision which forever changed the face of Scottish football: audaciously, they allowed their players to kick a ball in training. The decision came about following a club trip to England, as the *Fife Free Press* explained:

> During their English visit the Raith directors were very favourably impressed by a system of training, which is described as being alien to Scottish clubs, and which is to be adopted at Stark's Park next season. The principle of training, without going into details, is

ball practice of an unusual but very effective kind. Hitherto, ball practice has been an absentee from the training curriculum on the grounds that being away from the ball for a week imparted eagerness on the Saturday. So now we know the reason for a lot of things that were obscure to us before.

Rovers' early 1920s backline of Collier, Morris and Raeburn. Centre-half David Morris, rather than Alex James, is regarded by many as their greatest ever player. Morris won six Scotland caps and in 1924/25 captained his country to victories over Ireland, Wales and England.

The new policy came at the start of a charmed era at Stark's Park. The team finished third in Division One a year later, and over the following seasons regularly inspired in hard-hit Langtonians a joy that once a fortnight transported them from Kirkcaldy's economic woes to somewhere altogether different.

The architect of Stark's Park escapism was little over five and a half feet and suffered from chronic rheumatism. Alex James swapped Lanarkshire's coalfields for Fife's in 1922, his appearance in gigantic shorts bemusing and amusing Rovers fans. Underneath those and unbeknownst to them, James also sported drawers in an effort to warm his icy joints. He was brought east by Raith director Robert Morrison, a father figure deeply proud of his wily acquisition. Morrison had been wise in trawling fertile Lanarkshire for talent, with James' best friend at school the legendary Hughie Gallagher, with whom he'd later terrorise England at Wembley.

James made his Rovers debut at Parkhead in a 3–0 defeat against a Celtic side inspired by two other scintillating wee men, Willie Crilley and Patsy Gallagher. In the early days, his beguiling style frustrated Raith fans and management alike. As a match report in the *Fife Free Press* phrased it, 'James tricked himself and his own side as often as he nonplussed his opponents.' His talent was raw and not always useful to team play. After manager Jimmy Logan demanded that he track back when Rovers were not on the attack, James became incandescent. Quoted in John Harding's outstanding *Alex James: Life of a Football Legend*, the precocious forward later explained:

Alex James: cold body, electric feet.

I wanted to keep playing for Raith but I didn't want to be bound by rules and regulations about what I could or could not do on the field. What they wanted was impossible.

Dropped from the team and disillusioned enough to consider walking away from football, James' talent seemed irrelevant, a luxury item in a time of severe austerity. Following the return fixture with Celtic, a letter in the *Fife Free Press* spoke for those who saw no room for James' finesse:

There was a noticeable fault on the part of the Ashfield lad [James] all throughout the game. He seemed to think that it was up to him to give the Celts a lesson in trickery, and the result was that he sacrificed utility to the ornamental stuff. It is a failing which must be remedied if James is to be any more than a good for nothing sand dancer to the side.

At his lowest ebb James' heart was lifted by the timely intervention of Robert Morrison. He convinced the youngster to add perspiration to inspiration and fight for his Rovers place. Continuing the cinematic narrative, James began to settle into Kirkcaldy life, falling for a local girl, Peggy, who, far from being gripped by love at first sight had observed on meeting her future husband 'What, does that wee smout play football?'

With his difficult first season finished, James could look forward to 1923/24 and all the fresh hope August brings. Before that, Rovers were invited to play in the Canary Islands, a trip the players almost immediately regretted consenting to. As the squad boarded the *Highland Loch* for Buenos Aires via their island destination, all seemed well enough save for the stench of the boat's other cargo, chilled meat. Just after midnight one evening off the coast of Galicia, they were awoken with a thud. Their ship was sinking. Forward Tom Jennings remembered:

> Being good Scotsmen, we went below to grab our money before getting off the ship. Most of us were in pyjamas when we scrambled down the rope ladders into lifeboats. Spanish fishermen came out in boats to tow the lifeboats to the nearest village.

That village was Villa Garcia, and, according to Harding's book, Alex James did not think much to its credentials as a resort:

> We were landed on an island, the name of which I could never remember. I've always called it Cannibal Island for few of the fishermen on it seemed hardly civilised. They had absolutely nothing to give except two or three loaves of bread.

The shipwrecked of Kirkcaldy collected themselves and continued their tour before returning home and embarking upon the season that would prove the making of James. Shifted from inside-right to left, his brilliance was given room to breathe and prosper within Rovers' '£50,000 forward line', a name bestowed upon James, Bell, Miller, Jennings and Archibald following the serious reception given to a director's jovial remark about their worth.

Early in the season, James and his comrades triggered a 6–1 victory over Third Lanark, a draw at Parkhead and a 4–1 thumping of Ayr United. Langtonian lore holds that in the latter game, James rounded keeper George Nisbet, walked the ball into the net and walked out again. While not entirely following that script, the *Kirkcaldy Times* confirmed that James' goal was a special one:

> One of the most spectacular goals seen at Stark's Park for many a day. Twists and turns left four defenders absolutely dazzled and landed James in front of Nisbet with the ball at his feet. The pair eyed one another for a second or more and directly Nisbet made a move, the Raith man walked the ball into the net, leaving the goalie to wonder how it had been done.

Poor old George Nisbet; if it's not missiles it's some wee bloke in massive shorts leaving you on your arse.

James' gallus play often provoked savage responses from his opponents, though a man coated in Lanarkshire steel was unlikely to turn the other cheek. Twice in November 1923 retaliation led to scuffles and James' dismissal. On the second occasion, a home tie with Falkirk, his Stark's Park faithful scrambled onto the pitch to attack the guilty referee. In skill and passion, thick and thin, James was rapidly becoming the darling of Kirkcaldy. When his Raith side did lose, it was not their fault, but that of meddling officials or the lucky Old Firm. 'The Rangers have jam hingin' oot their een', remarked a fan in the *Fife Free Press* following a narrow home defeat.

In the New Year, James was applauded from the Tynecastle pitch after a virtuoso exhibition in Raith's first-ever win at Hearts, and hailed for

Alex James in later years as reserve team coach at Arsenal, by artist Mark I'Anson. The painting appeared in *Scotland's Dream Team*, I'Anson's 2003 exhibition at the Scottish National Portrait Gallery.
© Mark I'Anson

mastering successive victories over Glasgow's finest. His sorcery was allied to an increasingly vicious shot, part natural and part training ground persistence. James' Rovers finished that season, 1923/24, in fourth place. In just over a year, he had gone from disgruntled maverick to Fife idol.

With three of his £50,000 colleagues departed, James could do little to halt Raith's fall to a ninth place berth the following year. In spite of difficult surroundings, his game continued to develop apace and in the summer of 1925 English interest heightened. Shortly after what the *Fife Free Press* called 'one of the best exhibitions seen at Stark's Park for some time' against Airdrie, in the lounge of the now derelict Station Hotel, James signed for Preston North End for £3,000. He would later move on to Arsenal and become one of their, and Scotland's, all-time greats. As Britain observed the Queen's Coronation in June 1953, James slipped away through cancer. It is tempting to conclude James the footballer was ahead of his time, but perhaps he was of it. His magic was necessary in a harsh Scotland from which the people of Fife needed to escape, as JB Priestley wrote, 'through a turnstile into another and altogether more splendid life.'

Like neighbours Cowdenbeath, Rovers have churned out a fine line in escapist footballers. The egalitarian Fife Ian Rankin spoke of has allowed creativity to flourish. After Alex James came Norman Haywood's 47 goals in 34 games, overshadowed only by a Scottish Cup win for East Fife that same 1937/38 season. Following World War Two there was the mercurial Jim Baxter and record goalscorer Willie Penman. The cult of Penman was beautifully summarised in a 1993 essay by the Rovers-supporting novelist Harry Ritchie, writing in *My Favourite Year*:

> I'd been brought up on stories of these greats – how Willie Penman was so fast he'd once crossed a ball to himself... How, in a semi-final goalmouth scramble, a prone Penman had tried to blow the ball into the net. My Dad had a special affection for Penman, our record goalscorer and a 'character'. According to my father, Penman had once fallen asleep in the post-match bath, avoiding death by drowning only when a teammate noticed amid the steamy fug that Penman was missing. Another favourite story described how Penman had once been knocked unconscious and revived with the trainer's smelling salts, which Raith's record goalscorer promptly swallowed.

The Stark's Park of old. Those were the days, etc.

* * *

Rather than genius and folklore, Raith's most recent success relied on teamwork and cohesion. Jimmy Nicholl's mid-1990s side exhibited Fife characteristics previously more typical of Cowdenbeath, town and team: solidarity and belief in the unit. As Bayern Munich noticed, they could play a bit too. In 1994, Rovers, riding high in Division One, defeated Airdrie on penalties to reach a League Cup Final at Ibrox, where they would face Premier League Celtic.

In the week before the game, Jimmy Nicholl was visited by Tony Blair and *The Fife Free Press*, ever Rovers' staunchest backers, ran a souvenir special for the club's most important match since a League Cup Final defeat in 1949. Local businesses jammed its pages with urgently-adapted messages of promotional support:

If I can beat the cars, you can beat the opposition – St Katherine's Garage.

Go on and cut through the opposition' – Sawcare, Fife's largest saw service and suppliers.

The special also contained pictures of players handing out giant cakes at Victoria Hospital's diabetic children's ward, in retrospect perhaps not a brilliant decision. Inside the main paper, an editorial hinted at the barren economy of post-Thatcher Fife:

> Forget your worries, ignore the latest nasty letter from the bank manager, put your Christmas shopping list to one side, switch on the box and just bask for a while in the glory of little Raith Rovers hitting the big time, and heading for the clash that could yet see the Kirkcaldy club in Europe! It's the stuff every schoolboy's dreams are made of – and the stuff his Dad's and his Grandad's dreams are made of too...

Fast forward to Sunday 27 November at 4.45pm, and Rovers were 2–1 down with seconds remaining. Summoning the ghosts of James, Haywood and Penman, they pilfered an equaliser, held Celtic through extra time and won 6–5 on penalties. It was a rare, rare afternoon of joy for the 11,000 clad in blue there, and the many more back home basking 'for a while in the glory'. The headlines said it all: 'WE DID IT!' 'IT'S THE REAL THING' 'SAVE OF THE CENTURY CLINCHES CUP GLORY'.

Thousands gathered in Kirkcaldy for a celebration reception, with the local paper reporting that 'Fireworks, music and even free pies and Bovril were the marks of a grand civic occasion', a sentiment I agree with entirely. The team were piped onto the Town House steps to the strains of 'Fanfare for the Common Man'. Emotions ran high. After 111 years without a trophy to call their own, Rovers fans quoted in the paper could barely mask their excitement:

> I couldn't see a thing and there were a lot of bairns here who must have been disappointed.

and

> I was disappointed about how crowded it was because I couldn't get a good view.

Rovers' victory had been no fluke, but the result of several years of slow building. At the end of the season, Nicholl's hardworking, pass-and-move side caused further disappointment for local bairns by winning promotion. From the vantage of the Premier League they could enjoy a flirtation with European competition, and the visit of Jurgen Klinsmann's Bayern Munich. Europe's most expensively-assembled team won the first leg 2–0, but in Munich the Fifers inflicted a heart scare. Before half-time at the Olympic Stadium, Jean-Pierre Papin missed a penalty, and Danny Lennon, Cowdenbeath manager on the Saturday I visited, scored. Through the interval, awestruck away fans took pictures of a scoreboard which read 'Bayern Munich 0 v 1 Raith Rovers'. On bedside tables throughout Kirkcaldy, wedding photo frames were subsequently commandeered, their contents lovingly replaced with images of this new greatest day. Though the match ended 1–2, the *Fife Free Press* captured Raith's evening and sense of optimism:

> The players and fans partied long into the night, knowing that they had taken on one of Europe's biggest names and been far from disgraced. And there's always next year...

Stark's Park in the sun and manure avoidance.

However, within a decade the club had almost folded, and had it not been for the hard work and deep pockets of the Raith Trust ('Community, independence, democracy'), I would not have been following three blokes under a railway bridge in February 2010. It was under that same bridge that Rovers' club pavilion was carried in 1891, the top part of its gable being lopped off during the process. On Pratt Street, the men accelerated towards Stark's Park while I tried to strike the tricky balance between admiring the ground's architecture and not standing in horse manure. Behind the goals functional modern stands were rendered dramatic by the plummeting sun, while Raith's old main stand required none of the elements to make its character stand out. More a half-baked idea than a building, its L-shape nestles in a corner, impossible to expand upon due to its location on a ridge. Wooden seats run only to the half-way line, meaning residents of Pratt Street's two-up-two-downs have a prize view, or vice versa for those in the ground should inaction on the field turn them to voyeurism.

Low in the large stand behind the goal, I joined a few hundred others

A view of the quagmire.

cradling their eyes from the sun and took in the hulking McDermid Stand, named after another crime-writing Raith fan, Val. To the left, a long terrace squeezed in between the pitch and the railway line was empty save for shivering ball boys and a lucidly blue giant flag adorned with the borrowed slogan of Torino's Ultras, 'stregati da una fede' ('bewitched by our faith'). A week previously, over 7,000 people had been bewitched as the home side held Aberdeen to a surprise 1–1 draw in the Scottish Cup. Today, the home crowd was closer to the 1,000 mark.

Those that had turned up bellowed with startling zest as Rovers took to the bog in moody blue. ICT were, to use my favourite local radio phrase, 'going great guns' under Terry Butcher, a man I hadn't shared a stadium with since singing 'Terry, Terry Butcher, Terry Butcher on the dole' at Ayresome Park a decade and a half ago while he was managing Sunderland. For the first quarter of an hour, both teams showed an adherence to passing the ball, which seemed like inappropriate behaviour given the surface, a bobbly morass Worzel Gummidge would have deemed unplayable. Soon, teams home and away did the decent thing, thwacking the ball forward or into the crowd at every opportunity. I spotted advertising hoardings for the Scottish Nationalists and the Labour Party and wondered whether the Raith-supporting ex-prime minister would be here or behind his curtains. Home keeper David McGurn roused me by hollering 'DOUGIE. DOUGIE. GET A MOVE ON' with such volume and ferocity I presumed he was addressing a friend in the Ipswich area rather than full-back Dougie Hill.

Inverness' Stuart Golabek, still carrying weight from Christmas (1987), completed the attention-grab by bolting into a gloriously meaty challenge. As his foot connected with Raith's angular full-back Craig Wilson, it emitted a clacking sound of sheer, unbridled density. Supporters looked left to see if a train had derailed and seagulls dived for cover. For the 10 minutes up to half-time, Wilson just looked ill.

After a break in which I was stampeded by sweet fiend children crazily pursuing a Haribo fix, Rovers began the second half intently, albeit without intending to repeatedly roll the ball out of play. Forward Robert Sloan laboured and tottered, his cumbersome gait that of someone getting out of bed for the first time following an appendix removal. When players did flutter a glimpse of skill, more often than not they were tackled by the mud.

With 20 minutes remaining, Howling McGurn turned Howler, blasting the ball at ICT's Adam Rooney who sheepishly inserted it into the net as if expecting something to go wrong along the way. 'Rooooo-ney, Rooooo-ney' sang the newly boisterous Inverness followers behind the goal. 'Shut up you sheep-shagging filth' retorted the man behind me wittily. Goals two, three and four followed, not so much flowing as trickling in lame embarrassment. As each went in, more Raith fans left, and my neighbour revised his repertoire to include the positively Wildean 'I hope youse all fuckin' die'. The air prickled with volatility as home fans turned on their team.

With the whistle came relief as we stepped out of the ground and into a more splendid life of red sky over the deeply pleasant town of Kirkcaldy. There was nothing escapist about today, quite the opposite, but there was the comforting thought that life in the 'different' and democratic county of Fife goes on. As Ian Rankin knowingly put it once the last of his IPA had sunk in, 'I'll be back in Kirkcaldy next season'.

CHAPTER SEVEN

Greenock

Greenock Morton 1 v 2 Dunfermline Athletic, 27 February 2010

IN A VICTORIAN ROOM certainly free of alcohol and probably free of smoke, two joiners, a grocer, a steel riveter and a water inspector came together to plot. James Farrell, Matthew Park, Robert Aitken, Alexander Ramsay and John Barrie believed they had found a new vehicle for prising Greenock's impoverished out of their squalor and pushing them towards health and self-improvement.

Workers from the Highlands and Ireland had flocked and fled to Greenock, a town that created wealth and distributed it elsewhere. Any release from their overcrowded and filthy town was welcomed, with charabanc and cycling clubs bringing respite through weekend country-side trips. Now, it would be football that provided facilities and fresh air to give hope and exercise. Men and women who spent half the week bound in the shipyard or sugar mill and a quarter of it forgetting the strain through drink could now find a healthy means of escape. The new Morton Football Club would be a social liberator of the working class.

Crucially for the five plotters, Morton FC was a method of enticing people out of the pub; all were members of the Temperance Movement. Tellingly high up the list, clause two of the club's constitution decreed 'that all meetings in connection with the club be conducted on Temperance principles'. Morton's 1874 invention sprang from a context of other non-drinking schemes run by churches, clubs and sports organisations. The five were not alone in their belief that football could perform the same social role: early fixtures saw games against John Dunlop Templars and Morton Abstainers. As well as swapping dingy pub isolation for Saturday afternoon community spectatorship, Morton members could use its pitch for their own games and exercise through the rest of the week. It was a forward approach to self-improvement – Samuel Smiles with goalposts.

The Morton Five sought sponsorship for their new venture, and philanthropic former Provost Thomas Morton obliged. With his patronage, and the Five dwelling and playing football close to the street which carried his name, Morton Terrace, the club's handle came easily, and it wouldn't be until 1994 that the prefix 'Greenock' was formally adopted by supporters. Whether Thomas Morton's paternalism was motivated by compassion or a pat-on-head desire to rear a fit and sober workforce (he was, ultimately, a businessman), a football club had been born to help curb society's ills.

Five years after that foundation meeting, 'The 'Ton' moved to Cappielow, a slab of land sandwiched by the railway and docks. In accordance with the club's principles, the ground was immediately put to community use. Cappielow hosted public lectures, often on Temperance, cycling, athletics and women's football. The pitch was even put to use for grazing. For the 1910/11 season, goal bonuses came in the form of a live lamb, presented by a local butcher. Short on shepherding skills, the Morton playing squad generally left their animals on the turf until a buyer could be found. The last animal, Toby, exited dramatically, slipping into the team bath and drowning. A few decades on, screenwriter and Cappielow neighbour Alan Sharp watched training as the local rag and bone man's horse grazed by the players, an experience which sealed his love of the ground and fired his imagination:

> I'd slip into Cappielow to watch the endless track lapping that passed for training in those days and stay to watch the horse browse gently where my heroes trod. Magic. Even the word 'Cappielow' yielded its nugget of esoteric knowledge. Later it thrilled me in a manner I cannot explain to discover that it's an old Scandinavian word meaning 'a race between mowers' and conjured a Breughel-ian vision of a field being cleared by massive thewed men in Mortin strips in order to play the great game. And the Lord said, "verily shall ye clear this field and it shall be called Cappielow, and ye will pit doon yir jaikets and twelve will be half-time and twenty four the winner." And lo, as it was commanded so it was done.

From its opening in 1879, as Sharp knew more than most, Cappielow was an atmospheric theatre. Yet the ground's aura was never dense enough to veil underwhelming and ugly events on or off the pitch. In 1887, a *Greenock Telegraph* reporter slated a centre-forward who:

> again was as useless as ever he has been. The chief duty of a centre-forward I take to be that of shooting goals. That seemed to be the one thing he omitted to remember. He was far too occupied with opponents to see the ball or know where it was coming or going. He may have done a few good things in the course of the game but they cannot be recollected.

After a Cup tie with Rangers, that same newspaper described how a 'genial looking gentleman' had offered the words 'I think everything favours Rangers today' to the hefty Irishman next to him. In response, the gent received only the words 'ye're a loiar, Sor!' and a punch which knocked him to the ground.

As Greenock grew, Morton became a footballing force of distinction. With Glasgow on its shoulder, the club would never be a Goliath, but neither was it a plucky David. For 27 years from 1900, they remained in Division One, finishing second in 1917, and five years later becoming that seldom seen beast: a team in this book that actually won something.

In the season leading up to Morton's 1922 Scottish Cup Final against Rangers, George French had scored 37 goals. A town's hopes were vested in his golden boots, and when it was announced that injury would prevent him from playing, Greenock went into shock and the paper bemoaned French's withdrawal as an event 'like the loss of a Wellington before Waterloo.' Leaving the melodrama for others, the Morton team took the lead through a Jimmy Gourlay free kick and then matched the Blues in every department, including the one named GBH. With Waterloo still on the mind, the *Telegraph* depicted the bloodbath:

> With blunt plainness it was evident that nothing would be permitted to keep Rangers from securing a coveted goal in the second half. And thus one after another the Morton players suffered more than inconvenience and more than once the referee had to make a few judicial remarks to individual players. But there were incidents he didn't see. [Morton goalkeeper] Edwards came well out of the scrimmage at goal when it looked as if he were not only to be killed, but also buried.

Even without their Wellington, Morton held on. After the last whistle blew, the 'Ton players danced their way from the pitch singing 'When the Stormy Winds do Blow' and set about liberating some champagne from the Queen's Park cellar. There was to be no triumphant night out in Greenock as the club's board had kindly arranged a fixture with Hartlepool for early the next week. So it was that Morton came to celebrate their victory in a north-east town which hadn't seen such commotion since its infamous monkey hanging (cue letters of complaint from Peter Mandelson and Andy Capp). Hartlepudlians convened at the town railway station in great numbers, carrying the team to their hotel and cajoling a brass band into playing. It was a strangely appealing spectacle as the people of Hartlepool celebrated on Greenock's behalf.

When the Cup-winning team returned home, a record crowd of 23,500 awaited them at Cappielow. Their opponents were Celtic, who required a point to win the title, and a concoction of home jubilation and away tension resulted in an afternoon of chaotic violence. Defying police orders, Celtic followers brought with them countless banners and flags, hurled over the ground's walls and onto the terraces where they would become rallying markers. Cappielow heaved, with child spectators forced to watch the game from the cinder track at the field's edge. There, they saw Morton hold a 1–0 lead at the break in a skilful yet thunderous encounter against Patsy Gallagher's Hoops. As the players trudged off, a fight broke out behind one of the goals. The crowd parted down the middle into factions, leaving a gap on the terracing. On command, flag-clutching Celts stormed over the no man's land and into the Morton throng. The *Glasgow Herald* noted how 'Celtic Brake Club flags were in evidence within the enclosure, and these became very prominent in the disturbance.' Stones and bottles were hurled from both sides, while away fans in the opposite end tore across the turf to join the fracas. Thousands of onlookers poured onto the pitch, itself peppered with green and white paraphernalia, the spoils of a Morton raid on a further Celtic area. Many wiped blood seeping from head injuries. Bravely, the police and referee called the players back on to the pitch, a move that somehow brought about order of a kind, and emptied the playing surface.

Celtic ploughed on and got their equalising, championship goal, but as supporters flowed onto the streets afterwards, the trouble restarted.

Charabancs sat on the Port Glasgow Road waiting to carry fans east. However, as the *Herald* reported:

> A considerable number of the Celtic followers who took their place in them had apparently supplied themselves with ammunition in the shape of stones, and as the brakes moved off they started to use them.

In the other direction, Glasgow-bound passengers were ambushed by Morton fans on the way to Cartsdyke station, triggering a pitched street battle. There and elsewhere, shop fronts were smashed. At Paisley, a blade-wielding fan was removed from a train. A rumour circulated that Greenock shipyard workers, driven over the years to revenge by repeated violence from visiting Glaswegian fans, had anticipated the violence and all day carried with them sacks of rivets. The *Herald* was unequivocal in its condemnation:

> It was a disgraceful exhibition, and one dangerous to the public who had no concern with the football. One may hope that before another season opens the Scottish football authorities will take more stringent measures to prevent a recurrence of disorder of this description. There is a type of football fan who is bringing discredit on a great pastime, and football clubs themselves would gladly dispense with this support.

It wasn't exactly what the Morton Five had in mind.

Though failing to win the cup again, high times at Morton were frequent. After World War Two, to the chagrin of Ayr, Cowdenbeath and others, the 'Ton were placed in Division One regardless of poor pre-conflict performances. They reached the Scottish Cup Final again in 1948, taking Rangers to a replay which was lost 1–0. The two games had drawn more than a quarter of a million people to Hampden.

Cappielow was often home to some of Scotland's greatest talent. Tricky Billy Steel, through the

Morton's 1948 cup-finalists are in here somewhere.

week a clerk in Denny Town Hall, and on occasional Saturdays a Scotland international, first sparkled there. Steel was with Morton when he swayed through Rest of World defenders to score in a 6–1 Great Britain win. When Steel left for Derby County, his status as Morton's finest was taken, perhaps unusually, by a goalkeeper.

Signed on a free transfer from hated rivals St Mirren, Jimmy Cowan was in most Morton eyes their greatest-ever player. While still on active military service, Cowan made his debut at Easter Road and saved two Hibernian penalties. In Edinburgh, he was applauded from the pitch; to those there, it was already clear that this agile panther of a keeper was destined for greatness. If there was any doubt over how different Cowan was, supporters only had to arrive early for a game and watch him painstakingly marking in the turf a groove between the goal line and penalty spot, his way of geometrically calculating positioning and angles.

Cowan was instrumental in Morton's run to the 1948 Scottish Cup Final where, once again, they faced Rangers. In the first game and the replay, both watched by over 130,000 people, Cowan made unlikely and gymnastic stops. Masochistically brave, he hurled himself all over the area, on one occasion scooping the ball off the line as if pausing everything but himself with a remote control. When the Glaswegians did get their agonising winner at the end of extra time, Morton fans claimed it was only because Cowan had been blinded by the camera flash of a photographer. It was as if they didn't believe he could be beaten fairly.

A portrait of Cowan by Mark I'Anson, selected by the artist for Scotland's Dream Team.
© Mark I'Anson

Cowan's brilliance came to the attention of the English at Wembley in 1949. Against an onslaught engineered by Matthews, Mortensen and Finney, the keeper stood, hopped and dived resolutely. In waves England attacked, and

Cowan thwarts Stan Mortensen at Wembley and instantly regrets that second bowl of porridge.

Cowan repeatedly repelled. Up the field, his apparent perfection inspired Scotland's forwards to fashion a 3–1 win. At the end, Cowan was thrown in the air by his colleagues and paraded under English noses, his performance immortalised by the line 'Jimmy Cowan, the man who broke all England's hearts' in Morton's club song.

Though Cowan stuck with Morton through a spell in Division Two, England eventually called, and in 1953 he joined Sunderland. Having won 25 Scotland caps, soon after retirement he died, aged just 42.

Morton's next star wore a pork-pie hat and had a background in dealing tobacco for the Co-operative. Long a football man if not a Morton fan, Hal Stewart was elected to the club's board in 1961, a year in which the team finished bottom of the entire Scottish League. His business acumen and wheeler-dealer ways saved Morton from ruin, and there was little objection when he made himself director-manager, a new role that represented one of many Stewart innovations to football, suggested or otherwise.

Stewart reformed the club from top to bottom and inside out, somehow creating a viable operation out of economics that were part marketing genius and part Arthur Daley. Finding that Scandinavian players could be purchased for nothing and sold on at profit, he pioneered the import of numerous foreign players, Morton's 'Danish Invasion'. Stewart met the players in luxurious Glaswegian hotel suites, taking them to

Greenock only once the Is had been dotted and a line put through the øs. It was, on the whole, a successful undertaking. From the moment goalkeeper Erik Sørensen was listed on a trial game teamsheet as 'Mr X' to prevent other sides getting wind of Stewart's Nordic masterplan, the scheme caught the imaginations of both the Greenock and wider footballing public. The players themselves brought technical ability and ruggedness missing from Morton's fallow 1950s period, not to mention a 10-minute hat-trick against Celtic (Per Bartram in 1969). Stewart saw the importance of selling football as a commodity, advertising Morton through their brightly-coloured and regularly-changing strips. As Vincent Gillen wrote:

> Cappielow was the by-word for excitement and innovation. Morton joined the top flight of Scottish teams as a result of a mixture of psychology, gimmickry, kidology and sheer hard graft from Hal Stewart.

Tales of Stewart's scrimping are many. One year, players were offered a choice of Christmas bonus: a turkey or a pair of jeans. There was also a consensus among many at the club that supporters passing through one turnstile – 'Hal's Gate' – were not counted by anyone but Stewart himself ('We were on a crowd bonus – anything over 10,000 and we got a pound. It was always 9,700 or 9,100,' one player later said).

Whether visionary (it was claimed Stewart was the first to predict all-seater stadia and corporate hospitality) or archetypal loveable rogue, on the field his management, ably propped up by a skilled team of coaches, did the trick. 1963/64, a record-smashing season, saw Stewart's team win Division Two by a landslide. Morton took 67 of 72 available points, scored 135 times and won 23 games on the bounce. They also reached the League Cup Final, though were pummelled 5–0 against Rangers in front of 106,000 (another record, that of the League Cup's highest ever attendance). With Danish assistance and finishing excellence Allan McGraw, signed from army football and initially flown home from Germany for matches, netted 58 league goals, still the most in a Scottish league season. Down the years, McGraw would become Mr Morton, a Greenock idol who later managed the club.

From the mid-1970s into the '80s, new icons emerged at blessed Cappielow. In the dugout, charismatic manager Benny Rooney built a squad which, according to a 1980 edition of *Soccer Monthly*, could 'strike fear in the hearts of the Old Firm'. Indeed, the previous Christmas they had been top of the Premier League. His work was overshadowed, often literally, by a man whose name still sends Greenockians into a stupor: Andy Ritchie.

Rejected by Celtic having given Jock Stein a friendly one-fingered salute from the pitch, Ritchie joined Morton in 1976. Overweight but lanky and appearing utterly carefree, he appeared more the reluctant bass player than the supreme entertainer. Therein lied the rub with Ritchie: insouciant one minute, imperious the next, he could strike and curl a ball in defiance of physics, and feign with galumphing elegance like a world-beating outsize ballet dancer. A 1983 *Glasgow Herald* goal description summed up his peculiar knack:

> Towards the interval he scored a goal the likes of which will not be seen until he himself does it again. He was standing at the far corner of the box. He looked as if he had just come out from a stroll and to admire the grass. He then just hit the ball. He didn't seem to move but just hit the ball. To the east and south it bent through the air by four or five yards. That may not be possible but that was how it looked from the centre of the stand. Hugh Sproat in the Motherwell goal did not move to the left, nor did he move to the right. He appeared mesmerised. The ball screamed past him into the corner of the net.

For seven years, Ritchie captivated the Greenock audience, his whimsical skill a fortnightly restorative medicine for a public hammered by industrial decline, a modern heir to Crilley at Alloa or James at Raith. Insouciance gradually got the better of imperiousness, and aged just 27 Ritchie walked away from the game he had made others love. As a young man, he has since reflected, he needed guidance and reassurance but in the laddish isolation of football found instead cigarettes and alcohol. Still, Morton fans have the memories and, as Vincent Gillen put it, 'That goal against Aberdeen. He takes the ball, flips it over his head, controls it, beats two defenders and puts it past Leighton. Classic. I can still hear him rustle, hear him running.'

* * *

From double-breasted Dumbarton Rock to the point at which the Clyde gushes open, Inverclyde is a landscape of drama. On both sides of the big river, hills and mountains compete for attention, with a sprinkling of industrial cranes and old warehouses joining in. At Port Glasgow, cranes litter the sky and mercantile buildings sadly misused and disused speak of a Scotland that once looked out to the world. The train pirouettes around a curve, and then Greenock appears, an industrial town stuck on the side of a hill. Plonked in the middle appears to be the striking spire of a Spanish cathedral.

It's a mixed landscape of incline and industry that has always inspired over-the-top musings in writers and people with a keyboard like me. In one of my favourite passages, Thomas G Snoddy, author of *Round about Greenock*, used some lovely words to say 'it rains a bit and there are hills':

> It clings close to its moorlands. There are no easy pastoral landscapes about Greenock. Its landward parts are hills of heather reaching by long slopes up to considerable altitudes. It is here the sweeping showers of west country weather drench the moors and flood the brown burns that brawl in the lonely glens. These rains fall equally over the tenemented braes leaving the pavements white and clean, and establishing the remarkable record of at least 60 inches of rainfall every year. Wherever you go you see the hills; they look over the ridges of houses, between the tall chimneys and at the upper ends of the rising thoroughfares. The mountains beckon and will not let you escape: Perthshire, Argyleshire, Arran; Ben Ledi, Ben Lomond, Ben Ime, Ben More, Ben Cruachan, Goatfell – Greenock is on better speaking terms with these peaks than some of the people who live under their shadow. The result of all this is that your typical Greenockian is what he has always been, a kind of combination between a hand on a herring boat and a wanderer on the mosses.

Once my train had wandered through the mosses that separate Greenock Central Station from West, I 'de-trained' (the announcer's 'word', not mine) and walked aimlessly towards Fort Matilda because it sounded nice. The streets widened, trees exhibited themselves on parade and I admired the villas and town houses. This did not synchronise with the impression given elsewhere of a post-industrial, drug-ridden Greenock. Around 150 years ago high up in the west of the town, ship-owners, industrialists and investors had funded avenue upon avenue to scream their wealth. I should have been impressed, but I couldn't help thinking of those downstream that made them rich, and in any case, it reminded me a bit of Harrogate so I turned and drifted Clyde-wards. On the Esplanade bolshie winds threatened to blow cats into orbit but nothing could detract from the vast, poetic landscape of lapping dense water and bandit territory mountains beyond. In the 19th century, travel writer Robert Chambers was another sent dizzy by the locality, writing in his *Picture of Scotland*:

> A few miles off, across the Firth of Clyde, the untameable Highland territory stretches away into Alpine solitudes of the wildest character so that it is possible to sit in a Greenock drawing-room amidst a scene of refinement not surpassed, and of industry unexampled in Scotland, with the cultivated lowlands at your back, and let the imagination follow the eye into a blue distance where things still exhibit nearly the same moral aspect as they did a thousand years ago. It is said that when Rob Roy haunted the opposite coasts of Dumbartonshire, he found it very convenient to sail across and make a selection from the goods displayed in the Greenock fairs, on which occasion the ellwands and staves of civilisation would come into collision with the broadswords and dirks of savage warfare in such a style as might have served to show the extremely slight hold which the law had as yet taken of certain parts of our country.

I carried on down Union Street where further grand old dwellings stood up to be counted, eventually reaching the McLean Museum, a large grey stone building somewhere between a castle and a church. Its intact viewing gallery and varnished cases recalled Greenock's age of self-improvement, this time through enlightenment rather than football. The atmosphere was anything but starchy Victorian with emotive exhibits on shipbuilding through to socialism shooting straight to the heart of Greenock, and a coach load of French people busily discussing how best to translate the word 'rivet.'

As well as writing and talking about Morton, Vincent Gillen is a curator at the McLean, and a loyal advocate of his hometown. Having made a career out of studying Greenock's social history and spent his life locally, Gillen is well placed to try and capture the character here, and just what impact the unusual mix of geography has had. As he explained to me:

> It's isolated. It's all on the side of a hill. That in itself creates a distinct atmosphere and conditions in Inverclyde, because you can go up the road to Paisley, 17 miles and the language changes totally. Them with their 'see-ven', us with our full glottal stop. You're just out on that limb. The geography has shaped the character. You don't come to Greenock for any reason other than to go to Gourouck, or maybe the Highlands. The geography is also the wet, the rain. It's synonymous with rain. We tend to be this beaten down bunch, walking with a stoop to keep the rain off us.

As I left the McLean, the stoop was something I noticed immediately, and is perfectly represented on the front cover of this book. Shedding thoughts of retraining (well, training) as a chiropractor and moving here to make a fortune in spinal realignments, I walked through George Square, actually a triangle. There among the ascending spires rested the Baptist Church, home of a somewhat bitter sign reading 'If absence makes the heart grow fonder, lots of folk must love their church.' I turned right by the tallest of the churches, now home to a centre for self-defence classes, and headed down Kilblain Street, home of the Horseshoe Bar, one of very few pubs attached to a multi-storey car park. Ahead, a family of tower blocks attempted in vain to cover the hills behind, while the Oak Mall tried by sheer ugliness to draw attention away from the 'Spanish Cathedral' spire beyond. Outside the Westburn Bar, a man stood in his dressing gown smoking. Via an older walkway modelled on the abject perdition that is Stevenage, the Oak Mall vortex sucked me in. What I thought would be a short cut turned out to be a protracted episode in a shopping centre that refused to end. Inside, bearded zombie figures pleaded to be told where the exit was, and I'm pretty sure I saw Lord Lucan wandering about with a bemused look and eight or nine Primark bags.

After a three year stint working in Poundland, I somehow fell out of the centre and into Clyde Square. Immediately, my Oak Mall hell was forgotten as Greenock's wonder unfolded in front. The Municipal Buildings are startling in their own right as well as in the context of Oak Mall. Giant, unashamedly glamorous to the point of fussiness, the chambers and tower were built as a display of civic wealth, and a church to the new Victorian God, commerce. Close-up, or as close-up as you can get given its scale, my Spanish spire was even better; Mediterranean class and industrial prowess combined. When the buildings opened, the *Telegraph* remarked how they possessed 'every beauty but the beauty of economy'. Staring at them, I was profoundly grateful that not a penny had been scrimped. Given that they opened in 1886, when the east of Greenock was suffering from dire poverty, the *Telegraph* may have had a point.

Other detractors found solace in the fact that the buildings were never completed: on one end, a chunk the height and depth of the surrounding bricks and mortar is missing. Here once stood the shop of Robert Cowan, a man completely unwilling to sell his land. After several refused bids, the authorities finally gave up and built around his premises. Cowan's Corner became a revered part of Greenock, and remains so, though the eponymous owner's shop was bombed to smithereens during the town's two most traumatic nights.

On 6 May 1941, the Luftwaffe freckled bombs on Greenock. They created a ring of fire and in the illuminating glow caused by a burning distillery hit their targets with ease. A vital port and home to the Battery Park torpedo factory, the town was seen as fair game. When the 'all-clear' sounded at 3.30am, the entire area appeared to be on fire, with roofs blown from humble homes and the Municipal Buildings alike. An emergency edition of the *Greenock Telegraph* conveyed the news:

> One of the most intense raids in Britain was launched on Clydeside on Tuesday night. HE and incendiaries dropped on centre of one town over prolonged periods. Much damage due to fires. Defence services, aided by personnel of the armed forces, did magnificent work in rescuing buried people and extinguishing fires. All worked heroically even at height of blitz. Heavy barrage maintained. Flares dropped by Germans shot out by tracer bullets. In one case fleeing people machine-gunned by Nazi planes.

The next day, families scarpered to the countryside aware that a second wave of attacks was likely. From afar they witnessed the glow of their town being shelled from above again on 7 May. The next day's *Glasgow Herald* carried examples of the devastation:

> A family of ten was wiped out in one district of the town when a heavy bomb scored a direct hit on their sunken shelter, leaving only a large crater. The shelter had been specially constructed under a lawn and was entirely underground. When daylight came rescue workers found only torn pieces of clothing, a purse and a bank book which was charred and burnt.

Over two nights, 280 people died in all, with 1,200 injured. Figures in both categories would have been greater had not many scarpered for the country or hidden in nearby tunnels. More than 10,000 houses were damaged, with many occupants left instantly homeless.

Once the earth had cooled, Greenockians took some consolation in the fact that the parachutes used to land German bombs were made of fine silk. Putting them to good use, luxury skirts and shirts were soon being made and worn across town. Still, it had been a harrowing couple of nights that changed both people and place, as Vincent Gillen reflected:

> The Greenock Blitz is something that has marked the people, and although it only lasted two days, it was enough to change the face of Greenock. Fifty per cent or more of all houses had to be destroyed. If you walk through town now you'll see this concrete monstrosity, the heart of the town has changed beyond belief because of the bombing, and the '60s and '70s architecture.

It was in the shadow of such architecture that I peered at the Municipal Buildings and then right to the pinky-red walls of Wellpark Mid Kirk, a further classy edifice. Behind it on Bank Street, Thomas Kincaird, another of my bearded small town heroes, peddled his wares. Kincaird had moved to Greenock from Ireland as a 45-year-old in 1890. Named 'Tommy Matches' after his core product (matches, not people called Tommy), he suffered bullying at the hands of schoolchildren and adults, with the latter attaching 'charity appeals' to his cap. Tommy got his revenge by taking up the concertina and playing it appallingly and noisily. When asked to perform requests, he'd nod knowingly, and then continue with the din, an experience akin to watching a modern Ozzy Osbourne gig. After interrupting one funeral too many, weary residents clubbed together and purchased Tommy a more solemn barrel organ.

Pausing to look at a dark blue, green and pink fountain, I had a moment of empathy with Tommy as a beefy teen in a Rangers top exclaimed to his pal, 'Look, a fountain-spotter, the tube'. William Street spewed forth more frilly bits above doorways, and tragically derelict trading houses rotted at the back of the Municipal Buildings. Their colossal carcasses were occupied by seagulls choking on chicken wing bones scavenged from the KFC car park opposite. Told you it was romantic round here.

I followed tatty signs along a tattier route to 'The Waterfront', turning right in front of Clydeport's oversized Lego brick containers and continuing by a Tesco Extra, where many of their contents would end up. Sidling and sifting through the considerable chaff of a retail park, I reached Custom House Quay. Custom House was typical of Greenock: stunning splendour 50 yards from Carpetright. Gigantic Atlantic cruise ships dock here, though very few of their passengers pause to take in Greenock's history before heading onwards to the cities and Highlands.

That history is rich, and it is from here that Greenock grew. As Vincent Gillen said, 'The source of everything is the river. It's how it started. Connections with America, Canada, Australia; everything went through here whether it was trade or people. It's a Liverpool in miniature.'

Whether the trade was fishing, shipbuilding or sugar refining, Greenock lived by its harbour. Famous events were channelled through here too, from the Darien Scheme to World War Two, during which 2.5 million American troops docked.

Early on, Greenock was the home of free trade and commerce in Scotland, with little else given importance. When the poet John Wilson arrived to take up a schoolmaster's job, he was horrified to find magistrates had inserted a clause in his contract demanding he abandon 'the profane and unprofitable art of poem-making'. This atmosphere of unbridled and brutish capitalism makes the pursuits of the Morton Five and others admirable, and the achievements of James Watt, largely held as the town's greatest son, even greater than on first glance. Watt's statue was overcome by the silent creep of weeds when I visited, and the DSS built over the site of his house long ago. Still, there is a Wetherspoon's named after him.

* * *

On a puddly path between the docks and the motorway I set out for Cappielow, walking into spraying moisture that wasn't quite rain and hadn't blown from the water. The stoop began to make sense. Ignoring the welcoming pebble dash of the Barnard's Court Mission (slogan: 'A warm welcome awaits you to worship the Living God', which round here could well have been Andy Ritchie) I turned at Babylon (not another modern church but 'Fast food with flair') and entered the Norseman Bar. 'It's shite but we all go,' a woman in the street had said, which was endorsement enough for me. Ducking underneath two hanging lights invitingly smashed like pint glasses prior to an assault, I crept to the bar and ordered a drink and some Scampi Fries, of which there are just never enough in a pack. I took a seat next to the only other solo drinker, a man with a comb-over attempting the *Daily Star* crossword with all the intense concentration of a consultant performing brain surgery. As usual with these pubs and their once-a-fortnight clientele, there was a familiar contentment as football-only friends revisited in-jokes. Leaving the genial hubbub behind, I left thinking that indeed 'everyone' did go to the Norseman, but it was just the right side of shite, so to speak. Outside Cappielow, dads and sons pointed at things in the souvenir caravans and shivered beneath the cold blue sky and snowy hills.

Through the turnstile, Cappielow quickly became another ground to plant on my face a look of awe and an accompanying grin, possibly unsettlingly in the view of those nearby. After half a lifetime of Premiership functionality, here was another work of art sent to remind me that football was worth loving. To the left, a traditional Main Stand including walled-off directors' section with standard commotion at one minute to three; to the right, a deep terrace with painted iron bars to lean on and a corrugated roof; opposite, the open air benches of the Wee Dublin End, dwarfed by a crane aching to be put on a book cover. On a sparsely populated terrace that included a man wearing a Stetson, I remembered that it could be like this. Though the risk of injury or illness has significantly receded since it was written, Cappielow appealed to me for all the reasons it irked the writer of this 1948 letter to the *Telegraph*:

My desperate bid to have a photo included in a 'Spot the Ball' competition.

Sir, I pride myself upon being a member of Morton's 'Bread and Butter Brigade', one of those Spartans who regularly contribute for the privilege of acquiring fallen arches or staved toes at that 'bomb-hole' of a stadium, upon that pile of sticks and dirt which we flatter by referring to as terracing, or (on the other hand) sitting in that pneumonia conducive, corrugated iron object which serves as a grandstand.

Reclining on the back wall to drink in the panorama, I flicked through the programme and found a prime rant on the subject of the Old Firm from Morton chairman Douglas Rae:

I don't know about you but I am sick and tired of reading the trivia that is written about these two clubs and their players. Never a day passes when there is not one player or another extolling either what they are going to do to the opposition or what their team is going to do. Frankly I think that the space that is given to these two clubs is obscene.

The fury didn't sit easily in the Cappielow serenity, but perhaps that serenity was part of the problem Rae was writing about: over 10,000 had attended a recent cup tie with Celtic, the crowd undoubtedly boosted by local green and whites, while today's attendance did not bother the 2,000 mark. It was the same old story, one it seemed only Mike Mulraney at Alloa was willing to challenge.

After team-huddling with the awkward reluctance of teenagers at a ceilidh, Morton kicked towards the Wee Dublin End, once neighbour to Greenock's main Irish district. Dunfermline immediately attacked a Morton made frail and jumpy by the looming spectre of the relegation zone. For the 'Ton, dreadlocked Dominic Shimmin, once of Arsenal, held things together, time and again winning the ball and putting it to sensible use, the defensive version of a comforting hug. The teams over-passed the ball consistently and constantly to the point that I craved a centre-half's hoof, or at least something ugly to disturb the twee. As the half progressed, the away side became camped in Morton territory to the extent that the back four erected a tent and squabbled over who had forgotten to bring the tin opener. It made for near silence from the home supporters and a soundtrack of players hollering to be heard above the screeches of seagulls.

At half-time, I queued for a pie in the large terrace stand alongside the pitch. In front of me, a buxom old lady resembling a retired games teacher jogged on the spot to keep warm. Pie in hand, I moved to the collapsible condiments table and reached for the plastic ketchup dispenser. As I turned it upside down and gave it a shoogle, the top flew off and the wrath of a full bottle was unleashed on my jacket, hands and, more alarmingly, the nose of a child next to me. He wiped away the sauce with nonchalance, as if that sort of thing happened to him all the time, while I sought a cloth from the lady who'd sold me the pie. Instead, she emerged with a further, replacement pie, which was absolutely rubbish at soaking up ketchup from my coat. Watching football on your own can be a lonely, mortifying process.

Staying in the same stand for the second half, I was aware of people hostile to the scent of stale budget tomato sauce shuffling away from me. Their minds were momentarily distracted from the whiff when, quite remarkably, Morton scored. From a free kick, the ball hung in the air as both teams apparently slept. Unnoticed and not quite believing its luck, it carried on and bounced its merry way over the line. Perhaps now the

The second-half. Note distance to furthest neighbour.

home side could make Cappielow the 'fortress' manager James Grady sought in his programme notes. If they did, it had been modelled on a sandcastle trampled on by a tormenting overweight sibling: Dunfermline scored twice and easily held on for victory. As the sun set, fans trickled out of Cappielow and trudged home by the cranes and sugarmills of different times in Greenock. It was an occasion for being lulled by the comforting words of their greatest ever spokesperson, Arthur Montford, writing in *Morton, 1874–1974*:

> I can readily understand the desire of the fan in the street to support one or other of the 'big two' because success is nice. But fortunately supporting Morton isn't really about winning or losing, it's about loving the blue and white and it's talking about the Wee Dublin End and it's moaning about the pitch and it's about lots of other things as well.

CHAPTER EIGHT

Arbroath

Arbroath 1 v 1 Stenhousemuir,
6 March 2010

VISITORS TO VENICE fall for the city on seeing the Bridge of Sighs. With Barcelona, it's often la Sagrada Família. Similarly, when I saw DeVito's Nightclub, replete with *Twins*-era cartoon images of the fun-sized thespian, I knew Arbroath would do it for me.

Passing eight or nine hairdressers in the space of a few hundred metres, I heard several Polish voices while winding my way to the High Street, a pleasing reminder that even if indigenous young people were fleeing small towns, at least their places were being taken by a driven, rejuvenating bunch. On Market Place, I paid 30p to enter the Superloo and was soon glad I'd bothered. These turned out to be the most decorated public toilets in the world, the Brazil of bogs. Across the walls were proudly framed certificates proclaiming awards ranging from Dyson Loo of the Year to British Toilet Association Attendant of the Year. In some, toilet staff were photographed receiving awards from luminaries of the urinal world. Naturally, I entered with excitement, but while things were sparkling clean and smelt neutral enough, it wasn't the life changing experience I'd anticipated. As I washed my hands, the encounter went further downhill when a chap emerged from the cubicle, eyeballed me via the mirror and asked 'well at 30p, I wasnae just gonna have a pee, was I?'

If cathedrals and toilets can charge entrance fees, then Arbroath High Street should also be allowed to. Much of it is staggeringly beautiful, a real surprise. Maroon oil lamps and showy lampposts have been left intact and three-storey town houses are painted blue or red, cheering up the stone no end. There were shop names of endearing tradition (Goodfellow and Steven) and low level lewdness (Pert), though something about the dinnerlady Christian name stopped me from wanting to view Irene's Lingerie.

Walter Scott based the Fairport location of his *The Antiquary* on Arbroath, and much of it continues to echo a period drama film set. Nearly 100 years before 47 per cent of Scotland attached itself to JK Rowling and the Harry Potter franchise, the town was quick to exploit the concept of literary tourism. Several location guides were published, including 1904s *The Land of the Antiquary*:

> Everyone is conscious of the added charm of seeing with the eye scenes which have been made familiar to the mind through the works of some famous author; and readers of *The Antiquary* who visit the 'Fairport' of today will find, not only much that will make the past more real and vivid, but quite sufficient in the natural beauties of the district to afford delight in the present.

Unfortunately for Fairport, Scott and tourists, Haq's Newsagent was only added to the location relatively recently. Inside, a wall of varied magazine titles was bettered only by a wall of sweets in jars, among them my weakness: genuine Lion's Midget Gems. Had I not already seen the Danny DeVito theme club, this would have sealed my infatuation with Arbroath. Ordering a disgusting 200g, I savoured the noise of the sweets on the metal weighing jar and decided I really ought to stay in more. A short distance downhill was the Webster Theatre, once home of The Angus Black and White Minstrels. In an *Arbroath Herald* of 1903, I'd seen an advert for one of their shows, which included 'negro songs and dances' and 'plantation sketches'. Following up afterwards, I found the group had continued to perform blackface until 2005, making them the last in Britain to do so, at which point they'd changed their name to 'The Angus Minstrels'. The move received copious national press coverage, and for that week five years ago it must've been impossible to move for people leaving Haq's with their copies of the *Daily Express* tutting out the words 'PC gone mad.'

I turned the opposite way and walked upwards, towards the Abbey. On the way, I heard an old lady ask her two friends, 'Are Arbroath at home today?'. 'Aye,' one of them angrily replied, 'ye can tell because there's *men* about the toon.' This was either an uncommon occurrence in downtown Arbroath, or a coded salute to the fact it was International Women's Day. Feeling guilty about my gender, I walked on between yet more elegance and a Wimpy. In the window of Thomas Brown & Sons pet shop, a shakily written notice read: 'For Sale: 3 World War One medals, all named to same soldier with plaque and relevant papers.' It was a glum thought that these medals, fought and won in some horror show or other, were now being flogged in full view of empty hamster cages.

What struck me first about the Abbey was its colour, a crimson that begged for attention. It was as if, on founding the place in 1178, William the Lyon had asked his designers to give him something 'sassy, vibrant and fab-u-lous, girlfriend.' Overcoming the presence only metres away of cackling octogenarian feminists and the fetid whiff of Wimpy onions, the Abbey was peaceful, ancient and crumbling in an artful fashion. In this calm, even tweeting birds seemed an irritation worthy of an ASBO. It was here, of course, that Scotland declared its independence in 1320, eloquently demanding sovereign status and the right to charge an entrance fee of £4.70.

Having blown half my leisure budget on the Midget Gems, I surveyed the Abbey from behind cast-iron fences and continued on my way. On every corner, people gathered and gossiped in groups of three or four, a small town phenomenon lost in big city commotion. I passed the regal redstone public library and picture galleries, outside which a statue of Robert Burns stood guard to make sure no-one nicked any Maeve Binchys. Just when I thought Arbroath could improve no more, I emerged from the brightly-hued fishing cottages of Seagate at the Fit O' the Toon, a picturesquely crammed area looking out to rocks and then the lashing sea. Walking along a sea wall, I soon arrived at the harbours, part-working, part-attractive heritage sites. Boats rested and crustacean-mobbed creels were piled in their hundreds. Things were kept lively and relevant by seamen pottering on their boats and an abundance of bright, cheap and cheerful signs for Arbroath Smokie outlets.

The Smokie arrived here via Auchmithie, a village a few miles up the road. When the town council encouraged fishing families to relocate to Arbroath, the incomers brought with them their traditional method of cooking haddock and from there sprang an industry now covered by Protected Geographical Indication. They were joined by migrants from Shetland and Inverbervie, and together their labour made for a prosperous local fishing industry. Crucial in this were fishwives, the sharp-tongued class of tough women who sorted, smoked, heaved and sold their husbands' catches across town. Industrious and independent, Arbroath fishwives would follow the fleet across Britain, sailing to Scarborough and Great Yarmouth for their herring seasons, sometimes exporting their militant politics with them. Unfortunately, I was unable to taste the tradition they left behind as, somehow, 200g of Midget Gems had fallen down my throat and made me feel ever so slightly sick.

Fishwives. Come and have a go if you think you're hard enough.

Though Arbroath's two harbours are far from quiet today, at one time they buzzed along as the town's focal point. Ships arrived from and left for Portugal, Malta, the Black Sea, Jamaica, Uruguay and Australia. In 1840, Robert Chambers concluded that Arbroath was 'an eminently neat and thriving little seaport town; the harbour is neither safe nor spacious, but possesses considerable trade.' The diversity of activity here was encapsulated in regular Sunday night open air song and prayer sessions, still alive and kicking judging by a curious sign I saw:

THE HARBOUR AND FISH MARKET, ARBROATH.

B.9382.

Harbour hustle and bustle, 1960s-style.

Sunset Service Here at the Harbour, Every Sunday, 6.45pm. Bright Singing. Testimonies. Gospel Messages... Scotland, once known as a bible-loving nation was richly blessed and was home of famous inventors... Blessed is the nation whose God is the Lord.

Near the board bearing those words was another, which set the scene less idiosyncratically:

As you walk round the harbour, picture the hustle and bustle of days gone by – a world of schooners and brigs, grain lofts and woodyards, roperies and sailmaking lofts, ships' chandlers, ships' masters and sailors, fishermen and herring gutters. Imagine the smell of fish, smokehouses, tar boilers and creosote. And think back to when the harbour was so busy that boats often had to lie ten or twelve abreast.

While never operating on the scale of Greenock, Arbroath was important enough to feel under threat of attack at times, even if those doing the attacking didn't always know they were: in August 1914, a German schooner, the *Behrend*, sailed into the harbour with a cargo of oil cake. Having been on board for 24 days, the crew were unaware that their country was now at war with Britain, and on arrival the captain made a remark along the lines of, 'Oh, I thought I saw more ships than usual on the way.' By day, Boy Scouts guarded the impounded ship until it was time for the crew to be transferred to Edinburgh as prisoners of war.

A more knowing attack occurred in 1781, when a French ship, the *Fearnought*, anchored in the Bay of Arbroath and fired at the town. Its Captain, Monsieur Fall, followed up by sending ashore a series of notes that are best read in a slightly xenophobic accent somewhere between that of René on *Allo Allo* and one of the presenters from *Eurotrash*:

To Monsieurs Mair of the town called
Arbrought, or in his absence, to the
Chief man after him, in Scotland.

Gentlemen, I send these two words to inform you, that I will have you bring to the French colour, in less than a quarter of an hour, or I set the town on fire directly; such is the order of my master the king of France I am sent by. Send directly the mair and chiefs of the town to make some agreement with me, or I'll make my duty. It is the will of yours.

Slightly baffled, the 'mair' replied with a request for ransom terms, possibly beginning his missive with the words 'Lol. U R a laff'. The charming Fall wrote back:

> Gentlemen, I received just now your answer, by which you say I ask no terms. I thought it was useless, since I asked you to come aboard for agreement. But here are my terms; I will have £30,000 in sterling at least, and 6 of the chiefs men of the town. Be speedy, or I shoot your town away directly, and I set fire to it. I am, gentlemen, your servant. I sent some of my crew to you; but if some harm happens to them, you'll be sure [we] will hang up [in] the main-yard all the preseners we have aboard.

In the time between letters (bloody Royal Mail), Arbroath had armed itself and felt confident enough to implore Fall to do his worst, 'for we will not give you a farthing.' The enraged Frenchman let forth a barrage of cannon fire, none of which did much damage apart from, as one smutty contemporary account had it, 'burning the fingers of those who took up his balls, which were heated.' The *Fearnought* obviously began to fear something and sailed off in search of further comedic escapades, Fall shaking his fist as the people of Arbroath waved him away and the credits rolled.

I continued on to the Tourist Information Centre, housed in a trendy wooden new-build featuring a gallery, a restaurant and a Wealth Management Consultancy. Before I could shake my head and say 'how times change' like some rueful character on *Last of the Summer Wine*, the wind blew me onwards towards the Signal Tower Museum. Strolling by the deep blue sea I understood why Arbroath had once been known as 'Scotland's Sunniest Resort'. An advertisement from the 1960s printed in Arbroath Council's *Official Guide* summed up the eclectic charms on offer 'Every Tuesday at 3pm in East Coast Scotland's open-air pool' as:

> Miss Arbroath, Holiday Princess, Junior Miss Arbroath, Glamorous Grandma, Knobbly Knees, Eric Caldow (famous Scottish and Rangers footballer).

The Signal Tower was once home to the families of Lighthouse Keepers dispatched to operate on the deadly Bell Rock. Messages were conveyed via a pole and brass ball on the Tower's roof, and their content included birth announcements: if a pair of trousers was raised, a Keeper knew a son had been born to him; a dress was hoisted for girls, and a kilt was just confusing. Inside the cosy and proud museum, the industries which replaced Arbroath's fishing heritage (sail- and flax-making, engineering, canning, lawnmower manufacture) were accounted for in some depth, often via splendidly ugly papier mâché people. Leaving, I ruminated analytically that the Black's tourist guide of 1882 had been talking absolute bollocks when it asserted that there was 'little to attract the tourist [to Arbroath] except its Abbey.' In the distance, I spied floodlights, two of which appeared to be at sea.

* * *

The Red Lichties, nicknamed after the beam that once guided ships into the harbour and absolutely nothing to do with brothels, were founded in July 1878. Rugby players, curious about this new-fangled kicking game, met in the George Hotel and drafted a constitution with community involvement in Arbroath FC as its core value. Unlike Morton, there were no high morals, just a desire to give the town something to enjoy. A 1948 book, *The Story of the Maroons*, summarised the new club's essence and legacy:

> It was founded by Arbroathians who loved the game for the game's sake, and it is carried on today by men imbued with the same spirit. In an age when the game has, for better or worse, become highly commercialised, Arbroath FC is still run on its original lines, free from any question of gain or profit-making, concerned only with the game as a sport.

Initially playing in black and white 'spider stripes', the new club began with a 3–0 victory against Our Boys. In 1880, a community subscription campaign raised funds for Arbroath to purchase land at Gayfield, then occupied by a rubbish tip. A pitch was laid, and their home for life opened with a 2–1 victory against Rob Roy FC, or 'The Heather' as they were more commonly known. Three years on, Arbroath raised their first trophy, the Forfarshire Cup, after a victory against Dundee Harp at Rollo's Pier. When the result reached home, reported a local newspaper, 'no telegram had given such universal satisfaction since the fall of Sebastopol was definitely announced.' A 4–3 Scottish Cup victory against Rangers the following season should have represented the Red Lichties' greatest result to date, but the Glaswegians telegrammed home to claim they had been 'beaten on a back green', complained about the width of the Gayfield pitch and had the result annulled. Rangers won the rematch 8–1.

On 12 September 1885, Arbroath's name became eternally synonymous with the number 36. Their victory by that margin to Aberdeen Bon Accord's nil remains a British record and always will, unless another club comes up against a bootless outfit wearing belts and braces with their right-half in goal. John 'Jockie' Petrie netted 13 that day, and goalkeeper James Milne became so bored he sheltered under a spectator's umbrella. While *The Scotsman* understatedly described Arbroath's achievement as 'remarkable for some phenomenal scoring', the *Arbroath Guide*'s report appeared almost embarrassed in describing 'The most amusing football match ever seen in Arbroath.' One paragraph in particular outlined the 'farce' of it all:

> After Munro had put on the fifth goal a slight rest in the reckoning occurred, the Aberdeen men somehow managing to keep the ball for a short-time near midfield. Then the Arbroath forwards seemed to get thoroughly into the fun of the game, and before the call of half-time had scored another 10 goals. After the 13th had been got, the Aberdeen forwards had a momentary encounter with the backs near the Arbroath goal, but this was the only time they got away from their own territory.

In the second period Bon Accord did manage a shot, until it became 'a repetition of the first, five goals being registered within the first 15 minutes, and 16 during the other 30 minutes.' The *Guide* concluded:

> The Aberdeen men never seemed to be dismayed by the turn of events throughout the match, and to the close did what little they could to keep off their opponents. They cannot play football, but Saturday's lesson will have shown them how it was done.

Disregarding the validity of comparisons with later and modern football as it developed, it was a fine scoreline that announced Arbroath's arrival on the scene and has defined them since. Having said that, a thought should be spared for Dundee Harp: that same day, they defeated Aberdeen Rovers 35–0.

Soon after the Bon Accord gubbing, a player regarded as Arbroath's greatest ever made his debut. Ned Doig was a strapping, powerful goalkeeper, as well as, in the Victorian all-rounder hero tradition, a prizewinning athlete and accomplished musician. According to *Boy's Own* yarns recounted on his descendants' excellent website, as a teenager, he constructed a goalmouth from three beams, suspended a ball from a piece of rope and taught himself to punch the ball from all angles. Ned also made two dumbbells at a local foundry, placed one at either side of the goal, and dived to scoop each up in quick succession. He was soon able to fist a mere football incredible distances with frightening accuracy. The comic-book story continued throughout his career: his debut came when, close to kick-off, it became clear Arbroath reserves did not have a goalkeeper. 'Let Ned Doig play' went up the cry, and the teenager was sent for. Doig excelled and quickly became the talk of Arbroath. Match reports persistently flagged his performances, with the *Arbroath Herald* praising his 'skilful and dextrous movements', 'keenness of eye and deftness of both hand and foot' and 'masterly coolness'. In February 1887, he became the only ever Arbroath player to receive a Scotland call-up. The *Herald* saluted his accomplishment:

> This is the first time any northern player has received International honours and it is not a little to the credit of our town that the distinction should have been gained by an Arbroathian. Mr Doig has made rapid progress as only last season he was goalkeeper to the second eleven of the local premier team but he has proved himself to be a thoroughly reliable player and we heartily congratulate him on being called upon to occupy so proud a position in the football world.

Doig helped his country to a 4–1 win against Ireland. That same year in the Arbroath Annual Sports Day, he won the high jump, finished second in the mile handicap race and third in the 300-yard sprint. Twelve months on in the same competition, Doig, then employed in a flax and canvas factory, excelled himself, winning the 300-yard sprint,

Arbroath's high-achieving 1935/36 squad, five of whom regret throwing their maroon shirts into the crowd during exuberant celebrations.

The outstanding Dave Cumming in a lovely snug jumper.

skipping rope race and hop, step and leap. These days, this kind of restlessness is called ADHD. On Saturdays, he was soon renowned as the best goalkeeper in Scotland and beyond, the original cat. Bigger things awaited the local hero, and when in 1890 Sunderland offered him a chance to join their 'Team of All the Talents', he departed Arbroath.

A year after Doig left, Arbroath joined the new Northern League where they remained until the inception in 1921 of Division Two. From then on, they bobbed between the leagues, producing a number of notable, England-bound players on the way such as Preston North End's FA Cup Final-scoring George Mutch and Dave Cumming, one of my own team's greatest keepers. In 1935/36, Arbroath achieved their highest ever position of 11th in Division One during a campaign that included a comeback from three goals down at Ibrox in which, said the *Herald*, 'Rangers rocked, reeled and then collapsed.' After World War Two, the club were yet another shocked to find themselves abandoned to the lower division when football resumed. Written in 1948, *The Story of the Maroons* contained fresh upset at the Scottish League's decision:

> The late unlamented Adolf Hitler succeeded where the big guns of Scottish soccer failed. It was Hitler's war which ended Arbroath's career in the First Division... With victory, first over Germany then Japan, the question of peacetime football loomed large. It

is not within the province of this book to include any opinion on the 'politics' of Scottish football. Suffice to say that the undertaking, given at the outbreak of war, that victory would see the Scottish League re-started on the same basis as when suspended in 1939, was not implemented, and a new era yielded place to the old.

The 'relegation' decision had the positive effect of galvanising fans into organising for themselves a Supporters' Club. Their principal remit was to:

> Promote a friendly spirit between club officials, players and supporters... raising monies which shall be used in such a way as to be beneficial to the Arbroath FC as is deemed most necessary by the Supporters' Club after consultation with the Arbroath FC Committee.

The Supporters' Club pretty much *was* Arbroath FC. Emphasising its ethos of town representation, impressively for an era not known for equality its founding committee consisted of 12 women and nine men. The football club would sink or swim through the volunteers' efforts, and little has changed since.

Their commitment was rewarded in 1947 with a run to the semi-finals of the Scottish Cup, and five years later a record attendance of 13,510 for a defeat at the hands of old foes Rangers in the same competition. Proving their worth through the thin as well as the thick, the Supporters' Club played a pivotal role in raising funds after Gayfield's main stand was destroyed by a fire in 1958. In their *History of the Red Lichties*, Malcolm Gray and Stephen Mylles described how the drama had unfolded:

> Tragedy struck. The first warning that anything was amiss came around 3am when a little fox terrier called Susan wakened her mistress in a house overlooking the park. The playing pitch was illuminated as though by floodlight, but in fact a spectacular fire had broken out in the grandstand.

As if by way of reward for the Supporters' Club's endeavours, striker Dave Easson ended that season as Britain's top goalscorer above Jimmy Greaves and Brian Clough with 52 league and cup goals.

That second half of the last century was characterised by further to-ing and fro-ing between the divisions, and took in the extraordinarily lengthy

18-year reign of manager Bert Henderson. Whether through the efforts of the Supporters' Club or through the comfort of being an integral part of a fine town, Arbroath have long appeared a club comfortable in their own skin and, as those words crafted in 1948 had it, 'free from any question of gain or profit-making, concerned only with the game as a sport.'

* * *

After a walk by the sea up to Gayfield I crossed the road and entered the jammed Tutties Neuk pub, if only because the name sounded like a form of German pornography. There, one voice emerged above those of all others: that of the landlady, who appeared to be competing with the foghorns of nearby container ships. As a method of running a match day bar it worked a treat, though I was slightly concerned about the building's foundations. Clumsily filing through the turnstile and regretting the second hundred grams of Midget Gems, I was pleased to be greeted by balloons and a banner attached to a mesh fence, albeit for Betty on her 65th. It certainly trumped a crackly birthday wish on the tannoy betwixt Keane records.

In the club shop, an Aladdin's Cave had Aladdin grown up in Angus, the sociable woman behind the counter answered a proud new dad's surprisingly in-depth questions about Arbroath baby clothing with great humour and charm, and even endured a prolonged chat with me. Karen, I learnt, began attending her local team's matches aged 11 and joined the Supporters' Club committee in her 20s. Twelve years ago, she'd volunteered to run the shop, becoming another of the many fans who had buttressed the club since 1945. I'm slightly obsessed with these homely, lovingly-stocked outlets, chiefly because they make me nostalgic for Ayresome Park, where perm-haired Diane and tiny Derek with a limp would sell me postcards of Bernie Slaven for 50p and put highlights videos in the wrong boxes.

Of particular pride for Karen is seeing young people throughout the town ignoring the corporate polyester of Celtic or Manchester United and donning Maroons shirts:

Recently we had an open morning where we invited the Junior Lichties [under 12s season ticket holders] and they play five-a-side games on the pitch against the first team. It was brilliant to see how many had Arbroath tops on: more than 75% of the kids.

As I'd seen, the club shop was not just somewhere to buy 36–0 mugs and mouse mats ('we send those all over the world'), but a social hub:

> There's my regulars who don't buy a thing, but they come in every single time. They often want the gossip on new trialists, new signings, any info really. Every home game!

This cabin den is a key part of a community club. It's a brethren Karen is frequently reminded of through one of her other volunteering roles, that of programme contributor, as she explained:

> When I interview ex-players, the number of them that comment on how happy they were at Arbroath because it had that family feeling is extraordinary. Too many say it for it not to be true.

I bade the spectacularly friendly Karen goodbye, feeling a little bit better about the world and determining to make good use of my Arbroath fridge magnet.

While Gayfield didn't light up my senses like Cappielow, it possessed a quiet charm and open, un-segregated terracing on three sides. In the railway station earlier, I'd looked at a display of paintings completed by local primary school children. I particularly liked the one which said 'Gayfield holds about 7,066', but from this vantage it looked far closer to 7,067. Arbroath were in the middle of an ill-advised flirtation with the relegation zone, while opponents Stenhousemuir had little to ridicule from their position slightly above. Risking appearing on the end of season DVD, I stood right by the corner flag furthest away from the sea and saw Arbroath win an early penalty. Stepping up, forward Steve Hislop prodded the ball as if nudging a pet dog out of the front door. It didn't go in. Only a few minutes later, Arbroath took the lead with a shot that scythed through the penalty area and rippled the net like a shoal of herrings. 'We don't need penalties' sang the Gayfield faithful.

The away side came to life, ferociously pressing forward and earning a penalty, narrowly converted by Kevin 'Brother of World In' Motion.

So close I could smell the sweat. Putrid.

Arbroath noise turned to accepting and familiar bonhomie, though the consensus was disrupted by another bawling maiden. From behind the goal she howled 'Jimmy! Jimmy! JIMMY!' Amazingly, across in the main stand Jimmy replied with an 'Aye love?' 'FAGS!' came the answer. To my right, a very patient Dad read the 'A-Z of Footballing Cliché' to his young son so that one day he too could talk about good feet for a big man, low centres of gravity and pluralise single entities ('you see, your Stenhousemuirs and your Arbroaths of this world cannae just go out and buy anyone').

At the break, the 150-or-so home supporters gathered behind the goal moved off in a herd, trudged behind the main stand and took up position in the opposite end. The 35 away fans that had been there did the same in the other direction. It was the first half-time mass migration I had ever seen, apart from the time an overweight Branco stormed out of the Riverside never to be seen again. As a long term subscriber to the wisdom of crowds, I followed them and took up a position at the back

Somewhere beyond the sea Arbroath huff and puff for a goal.

of the enclosure close to Pleasureland funfair and amusement arcade. When later an errant shot landed on its cold tin roof with a thud, those around me let out a gasp as if fretting for the heart rates of angina-suffering grannies on the slot machines.

Arbroath pushed and pressed with moments of quality bringing nods of approval. Desperately seeking forgiveness, Hislop threatened repeatedly and low-socked loanee Callum Booth jinked up and down the left flank. I moved over to his side and watched a few yards away from the North Sea, a ridiculously thrilling experience. In a ground renowned among fans as the coldest, this was the most perilous spot and the one in which club shop Karen had long stood with her family:

The worst I remember it was one year Cowdenbeath came to visit, and it was blowing a gale, it was raining, it was high tide and you could taste the salt water coming up as the waves came over. That was very cold indeed. But you get used to it.

Today the sea remained calm and the winter blue sky was far too polite to freeze anyone. The main danger for me was distraction and the way in which hearing waves crash against a wall while watching a thumping two-footed tackle confuses the senses. Stenhousemuir's Willie Lyle earned a red card for the worst of those tackles, and his victim, the buccaneering Booth, will long be finding bits of stud in his leg. That was the away team's second dismissal, yet Arbroath seemed to slow down against the nine men, presuming a winning goal would arrive. It didn't. At the game's end, players slumped to the ground in exhaustion and supporters cursed the manager for not introducing more firepower.

I walked back by the sea and forgot all about football in a manner impossible down south amid the in-your-face nature of Sky Sports News across every post-match pub. In any case, DeVito's would be open in a few hours.

CHAPTER NINE

Dingwall

Ross County 1 v 1 Dundee, 27 March 2010

HIGH ABOVE DINGWALL, a lone turret rises above a graveyard. Its isolation suits the subject for whom it was put there, so excluded from mainstream history has Hector Macdonald been. The crofter's son who became a Major General was once a hero. Through the century since his suicide, the silence over Macdonald has continued in death the class discrimination and homophobia he suffered in life.

On the morning of 25 March 1903, in a Paris hotel room Macdonald tidied his belongings, hung up his jacket and placed his boots out of sight underneath the bed. He then raised a pistol to his right ear and shot himself.

Macdonald's death ended a triumphant military career. Having joined the Gordon Highlanders aged 17, bravery and tactical brilliance saw him climb through the ranks in a period where buying high army office was the norm. The working-class Dingwall man's meteoric ascent irked whole sections of the military Establishment; how could this dour plebeian come to be ordering around the aristocracy? Sprinkling salt on the wounds, Macdonald had what could euphemistically be called 'homosexual tendencies' at a time when being gay was equated with being a paedophile. Wherever he served in the world tittle-tattle and insinuation plagued him. A letter in *The Times of Ceylon* published shortly after his arrival as military commander of what we know now as Sri Lanka was not unusual:

Hector's Dingwall turret.

You know, we heard a whispered rumour that he does not like ladies, and possibly may have been pleasantly surprised to find he had dropped on a spicy little isle where ladies are few and far between.

Rising above this context, Macdonald excelled militarily. At the Battle of Omdurman in Sudan, he saved the skins of Lord Kitchener and his troops. Actions in the second Boer War and Afghanistan saw him knighted and transformed into a Scottish icon: Fighting Mac, one of their own who had risen and now got to order the posh English around. When he was awarded the Freedom of Dingwall in May 1899, a crowd of thousands convened to salute their finest export.

Hector Macdonald taken by G Lekegian in Egypt, c.1898.

On Macdonald's arrival in Sri Lanka, things began to go awry. Islanders gossiped about his relationship with the teenage sons of a friend. Then one day in a train carriage, he was allegedly caught 'with' four young boys. Rumours that further accusations would soon come to light swept through the island and the army. Macdonald was dispatched back to London to await his fate where, wrote Ronald Hyam in *Empire and Sexuality*, he 'was probably told by the King that the best thing he could do was to shoot himself.' Within the military leadership, an atmosphere of *schadenfreude* reigned – the cocky upstart was at long last getting his comeuppance. Learning he was to be sent back to Sri Lanka to face a court martial, despair engulfed Macdonald. Should these allegations – never substantiated – be proven, his beloved career would be over.

En route to Sri Lanka, Macdonald checked in at the Hotel Regina in Paris. After a night's sleep, according to his biographer Trevor Royle, he breakfasted before examining the day's newspapers. One headline in particular caught his eye: 'GRAVE CHARGE LIES ON SIR HECTOR MACDONALD'. Fighting Mac realised that a scandal previously confined to the military had gone public. Perhaps in his gentleman soldier eyes, suicide would amount to 'doing the right thing.'

The Scotsman reflected that news of his death

Created in Edinburgh the keenest surprise and regret, the sad intelligence quickly spreading over the city and causing intense excitement. Throughout the South African Campaign... his career was watched by the citizens with the utmost interest, his name being quite a household word.

Their Inverness correspondent wrote of the reaction in Macdonald's native Highlands:

The report of the suicide of Hector Macdonald caused something like a shock, as he was personally known to many in the town, and was regarded with quite peculiar pride by everybody. His last visit to the north of Scotland, after his magnificent handling of the Soudanese troops at the Atbarand Khartoum was like a triumphal progress through the Highlands. Wherever he made his appearance, thousands flocked to see the renowned Hector, and his bluff manner and characteristically Highland face and form made him the Highland hero of his day and generation.

The grieving public would not be given the chance to offer Macdonald a send-off. Secrecy cloaked the return of his body to Scotland and, most unusually, he was buried at six o'clock in the morning. Only a handful of people were there at the Dean Cemetery on 30 March; it was almost as if there were something to hide. In the following night's *Glasgow Evening News*, author Neil Munro offered his interpretation:

It must be rarely, indeed, that Edinburgh has known of a six o'clock funeral. The Princes Street scavengers stared as the hearse trotted briskly past them, its dozen cabs behind; workmen walking on the bridge high over the Village of Dean looked and wondered, but they did not know that this was Hector Macdonald. How could they? He was being disposed of secretly – for so it was ordained – against the Will of all Scotland: the greatest precautions were taken to prevent the public from hearing where he was to go.

Throughout the following week, enormous crowds queued at the cemetery to pay their respects. A feeling grew in Scotland that Macdonald had been betrayed by the dastardly English. While down south his papers were lost and his existence gently airbrushed, Scots set about creating a lasting memorial, erected in Dingwall in 1907.

Macdonald's memory has also been maintained in print, firstly through Trevor Royle's estimable *Fighting Mac: The Downfall of Major-General Sir Hector Macdonald*, and recently in Jake Arnott's mesmerising novel *The Devil's Paintbrush*, in which Macdonald plays the lead role. I asked Arnott, an English novelist known for writing about 1960s London, what drew him to this sadly neglected son of Dingwall:

> I came across Hector Macdonald and realised there was something else there, something different, which was a genuine tragedy. It was a tragedy in the Greek sense that he rises up, and then he rises too far and then he falls. He's brought down by his own nature really. It's like Othello. This is somebody who was a great general but will never belong. Othello never belonged because of his colour, Macdonald never belonged because of his class.

Interestingly, Arnott saw the class factor as being far more important in Macdonald's downfall than his sexuality:

> This is where it becomes a tragedy rather than anything else: it's because of his background. It wasn't his sexuality that brought him down, it was his class and all through his life that was the case. You weren't expected to live on your wages as an Officer in the British Army. It was expected you'd have your own means. People would be drummed out for being too middle-class, let alone working-class. He was used to show that this was the new age of meritocracy when you didn't have to buy your rank. But of course he suffered terribly for that.

That did not mean Macdonald's sexuality was accepted, and in his research Arnott found that some Scots even explained it away as an English smear. Whatever the politics, he lamented the lack of recognition his subject has received beyond the Dingwall turret:

> The really sad thing about Hector is that he disappeared. There's not a single monument to him south of the border. At that time, the Empire heroes were the single-name celebrities, and yet he's disappeared. He was the greatest fantasy and the worst fear of the Empire.

* * *

By the Macdonald Monument a murder of crows swooped far too close to my head for comfort and made the noise of a thousand nails scraping a blackboard. Panicking, I tripped and kicked my way down the gravel path between graves, looking like Frank Spencer in a Hitchcock film. From the cemetery's foot I looked down on Dingwall, a small town made slighter by the scale of its glorious mountainous surroundings. Towards the Cromarty Firth I could make out stewards putting on their fluorescent uniforms in the car park of Ross County's Victoria Park. From the long and winding road down to town, Dingwall's Tesco superstore appeared to be the same length as the entire High Street.

On the town notice board a flyer offered children the chance to 'play games, do challenges, crafts, sing and learn who Jesus is'. I liked the tacked on bit at the end, a written equivalent of quickly coughing through bad news. Along the High Street, there was a modesty in the architecture suggestive of a town never wealthy yet never poor. Its history was more titbit than epic: the word Dingwall came from the Norse for 'Hill of Justice'; the town was called Bailechaul in Gaelic, meaning 'place of the cabbages'; Macbeth might have been born here. It was pretty but plain, lacking the gripping architectural ups and downs of industrial Scotland. The 1885 *Gazetteer* captured the locale's restrained ambience well, offering that:

> The burgh, lying snugly among rich clumps of trees, at the entrance of Strath Peffer, chiefly consists of one main street, a mile in length; and, while the majority of its houses are irregularly disposed and unpretentious architecturally, still there are several very handsome modern residences.

In 1724 residents had painted a grimmer picture, desperately pleading for attention from the Convention of Burghs on the grounds that:

> the town is almost turned desolate, as is weel known to all our neighbours, and there is hardly anything to be seen but the ruins of old houses, and the few inhabitants that are left, having no manner of trade, live only by labouring the neighbouring lands, and our inhabitants are still daily deserting us.

They were eventually granted a small harbour that meant life in Dingwall was upgraded to solid if unspectacular, the town version of a dependable defensive midfielder. In an unfamiliar bout of abandon, the elders did spend a tidy amount on the Town House. Its proud clock tower now performs the important function of trying to stare out Tesco's brash lettering behind.

With Dingwall so physically and historically discreet, colour would have to come from its citizens. In a series of columns in the *Ross-shire Journal*, Jack Sinclair brought to life the town he had known as a teenager early in the last century. It was a time of artistic and inspired nicknames such as Ma Jaw, Murdo the Bird, the Ferry, Ken Spun ('a name commemorating the gyrations of Ken homeward bound from the Caley Bar after closing time'), Beelack, Scooch, Dobbler, Jock Snowdrop, Swallow the Wheel, Swallow the Wheel's Wife and Swallow the Wheel's Wife's Man. Sinclair told of a High Street brimming with well-drawn characters and their animal accomplices such as:

> The bearded quiet-spoken gentleman wearing a distinctive hat of the type favoured by Winston Churchill. With several small grazings around, he moved his sheep from one to another in a strange way. We were used, in those days, to flocks of sheep being driven along the street with a multiplicity of barking dogs, heading to and from the auction marts, but my old friend walked in front followed by his sheep. Thus we were able to understand the scriptural phrase – "he shall lead his flock like a shepherd."

Even living this peaceful life, reality was not inescapable. A contemporary of Sinclair's, Alex Rind, recollected that their idyllic world had been punctured by tidings of tragic events at sea. News of the *Titanic's* sinking was mysteriously accompanied, as he remembered:

> I vividly remember how some of our neighbours wrung their hands in sorrow when full details of the disaster became known. And as though to add a note of poignancy to an already lugubrious mise-en-scéne, a youth in his late teens drearily and repeatedly played the 'Merry Widow Waltz' on his melodian. I could only see his figure vaguely in the fading light of the afternoon. Who he was or could be I cannot tell, and I never set eyes on him again.

I can now reveal that the young man was head hunted by *Sky News* to lead their Department for Completely Inappropriate Soundtracks and Graphics.

Like most of the places I'd visited, Dingwall's High Street looked tired in places and was undoubtedly browbeaten by the parallel presence of that megalithic supermarket. It's a standard gripe, but nonetheless a valid one. Removing ideology from the equation entirely, the centralising of business into one turgid hub is just *boring*. The Dingwall High Street Sinclair and Hind knew overflowed with independent shops, each loved by their owner and proudly turned out. A 1930s directory of Dingwall I flicked through listed 51 'leading businesses' including the Picture House ('now 100 per cent talkie'), Wishart's Electric Bakery, Lemon and Co off-licence and The Temperance Café. As Sinclair himself noted,

> At that time, the word 'supermarket' had not been thought of and we had six grocers, three bookshops, three shoe shops, three chemists, three saddlers, four bakers, three drapers, a milliners, and a taxidermist with the inevitable stuffed wildcat in the window.

Fearing this chapter would not have quite enough talk of cemeteries, graves and monuments, I walked through the grounds of St Clement's Church, bouncing on years of undisturbed foliage. I stopped to look at a section crowded with tiny gravestones, each etched with two or three initials and a year. It would have been a moving sight, but behind me a rotund Grotbags type was hurling empty wine bottles into the Tesco recycling bins with Olympian force. Being here reminded me that Jack Sinclair told a story about the deeply religious identity of his Dingwall. One August Communion, he and his Dad had spotted a devout man returning from church,

> Who in response to my father's polite greeting, "a fine day Mr McN...," said in a solemn tone, "This is not a day to be speaking about days." I am still pondering this profound observation.

Next to the church I took a quick look at the leaning tower of Dingwall, a 57-foot obelisk dedicated to George Mackenzie, first Earl of Cromarty, 'thrown slightly off the perpendicular by an earthquake of 1816' according to the 1885 *Gazetteer*, but was quickly distracted by the cheerfully punning Hong Kong Foodie takeaway behind. The sun streamed down and cheered up the town, though my own mood was lowered by the depressing spectacle of an old lady sitting alone in Wimpy morosely sipping tea. This made me want to cry a little, so I tried to imagine that she deserved it, perhaps for crashing bottles into a recycling bin.

Inside the newsagent, a man with an Essex accent, the golden skin of retirement and darkened glasses purchased the *Daily Mail* as if by contractual obligation, and I grew concerned for the education system when the young lad in front of me happily paid 34p for three 10p mixes. I walked towards the railway station, now home to a Christian Bookshop. I'm never sure if that means they sell Bibles or are run on religious principles, so that shoplifters are forgiven. Judging by the response to my question about Sunday opening hours, it appeared to be the latter. With roads into Dingwall poor until relatively recently, the station was for a long period the town's main outside connection, as Jack Sinclair reminisced:

> The station was the hub of trade and commerce and everything and everybody moved by rail. Folks had time to converge on the station, especially for the mail train. Under the glass roof there was always a vast army of trolleys and hurleys laden with parcels, hampers, boxes, even young calves in sacks, with only the head protruding, and two brown eyes registering panic and alarm, and maybe hunger not really allayed by small boys who offered a grubby finger to suck.

* * *

These days, one of the station's buildings is home to a bar, The Mallard, though what trains have to do with ducks I'll never know. Entering, after the emptiness of the High Street I was aghast to see so many people. It was as if I'd stumbled into the only speakeasy in town, albeit one containing rosy-cheeked men in Dundee tops. Worryingly for someone with most of his own teeth, I realised the racket they were making was annoying me, and soon left. This was either a side effect of a relatively peaceful season, or jealousy that despite the rewards of travel, the tranquillity of solitude could never match the vocal unity of partisanship. That and the fact the Guinness was shit. Across the road in

The National, where Hector Macdonald had once worked as a stable boy, the barmaid twice asked if I required 'anything else?', and my inner Robin Askwith wondered just what kind of establishment this really was.

Here, things were more serene but equally animated as Ross fans debated travel plans for their forthcoming Scottish Cup semi-final against Celtic. Notwithstanding Dingwall's 5,000 population, they'd been allocated 8,000 tickets. With Hibernian recently beaten in the quarter-finals, and a top-of-the-table derby with Inverness Caledonian Thistle imminent, there was much to anticipate.

Reading the papers, I found the headline 'Man found with dope at dance' to be harsh on the poor woman he was tangoing with, and shook my head at the news that 'The enduring popularity of toyboy rockers Showaddywaddy has prompted Strathpepper Pavilion to release an extra 200 tickets for their gig in May.' In total, that would mean an attendance of 750, or 122 more than had been at Cowdenbeath and Albion combined when I visited.

Still, judging by the numbers stomping to Victoria Park, the crowd at that retro retro night would be trumped by today's. Crossing the railway bridge, I became aware that all around me grew something often missing this season: atmosphere. Both of these sides had their eye on promotion, and a healthy number had trekked from Dundee to tell us all about it through the medium of song. For all the architecture of Somerset Park and Cappielow, the community ethics of Alloa and Arbroath, the thought space of a Montrosian half-time, I hadn't half missed a thousand people belting out 'the referee's a wanker'.

With no cash turnstiles, I stood in the queue for a ticket and studied a shiny sign bearing the club's Code of Conduct. I was struck by the words 'The following behaviour is not acceptable within the stadium: to refrain from any Racist language or behaviour.' Did that mean my usual tactic of not being racist wouldn't be tolerated?

A stag's head hung above the entrance to the ground next to an appeal total thermometer at its maximum, something I'd never seen before, showing that fans had raised £60,000 to 'Save Our Staggies'. I soon learnt that none of this had anything to do with local deer fans, and that 'Staggies' was in fact County's nickname. Inside the tight, unblemished ground the din continued, benefitting hugely from another PA system in 'resting' mode. Passing along the back of the packed Jail End (the jail building remains only as flats) where youthful supporters sang of Hampden, I settled in the largest seating area opposite the functional West Stand.

From the off, the tempo was unlike anything I'd seen all season. The play ebbed and flowed, encouraging followers at both ends to roar their collective approval. Rain lashed violently and intermittently, watering the playing surface and adding zip. Even better than all that, I realised the barrel figure in goal for Dundee was none other than Tony Bullock, once of this parish among others. Bullock was born in deepest rugby league territory and as a youngster clearly bulked up to fit in. Today, his rasping, ranting voice harked back to an industrial north of lock-outs and matchstick men and dogs. Until he signed for Ross, sweet old Dingwall had never seen the likes. I'm sure I detected fondness for Bullock in the ribbing he received from his old fans in the Jail End, and Dundonian adulation was obvious. They may have been cheering on Caniggia and Ravanelli only a few years back, but now nothing beat a bit of Bullock.

In several hundred football matches, I'd never caught the ball on those occasions when it entered the stand. On the whole, I was glad about this: aware of my limp throwing abilities, I knew it could only end in derision rather than the chants of 'sign him up' I'd heard greet champion hurlers, especially the one at Middlesbrough who'd caught Bryan Robson squarely and powerfully on the back of the head towards the bitter end of his managerial reign. This all changed just before half-time when, with no-one else near, the ball bounced between seats and settled next to me. Those nearest implored me to pick it up, and a boy of primary school age looked at me as if I'd just snapped his Buzz Lightyear figure over my thigh. I leaned over, picked up the ball and stood up, sending my notepad flying from my lap and into a puddle. On receipt of the ball (which, for some reason, I tried to spin), the Dundee right-back, Eric Paton, let out a kindly 'cheers pal'. He was either polite or felt desperately sorry for the geek with the soggy pad.

Thankfully, attention quickly moved to the similarly ridiculous figure of Ben Hutchinson. Fairly tackled, the Dundee forward performed the opposite to a snide dive, deliberately labouring to the deck and then writhing in sluggish agony like a drama student impersonating a slow

From the Jail End, another 'Spot the Ball' entry.

A free-kick is swung in shortly after my throwing heroics.

motion replay. The referee did his bit for the atmosphere by awarding a free kick for Hutchinson's efforts, before whistling the end of a decent first half.

I moved to battle for a space in the Jail End. Through the break, those around me stood in rare silence, mentally noting every morsel of the Hampden ticket and travel arrangements being laboriously read out over the tannoy. Beneath outward appearances, enthusiasm was not universal. A sturdy septuagenarian with cheeks the colour of offal was asked whether he'd be journeying to Glasgow for the big game. 'No chance,' he replied in the kind of sonorous voice that could so easily have powered the Large Hadron Collider, 'it'll cost a bloody fortune *and* they'll get beat.'

As if begging him to mutter 'bloody typical', Dundee took the lead early in the second half when slow-dive Hutchinson took the ball down on his chest and crashed it in. The noise from the Dundee end grew as the travelling army began to smell promotion and the reinstatement of city derbies. The Staggies pounded Bullock's goal, but the keeper defied his waistline to save time and again with sprightliness. As the clock advanced, Ross manager Derek Adams located his 1920s coaching manual and moved to a five-strong forward line. They raided until finally, with four minutes left, an equaliser was pillaged.

* * *

'What you going there for? They've no history,' said some of my fundamentalist football friends when I told them I was going to see Ross County. There were two answers to this: number one, they did have history, just not in the Football League; number two, after visiting so many clubs whose best days were usually 90 years behind them, I wanted to see what a club on the up looked like. I was also interested in the relationship between Ross and Dingwall; it was clear elsewhere that industrial society had led to the creation and support of football clubs, but what of such an agricultural, seemingly comatose area?

In part due to the popularity of golf, bowls, cricket and rugby, football was never king in Ross-shire as elsewhere, but did provide another outdoor pursuit for a people who appeared allergic to being indoors. Jack Sinclair recalled hundreds turning up to watch Dingwall's two main teams, Thistle and Victoria United, after World War One. With no turnstiles, there was 'lots of movement in the crowd as the hat came round!' Sinclair also recited ingredients of his favourite United team, constructed entirely by more Dingwall characters:

> 'Tackets' in goal, a specialist at punching clearances, and a terror to any opposing forward. At the back, Willie Morrison had experience in the English League; 'Rabbit' Urquhart; Jock MacMillan, for long a defender; big 'Dai' Maclennan, a great goalscorer, and occasionally Willie Dewar, the Town Clerk with twinkling toes, who, we were told, had at some time played for Heart of Midlothian. Jock Mackay was on the right wing and had a peculiar aptitude for scoring from the most unlikely angles.

Rather than an escape as elsewhere, early football in Dingwall was a continuation of normal life and community ritual. Working outdoors through the week, inhabitants stayed there to play and watch sport at the weekend. In 1929, those that took football a little more seriously realised that the town was too small to support a reasonably successful Highland League team, and decided to extend ownership and belonging to the wider region. The result was Ross County. Reflecting their surroundings, County took their nickname from the badge of the Seaforth Highlanders, a neighbouring army regiment. Many Ross-shire men had fought and died with the Seaforths in World War One, including players from Thistle and United. Reflecting the extent to which football was embedded in Dingwall's recreational habits, they constructed their new ground in the middle of the town's municipal park.

The Staggies won the North of Scotland Cup in their first season, and reached the last 16 of the Scottish Cup in 1933/34. By 1966, a year I wish English football commentators would mention more, they had etched themselves into county life to the extent that 8,500 people, a record, attended a Scottish Cup match with Rangers played on a Monday afternoon. Then, as in the cup run of 2010, a zealous core support was supplemented by thousands of others from across Ross-shire as the club became a beacon for regional identity.

After snaring back-to-back Highland League titles in 1991 and 1992, Ross felt bold enough to apply for membership of the newly extended Scottish Football League. On the club's day of reckoning, chairman

Hector MacLennan travelled to Glasgow with secretary Donnie MacBean. MacBean later told the County website:

> [We] travelled down by train and took the opportunity to go over our presentation and draw up some cue cards. I don't mind telling you that I was nervous – especially when we arrived and saw that other teams had gone to great lengths such as having pipers playing and fancy video presentations. Having got over the urge to turn around and jump on the first train home, Hector and myself stood up and made our pitch – we had done a lot of work and were confident of our facts, and I think that must have been what swung it in our favour.

Along with Inverness Caledonian Thistle, they had pushed their club on to a new level, and it would soon go further. Now, the main challenge is breaking into another elite, the SPL, and everything seems to be in place for that to happen. Refreshingly, Ross County are mid-project, their best days ahead. Bucking the trend of most other clubs in this book, support may not yet have peaked. Escaping industry meant Dingwall avoided the economic decline that blighted those clubs' towns. With the steady rise of Inverness Caledonian Thistle too, could it be that the future of smaller-team football is brighter the further north you go?

CHAPTER TEN

Cumbernauld

Clyde 1 v 2 Stirling Albion, 20 April 2010

SOON AFTER MOVING to Scotland, I felt I had the hang of things. St Mirren were from Paisley, St Johnstone played in Perth, East Fife's hometown was Methil and no-one knew anyone who had ever eaten a deep fried Mars Bar. Then one day on the train from Edinburgh to Glasgow, I spotted a medium-sized new build stadium somewhere in between. This, it turned out, was Broadwood, Clyde FC's Cumbernauld abode.

On a journey earlier in the season, I'd asked a train guard to where exactly I should travel for most easily accessing Broadwood. 'You should set alight at Croy,' he had said, baffling me into silence. Risking spontaneous human combustion, I disembarked there late one spring afternoon and immediately found myself alone. Fellow passengers had disappeared into waiting cars for lifts, and Croy seemed to be little more than a car park with a railway station. Attached to the bus stops on both sides of the adjacent road were Perspex cases advising of bus times to Kilsyth. In weakening sun I resolved to walk on to the next set of stops to search for a destination that sounded less like 'Kilsyth' and more like 'Cumbernauld'.

After 10 minutes it soon became clear that either I'd turned the wrong way and lost the bus route, or the conductor's Croy answer had been the equivalent of asking the cocky new apprentice to pop down the shops for tartan paint and a long stand. The more I said the word 'Croy' to myself, the less it sounded like a real word, never mind a place, and if I'd turned back to find the station had vanished I wouldn't have been astounded. But go back I didn't. To the warped male psyche in an unknown place, that is defeat and reneging on a mission of survival. Indeed, walking through a Cumbernauld industrial estate was probably how Ray Mears got started.

Soon, paths dissolved into grass verges and a torrent of cars whooshed by. After 15 minutes, I spotted a Tesco and the insipid outline of a roadside chain pub. At first I thought this must signify civilisation. In reality, it signified another roundabout. Road signs, with their references to area numbers and 'The Village' refused to help. After an underpass and a mild contemplation of my life's direction I stumbled into Cumbernauld Community Park, welcome firstly because it contained the word 'Cumbernauld,' and secondly because it turned out to be charming. Trees silenced the traffic and the hilly green rolled out ahead. Still, it wasn't where I wanted to be, and after sensing two nearby rabbits were mocking me for being lost, I carried on, eventually reaching Eastfield Cemetery, a forest and then the A80 motorway. From the opposite side, tower blocks surely belonging to Cumbernauld peeped out above trees like ugly trolls on the other side of a river. With nowhere to cross I grudgingly retraced my steps for a while, inwardly weeping and regretting a late decision not to pack distress flares.

A different turning took me at last to bus stops, and after decoding timetables it seemed there would be a bus in 23 minutes. As 20 and then 21 minutes elapsed, a succession of loud unsighted 4x4 vehicles had me rising to my feet in anticipation of a bus and then dejectedly sitting again. Never had a man wanted to board a bus marked 'Cumbernauld' as much as I did then. At last, the lesser-spotted number 34 chugged up, its rosy-cheeked driver my saviour, albeit one whose heroic soundtrack consisted of a Real Radio phone-in. My rescue vehicle rattled back and forth through many of the directions I had already been in, passing Tesco, now a vague memory from what seemed like days before. Out of the window the newest of Cumbernauld new town whizzed by, its house sizes and styles ranging from Brookside Close to Hertfordshire footballer. Spaced out and with grass dominant, it aped the comfortable monotony of all suburbs, with shops, pubs or any community hub absent.

We spluttered downhill, bypassing the original Cumbernauld village (presumably 'The Village' of useless sign fame) and the well-regarded theatre. The driver slowed towards the town centre and invited me, the last remaining passenger, to depart at the bus station. Entering, I realised he had not only been a valiant knight, but one capable of time and place travel too: judging by the station's design, it was 1972, and I was in Budapest.

I'd like to write that Cumbernauld's creators had not been going for this Soviet look, but I'd probably be wrong. Theirs was a scheme of soaring ideals once lauded for its ambition but since lamented for its appearance. It was a social and economic experiment every bit as worth studying as anything produced by the Kremlin. Half a century ago Cumbernauld was a concrete dream aimed at transforming society. It was Robert Owen's New Lanark for 1956, only with more parking spaces. Overcrowded Glaswegians would be transferred here, spirited away from the grime of that mean city, from tenements to garden homes. City culture would be no match for provincial consumerism: Cumbernauld had Britain's first shopping mall. In fact, Cumbernauld *was* Britain's first shopping mall; its town centre remains, for the most part, indoors.

* * *

The New Towns Committee launched by the Labour government of 1945 was charged with springing millions of Britons out of city squalor and human congestion. The Committee's first report conveyed the scale of change required:

> It is not enough in our handiwork to avoid the mistakes and omissions of the past. Our responsibility, as we see it, is rather to conduct an essay on civilisation, by seizing an opportunity to design, evolve and carry into execution for the benefit of coming generations the means for a happy and gracious way of life.

The vision for Glasgow was set out a year later in the Clyde Regional Plan, a hefty handbook for dispersing over 500,000 Glaswegians. Half would be moved to peripheral areas of the city, and half to the new towns at Cumbernauld, East Kilbride, Bishopton and Houston. In *An essay for today: the Scottish new towns 1947 to 1997*, David Cowling articulated the optimism of the movement:

> The New Towns were to be at the leading edge of a buoyant sense of enterprise and self-belief within our society. Emigrants from the crowded urban areas, freed from the unhealthy city core, were to be pioneers in new communities of opportunity in the nearby countryside. Beneficiaries of healthy fresh air, open space, trees, easy access to the fields and hills, and participants in a new

'clean' industrial future. They were to be harbingers of a national liberation from the 'dark satanic mill.'

In December 1955, the Cumbernauld Development Corporation (CDC) was instigated and charged with delivering Scotland's most ultra-modern new town. Forecasting a population of between 50,000 and 80,000, the CDC appointed architects and engineers from across the world to design and build the future in the middle of the Lanarkshire countryside. They produced a suitably futuristic and pioneering blueprint of satellite neighbourhoods clustered around a hilltop 'Town Centre'. Those neighbourhoods were linked to the Centre by a series of walkways, paths and underpasses so that traffic need never be encountered. As a CDC factsheet published in 1968 put it:

> This is a pedestrian shopping centre, and the success of such centres elsewhere has proved that people like to shop away from the noise and danger of motor roads. The hectic struggle in crowded streets is replaced by the pleasant conditions in the vehicle-free areas where shoppers can stroll and chat.

The Centre catered for all their life and retail needs, a forerunner of the 'everything under one roof' mantra running through shopping malls today. There were shops, banks, a Post Office, pubs, restaurant, hotels, a library, churches and numerous community spaces. All were stacked layer on layer and supported by *Jetsons*-style stilts, with unapologetically sci-fi addresses (J4–09, Centre North; K4–54 Centre South; J4–10 Centre North...). On the Centre's top floor sat 35 penthouse apartments, at their opening rumoured to comprise the most expensive public housing in Britain.

A carefully-planned road system meant traffic wardens and pedestrian crossings were not needed, and Cumbernauld's accident rate was a fifth of the national average. Though accommodation varied from tower block to town house, all dwellings – 90 per cent of them council-owned – were grounded on the principles of maximum light, space, privacy and greenery. 'In Cumbernauld,' claimed a later factsheet, 'a compact, urban way of life is combined with a constant awareness of the countryside, penetrating the heart of the town.' The aim was to build no house more than a 15-minute walk from wide open space. For Glaswegians raised in the grimy struggle of a post-war city this was a project worth buying into; as the CDC continued, 'Everyone in the town has come as a volunteer, for the good life that the town offers, so they all have a stake in its economic success.' Those wishing to move would first have to meet Glasgow Corporation's overspill criteria, and once in Cumbernauld the CDC's housing policies. A lengthy and meticulous tenants' code was established, covering every aspect of life in the new town from bins and smokeless air to 'The care of a bath' ('The bath should always be cleaned immedi-

Concrete dreams on the birth of Cumbernauld.

ately after use, preferably while the bath is still warm.') and pets ('It is emphasised that the prior written permission of the Corporation must be obtained before a pet is brought into the dwelling'). In return for subscribing to the dream, new residents received housing of a standard far improved on what they had known in Glasgow.

It was a bold, sometimes overbearing plan to forever change life in Scotland. Students and scholars of architecture and sociology converged to witness the experiment in action. In 1967, Cumbernauld's 'town centre of the millennium' won the American Institute's award for Community Architecture, their fulsome citation hailing Cumbernauld as:

> Undoubtedly the most comprehensive project of community architecture to date. Rarely has a group of architects and their allied professionals and consultants produced a more carefully developed scheme on this scale. Throughout the project evidence is found of devotion to the overall problem and superb skill in urban design.

Economically Cumbernauld thrived, with new industries and businesses enticed by tax incentives and a ready-made labour force steeped in the Clydeside work ethic. The population snowballed, prompting revisions of earlier predictions and planning alterations. In the early 1980s, a television advert was screened to celebrate a town on the up. Its message clearly worked as now, whenever Cumbernauld is mentioned, it is obligatory for any Scot to reply 'what's it called?' It was by no means utopia, but the CDC had dared to dream and then make real much of their design for life.

Architecturally and socially, though, that design was not necessarily a good one. Criticisms were many: the Town Centre was made out of crude concrete rendered only marginally less brutal by a paint job soon after it opened; from 1982, many of the surrounding buildings were deemed structurally unsound and demolished; walkways and open, wall-less malls became wind tunnels; those malls failed to attract big name shops to take up occupancy; the penthouses emptied as wealthier residents moved to the large houses on the outskirts I passed on my magical bus journey; Glasgow communities were split and found Cumbernauld's labyrinthine layout anti-social and difficult to navigate.

In 1980, the words of architects Philip Opher and Clinton Bird encapsulated the disdain in which the Town Centre was now held across Scotland:

> The megastructure – stranded between two windswept and desolate areas which are likely to remain undeveloped for many years to come – seems like the folly of some mad 20th century eccentric.

Over the last decade, the Town Centre twice wrested the Plook on a Plinth award away from Coatbridge and was voted 'the worst building in Britain' on Channel 4's *Demolition*. Leaving Budapest 1972 on a spiralling walkway, I went to find out why.

* * *

The first words to remember when entering Cumbernauld Town Centre are 'yes, this is it.' The shopping mall is not a Greenockian hell hole that leads to something better outdoors, it *is* the town, save for a few civic buildings across the road. This is post-apocalypse indoor living. Spread over a number of bending and twisting levels are 'streets' cheerily named after rivers. There's Esk Walk, Forth Walk, Allander Walk, Avon Walk, Tweed Walk, Spey Walk and Clyde Walk, suggesting the word 'Walk' was on buy one get one free at the sign maker's. All suffer from the dim lighting of a railway station toilet and low mishmash mesh ceilings. I crossed the dark brown stilted sky tunnel over the dual carriageway to the north side of town and looked at murals painted outside the closed library. Recently hung and depicting vibrant local scenes, their bright-ness seemed sickly and irrelevant in such shabbily dark surroundings, but at least those who had painted them appear to have retained some of the optimism Cumbernauld was founded upon. Disorientated by the sight of a live plant (it was that kind of atmosphere), I pressed on to Cumbernauld's newest addition, the Antonine Centre, a much-needed shopping mall by the people who took coals to Newcastle and flogged ice to Eskimos. There, the light was far brighter, more like that of a drug rehabilitation unit, and teenagers flirted outside the closed Zumo Fresh Smoothie Bar.

Outside the Antonine, people were gathered in groups chatting. I walked by the bustling Tryst Sports Centre and pondered the rarity of seeing a British town not dying by sundown or collapsing under the weight of Happy Hour. In the housing area south-east of the Centre, the liveliness continued with scores of people old, young and in between using the outdoor spaces. By playing their games under them, children had made the ubiquitous underpasses far from intimidating. All in all, I couldn't help but notice that, despite being among housing resembling primitive tumble driers, people seemed content. The happy noises of kids playing and grannies gossiping with Glaswegian lilts made the experience I'd been so heavily forewarned about a not unpleasant one. It could be, of course, that they were happy *in spite* of their surround-ings. Either way, if I'd closed my eyes and ignored the man calling his dog a 'fat baw heid', it might have been utopia.

Back over towards the Centre, I paused to look at Cumbernauld College, one of very few excessively futuristic buildings remaining here. With its jagged pagoda edges and squashed centre, the side profile of the College looks a lot like Bagpuss, another 1970s creation that frightens me a bit. Beneath it a disturbing sculpture suggestive of a baboon's back-side with giant wasp's eyes commemorates a visit by Princess Margaret, appropriately. Staring up, the sheer vulgarity of the Centre at last became clear. Lanky clumping legs and a long body make it look as if it may walk off and stamp on some cars at any point. The closest thing to it is a *Star Wars* AT-AT Walker painted in dank brown and cigarette ceiling yellow. Underneath, cement and glass cubes of differing size jostle to be the ugliest. Even with the hideousness I liked looking at it, perhaps in the same way people slow to look at accidents or buy the records of Michael Bublé. This was the future, even if it never happened. It was a different path we could have taken, and I found being around this derailed Shangri-La enthralling, similar to stumbling upon a Wild West film set reconstructed in the middle of a desert. It was a living breathing heritage park, like going to Beamish and being reprimanded by Gladstone for wasting bread on the ducks.

The Centre is now bookended by an Asda and a Tesco, both open 24-hours. The free market identikit has cancelled out the planned one. I would have stood and pondered the irony of this but a more urgent matter pressed: how on earth was I going to get to Broadwood?

* * *

Clyde FC's journey to Cumbernauld took even longer than mine though probably involved less having to pee in the woods. The club began life at Bridgeton's Barrowfield Park in 1877 when, so the story goes, a group of rowers were looking for a sport to occupy them in the winter months (that's rowers as in people with boats and oars rather than argumentative so-and-sos, who can carry out their cantankerous hobby in all seasons). Barrowfield Park was part of a sporting and social hub in Glasgow, with tennis and cricket matches, musicals and plays hosted locally. Football was an extension of those apparently middle-class recreational pursuits; surprisingly for a club on the banks of an industrial river, Clyde's origins were far closer to Ross County's than Morton's.

'The Bully Wee' (no-one is quite sure how they got the nickname) played for 20 years at Barrowfield before moving on to Shawfield Stadium in Rutherglen, actually a horse-trotting track. In 1906, Clyde were promoted to Division One and more than held their own, finishing third just three years later. By then the celebrated Mattha Gemmell had worked his way to the role of coach, having served the club as a player,

The Centre and Tesco strike a pose like some kind of complex metaphor
I can't be bothered to work out.

and then a groundsman, though first and foremost as a fan. Living most of his days in Main Street, Bridgeton, he had watched the club from its earliest days and retired only in 1945. Famed for his tobacco chewing and accuracy with a spittoon, Gemmell was endearingly gallus. On being offered the coach's job at Queen's Park, he responded by accepting on the condition that he 'goat away every Setterday tae watch the Clyde.'

The early sides Gemmell trained enjoyed a prolonged golden epoch, if not a trophy-laden one. From 1909 to 1913, Clyde moulded the bridesmaid template, returning home unsuccessful from two Scottish Cup finals, two semis and a quarter. In 1912, 48,000 people watched an infamous second round home tie with Rangers which highlighted the threat to Old Firm dominance Clyde now posed. With a quarter of an hour remaining, *The Scotsman* reported,

> When Clyde were winning by three goals to one, a collision between two opposing players occurred, and immediately a section of the crowd on the south-west corner invaded the field.

One of their number struck a Clyde player, and was promptly arrested. Thereupon many hundreds more of the spectators crossed the barriers into the field, and a scene of confusion ensued, the four mounted police and some 30 other police on duty being unable to exercise any control over the crowd. The referee and players apparently realising that it was futile to endeavour to proceed with the game, retired to their own quarters. Some 15 minutes later it was announced that the game had been abandoned.

Clyde were outraged and insisted that Rangers forfeit the match rather than take up their right to a replay. The Ibrox side gracefully withdrew from the cup, allowing the Bully Wee their passage to a second use of the bridesmaid dress.

In World War One, Clyde were devastated by the loss in action of five players. It signalled the start of a bleak period where success was sparse and finances precarious. To stave off liquidation, in 1932 the club's board decided to make profitable use of Shawfield's racing track. Founding the Shawfield Greyhound Racing Company, directors purchased the ground and leased it back to the football club. With crowds numbering three times those of Clyde matches, the income generated by the dogs subsidised the football club. Shawfield was also leased out for boxing matches, including a 1937 World Flyweight Championship bout watched by 36,000.

Kept on course through the doldrums and out of the other side by the ever-present Mattha Gemmell, Clyde finally got their hands on the Scottish Cup in 1939 under the stewardship of Paddy Travers. Startlingly given the score, star man in their 4–0 crushing of Motherwell was goalkeeper Jock Brown whose impeccable first half performance gave the Bully Wee a platform on which to build. Quoted in Tom Greig's *The Bully Wee*, Brown recounted his team's pre-match build-up:

For the semi-final and final rounds we stayed in Troon, trained on the sands and played pontoon till 3am. On the day of the game we travelled up from Troon, had lunch in the club at Shawfield and proceeded by bus to Hampden. For the record I wore a yellow jersey with a blue cap. Snappy dresser, eh?

His side were played onto the pitch by the Glasgow Gas Department Band's rendition of 'I Belong to Glasgow' as 95,000 fans, many in Clyde-white glengarries, looked on. At half-time, the deafening noise created by the crowd drowned out a speech expressing the advantages of national service by Provost Dollan. For the benefit of those lost in ale and atmosphere, Jock Brown narrated the action:

> We elected to play against the wind and survived a fierce 30 minute spell of Motherwell pressure. Our pivot, Eddie Falloon, all 5'6" or so of him, got his head in the way of a pile driver. He was still dazed on the ground when Dougie Wallace scored at the other end. He took a deal of convincing that we were ahead. We had two fast-raiding wingers, inside men with polish and finishing power and Willie Martin our big centre was deadly in the air. I felt the neutrals in the crowd were with us and in the second half with the wind behind we went to town. Final score 4–0!

The Scotsman offered praise for Brown and his team:

> Clyde, in weathering a difficult first half in which a strong wind was heart-breaking for defenders, gave a splendid display. Falloon dominated the goal area despite his lack of inches... Brown was confident and made a number of good clearances.

The team travelled back to Shawfield for champagne-soaked celebrations and to negotiate the collection from a Glasgow jeweller of complimentary gold watches. Brown depicted the glee felt by the man who had waited longest for that moment, Mattha Gemmell:

> Oh, he was a happy man that night. He kept saying, 'Ma boys did it! They did it! I can hardly believe it.' I think every player that night was as delighted for Mattha as he was for himself. You know I often wondered how frequently Mattha himself went without his wages. He would never say. That man loved the Clyde. We all did.

After World War Two, with Gemmell in retirement but on the Shawfield terraces, Clyde built a reputation for attractive football.

The mercurial Tommy Ring does moody indie band singer look.

Their style had substance: twice in four seasons the Scottish Cup was brought back to Rutherglen.

In the 1955 Final, Clyde's revered forward line of Johnnie Divers, Archie Robertson, Ally Hill, George Brown and Tommy Ring took on Celtic. Equally important to that side was Harry Haddock, a gentleman full-back who refused to bring down opponents ('it's an admission of weakness if you have to foul a man to stop him,' he once said). Haddock was famed for his forward sojourns, then deeply unfashionable as he explained:

I had a tendency to overlap and no-one, including the manager, could understand it in my day. A full-back was expected to stay in his own half and boot the ball away. Many a time I got my knuckles rapped for attempting an overlap.

The BBC showed the final, making it Scotland's first live televised domestic game. It was refereed by a man whose name meant a career in officialdom was inescapable, one CE Faultless. Commentator Kenneth Wolstenholme saw Celtic take the lead and hold on until Clyde scrambled a corner with just three minutes to go. Writing in the *Sunday Mail*, RE Kingsley described what happened next:

I couldn't read his [corner taker Robertson's] mind. But I guess he decided there was too much height in that Celtic defence for a normal ball – so he'd drop it in as near the crossbar as possible, and hope for the best. The best was even better than he'd hoped for. That ball hung just under the bar as Bonnar's groping fingers clutched desperately for a purchase – then drifted down the back of his hands and over the line. Robertson stood transfixed on the corner spot with his arms stretched upwards in dumb token to the fates. His pals soon broke that up. He was lost in a human hug-me-tight. Result, we had all the Clyde team near the Celtic corner flag – the Celtic team wringing their hands in and around their own goalmouth – while referee Faultless could be seen dribbling the ball on his owney-oh up to the centre-spot.

In the face of an under par performance, Clyde had forced a replay.

Reports of the 1955 cup finals are, as so often, more interesting for their content concerning off-field happenings. In a fierce sports editorial, the *Glasgow Herald* lambasted the presence of Irish tricolour flags and their incendiary effect:

> Despite the requests of the Celtic management, this flag continues to be carried and waved. What is worse is that more flags of the kind than ever were seen at Hampden on Saturday... I now seriously suggest that if the creatures who under the flags of Eire disgrace the club which they profess to support continue to do so Celtic should put the club's tricolours "in cold storage". On Saturday – and not for the first time – a ceremony before the kick-off was ruined by the flag-wavers seeking to destroy the effect of the National Anthem and behaving in a fashion that can fairly be described as inciting to riot... It is not an offence in itself to wave the Eire flag or any other, but it is an undisputed fact that shocking behaviour invariably accompanies the waving... It is additionally distressing to know that some of those who behaved deplorably are visitors from Belfast whose regular appearances at Celtic's important games should be summarily stopped.

For the replay, the same newspaper noted that the situation had changed after 'The police took immediate steps to ban the Eire flag which, however, was almost conspicuous by its absence.' This time, in a much-improved game, the football did the shouting as, said the *Herald*, 'Clyde won the cup deservedly, though they withstood a terrific barrage in the final five minutes.' Pouncing on a rebound, Tommy Ring had scored the final's only goal. 'Oh, how Bridgeton and Rutherglen danced and sang last night when Clyde brought the Scottish Cup home to Shawfield,' enthused the *Daily Record*, 'What a victory night it was!' On its way to the ground for those celebrations, the team bus had taken a detour

After calling in on Mattha, Clyde bring the cup to Shawfield.

to 236 Main Street, Bridgeton. From a tenement window, an old man named Mattha Gemmell saluted his visitors with a handkerchief.

As in 1939, the 1955 victory was masterminded by forward-thinking manager Paddy Travers. Perhaps emerging from the shadow of his retired coach Gemmell, Travers' view of how football should be played was stamped all over the latter team. Taking their lead from emerging Hungary, Clyde became famous for their slick, silky play. Travers pioneered preparation techniques including Saturday morning warm-up training. He punished players for allowing the ball to go above knee height, and encouraged them to take jobs so they would appreciate the beauty of football.

By the time of the Bully Wee's 1958 cup capture, Travers' assistant Johnny Haddow had taken over and continued the theme, his mantra summarised thusly:

Football must be played on the ground, the ball never passed higher than a few inches from the pitch. In all training matches, it will be a foul if you don't keep the ball low. The air is for birds and sputniks, not footballers.

Against Hibs in the Final, a John Coyle goal meant a trio of cup wins for Clyde. From the dog days of the 1930s, the club had been transformed.

Keeping with the narrative of most teams in these pages, Clyde's halcyon days could not last. Tom Greig put it most succinctly, writing 'Since the 1958 cup win the story of Clyde has been less than encouraging... Mostly it has been a recurring story of disappointment with relegation being high on the list.' When the good times did return, they were fleeting and beset by administrative ill-fortune; in 1967, Clyde finished third in Division One but were barred from taking their place in the Fairs Cup because another Glasgow club, Rangers, finished above them and took the city's only allotted place. Protestations from the Bully Wee that they belonged to Rutherglen fell on deaf UEFA ears.

Falling gates and declining revenues had by then forced the Clyde board to survey their options. A move to the new town of East Kilbride was mooted as early as 1966 – there, went the logic, a large population without football would rally to the cause in great numbers. Attendances continued to plummet into their low hundreds throughout the 1970s, and writing in 1977 Tom Greig explained the club's position:

> The reasons for the decline are not exclusively connected with the lack of success on the field, television or the increased mobility offered by the motor car, popular excuses offered by clubs when declining gates are mentioned. Shawfield sits in a triangle that lies 70 per cent in Rutherglen and 30 per cent in Glasgow. There was a time when such a location drew on a heavy population in Gorbals, Oatlands, Bridgeton, Burnside, Dalmarnock, Hutchesontown and Rutherglen. Then the domestic face of Glasgow changed and thousands of families found brighter prospects in new housing areas and towns far removed from Shawfield and many of the houses left behind by the Glasgow overspill were demolished.

By 1986, Clyde's greyhound landlords were no longer connected to the football club. They served their tenants notice, and on 28 April the Bully Wee defeated Alloa 4–2 in the last game at Shawfield. Writing in *The Shawfield Story*, Dave Coupar illustrated the scenes played out under the ground's infamous Tote board, a dominating presence indicating the stadium's primary function:

> The fans on the terracing danced, sang and grabbed everything that wasn't nailed down, plus a few bits that were. There was

nostalgia galore in the old Shawfield stand as the great romance came to an end. They rolled out the Clyde heroes of yesteryear like Harry Haddock, David White, Neil Hood and even Disc Jockey Dougie Donnelly took a half-time bow… And as the final whistle sounded, the terracing emptied as the fans poured on to the hallowed turf for the last time, surrounding their heroes and digging up prodigious amounts of the field. The party then spilled over into the local hostelries, with many a supporter spotted clutching a substitute number board or a bag full of grass.

For the next five years, Clyde shared Partick Thistle's Firhill. Coupar had foreseen how desperately unpopular that partnership would be, writing in 1986, 'As to the future, many of these fans will trudge their way to Maryhill every second Saturday, while others have vowed never to darken Firhill's doorstep.'

At the start of the 1990s, the CDC approached Clyde and proposed a move to Cumbernauld. For the public and private bodies involved, luring a League club to the new town would mean raised profile and more chance of finance to build a municipal stadium. Clyde would benefit from a growing and captive audience hungry for football, many of whom had arrived from the razed tenements of Rutherglen and its environs. With a 50-year lease agreed, work on Broadwood Stadium began on a site in the west of Cumbernauld. In the meantime, the nomad Bully Wee moved on again, this time to Douglas Park, home of Hamilton Academicals. Broadwood was funded by the CDC together with Dumbartonshire Enterprise. Costing £6 million, it was to be the springboard for a further £50 million business and retail development in that part of town.

In seeking out-of-town relocation, Clyde were following football's perennial motif of clubs being shaped by the society around them. Just as Cowdenbeath and Raith had grown to bring about release for the industrial working class, Morton had been created in the spirit of Victorian paternalism and Ross as an outdoor pursuit, so Clyde would have to go where the people and money were in order to survive.

* * *

Back over in 1972 a coach driver assured me Broadwood could be reached by taking a bus to the Craiglinn Interchange, which sounded like it had something to do with sex reassignment surgery. The number 147 wound its way through the kind of spaghetti housing estates that cause Sat Navs to be signed off with executive stress. On lampposts, next to signs promising weight loss political parties advertised their wares ahead of the imminent General Election. At Craiglinn, following a quick and unsuccessful search for Hayley from *Coronation Street*, I negotiated another underpass and emerged on a path with Broadwood at its end.

In the spaces around the stadium, that £50 million of investment appeared to have been spent creating empty muddy fields and a large pond, or loch as you Scots prefer to call them. There was simply nothing around: no pub for fans to congregate in and build rapport; no local newsagent boosted by match day sales; and very often naught as luxurious as a pavement. Up bumps and down potholes, I reached a stadium that appeared to have weathered well and was as aesthetically rewarding as an early-1990s ground could be. Above the main entrance, attached to the large 'B' in Broadwood was a graphic of an analogue stopwatch, stuck in time like the Town Centre. Underneath it, the 1878 and sailing ship on Clyde's badge sat uneasily, like an elderly relative at an 18th birthday party.

An attempted arty shot of Broadwood. Cumbernauld does that to you.

Though only a few hundred were expected at tonight's game, the large car park was packed and a traffic jam blocked the main thoroughfare. Unfortunately, the abundance of lycra and leggings suggested drivers were heading for the Broadwood Leisure Centre or the Gymnastic Academy rather than a Scottish League Division Two game.

Very few fans were in evidence, their loitering curbed by the risk of ladies late for step aerobics mowing them down. The wind howled through the concourses inside the ground, their smooth silver plastered concrete walls adding to the chill. I climbed the stairs and took a seat above the players' tunnel. Opposite and to the left were stands only ever used now for Old Firm cup visits, empty as the penthouse apartments in town. Behind one goal was an imposing metal structure modelled somewhere between a maximum security prison in Baltimore and a giant air vent. Thirty feet high and the width of the pitch, it had the intimidating effect of making the warm-up look like exercise time in the penitentiary yard.

The largest groups in the Clyde crowd were teenagers taking up the £2 entrance fee for under 16s, middle-aged Shawfield travellers and pensioners who had chased the Cumbernauld dream. Again football reflected social trends; so many of the young adults who had grown up in Cumbernauld had now made the reverse trip of their parents' and moved back to Glasgow or further afield.

Clyde ran on to the kind of mild applause usually reserved for irritating street entertainers. With three games to go, they had claimed squatters rights in the division's basement. Only nine points for them and none for Arbroath would bring salvation. The programme editorial was far from bullish at Clyde's chances:

> We effectively surrendered any real prospect of avoiding relegation
> to the Third Division a fortnight ago... we are determined now
> to play out the season, take a break and come back in July with a
> squad capable of winning back the fans after a wretched season.

Stirling Albion, meanwhile, had spent the months since their failure to equalise at Recreation Park tussling with Alloa for first place. The Binos were followed to Cumbernauld by an army made rowdy when they took an early lead. Reacting, Clyde began to channel everything through Adam Strachan, a spindly, skilful winger with shorts pulled too far up his stomach. His persistence encouraged those around him, five of whom believed themselves good enough to wear white boots. One certainly appeared to be: with 19 minutes gone, Willie Sawyers plucked the ball from the air and half-volleyed it into the net from a distance. In the summer, Sawyers had been picked from 100 trialists and offered a contract with the Bully Wee. Leaving Maryhill and his job at Optical Express behind and taking his boots to Broadwood, his was a story redolent of long ago or an awful film starring Sean Bean.

Not one for romance, the referee reacted by awarding the away team a suspect penalty. When that was saved, the Clyde fans rejoiced with more fervour than I had seen from any supporters all season. It was as if a first drop of rain had fallen upon their drought-afflicted lands; at last, something had gone their way. Spurred and inspired by the vision of Strachan, Clyde zipped the ball around as though they had finally remembered the purpose of football. 'If only we'd played like this 30 games ago,' said the man next to me to avert the risk of anyone enjoying themselves too much.

It didn't last. As the second half wore on, Stirling dominated and the histrionics of their floppy blond forward Iain Russell failed to charm those in the stand. 'He's the kind of man you'd want in your own side' said my neighbour. 'Aye, then I could boo the wee shite every week,' replied his pal. Inevitably, Russell scored a fine winning goal, securing Clyde's eviction to Division Three.

Under broken streetlights somewhere in a town of broken dreams, I walked downhill, hoping that Croy still existed.

CHAPTER ELEVEN

Dumfries

Queen of the South 2 v 2 Airdrie United, 24 April 2010

PICTURE THE SCENE. March 1919. A crowd, ready to live again after the trauma of war squeeze into dusty old Dumfries Town Hall. A meeting has been called that could bring some relief to those who were injured in service, and rare pleasure for those who lost family men at the Somme and in every other hateful quagmire. This time, they have gathered not to hear about an emergency loan scheme or a relief fund, but football. Members of the Arrol-Johnston car factory work team and the boot boys of the Fifth Kircubrightshire Rifles have come together to propose a new club. It would mean business, a serious outfit above the friendlies-only malarkey of pre-war football in Dumfries, one to put the town in the League and on the sporting map. Their success could just give hope to the returning war weary and those weary for war's non-returnees; something to believe in again, something to rally around. If not, that club would at least provide Palmerston fields for their children to dream on. At the end, they have a vote. Their new club shall be called Queen of the South.

The name Queen of the South had been plucked from an address given to charm the town in 1857. Poet David Dunbar was standing in the general election and coined the term to describe his prospective Dumfries constituency. From the start, 'The Doonhamers' played at Palmerston Park, the Rifles' drill field. They entered the Western League and highlighted their credentials for a place in the national version by supplementing fixtures with profile-raising challenge matches. A scouting network was established to bring players south and soon snared a rough black diamond from the coalfields of Lanarkshire.

Early in 1921, Alex James' old school pal Hughie Gallacher left Bellshill for Dumfries. Gallacher scored four times on his debut, a friendly against St Cuthbert Wanderers, and all the Queens goals in a 5–2 destruction of Dumbarton soon after. The *Dumfries and Galloway Courier and Herald* gave him special mention:

> From the first kick until the last, he showed exceptional dash and had the unusual record of scoring the whole five goals. He was continuously the source of great danger and showed no mercy with his rocket shooting.

Goals followed against selection sides from Glasgow Railway and Queen's Park. By the season's end, Gallacher had netted 19 times in nine games. It was clear the 18-year-old was destined for big things, but Queens hoped he would bloom at Palmerston before that. That summer, Gallacher was struck down with double pneumonia. Among those visiting him with grapes and copies of *Take a Break* in his Dumfries hospital bed were directors from Airdrieonians. Impressed by Gallacher's performance and overhead kick in a reserve match against their side, they came bearing a contract for him to sign. Free from contractual obligations to Queen of the South, Gallacher summoned the strength to place his signature on the dotted line. In a letter quoted in Iain McCartney's *Queen of the South: the history*, the board of his former club attempted to secure compensation for the exit of their prize find:

> It was with great surprise that the above club learned that you had signed on Hughie Gallacher while he was lying in the Infirmary. However, the Deed is done, and you have certainly made a big gain, while we have sustained a great loss. In fact it is a bigger loss to us than perhaps you realise. It is the old story, a struggling, provincial club, a good player, the investment lost. Mr Chapman, it is very hard on us especially when the player has cost us a lot of money, at least a lot to a club like us, to lose without so much as 'by your leave'. Mr Chapman, surely the above club are entitled to some recompense after what they have done for this player.

Despite Airdrie's promise to hand the Doonhamers 'a donation in respect of this player' once they had seen 'the strength of his abilities', no recompense was ever received. Seven years later, Gallacher was tearing the 'Wembley Wizards' asunder with his old schoolmate James.

Two years after his exit, Queens were admitted to the new, short-lived Division Three. In their second season, 1924/25, the club gained promotion by virtue of goal average and settled well in Division Two. In 1933, they entered the last game of the season with a chance to complete their rise. Victory over champions Hibernian at Easter Road, and a dropping of points by Dunfermline, would mean Division One. As kick-off drew near for the game in Edinburgh, it became clear that centre-forward Jenkins was stuck on a broken-down train and would not be playing. Unruffled, the away side scored after four minutes through Tommy McCall, the left-winger's 32nd strike of the season, and soon doubled their lead. It was a result they held until the final whistle, though their fate would not become clear until the following Saturday, the date of Dunfermline's final fixture at King's Park. That day, Doonhamers amassed outside town newspaper offices to gather word of events in Stirling. Dumfries came to a tense standstill as supporters and those caught up in the fever stood waiting for news to drift through. Late in the afternoon, a telephone at the *Dumfries Standard* finally exhaled its shrill call: King's Park had won by two goals to one. The town exploded.

The team excelled in Division One, finishing fourth in their first season and only once in the next 25 years tasting football in the lower league. Pride in the relatively new team grew; within their first two decades of life, they had become mainstays in Division One. One man who personified Dumfries' love of Queen of the South was Billy 'Basher' Houliston. Houliston was born close to Palmerston though never played football seriously until joining the RAF where he played for military teams across Scotland. His exploits as a barnstorming inside-forward courted the attentions of Queens. In a trial game against Celtic, Houliston scored and in doing so acquired a full-time contract. Swashbuckling, ready to shove goalkeepers of all sizes into the net and possessing deft goalscoring prowess, he rapidly won the affections of the Palmerston congregation. His reputation spread: Houliston spurned a move to Celtic to remain in his home town, and became the first – and last – Queen of the South man to play for Scotland while at the club. Upfield from Morton's Cowan in goal, 'Basher' was centre-forward during the 1949 win at Wembley. 'If Houliston appeared over-robust at times,' said the *Daily Mail* of his performance that day, 'it must be remembered that football

Billy Houliston (left) with Rangers'
George Young. Yikes.

is a man's game. His manliness had the desired unsettling effect on the defence.' He must have done something right: at the final whistle, England fans booed him from the pitch.

Houliston's career ended abruptly. After suffering an ankle injury on a playing tour of the USA, he struggled to recapture the physical fitness so central to his game. 1952 saw his release from Palmerston on a free transfer, though he soon returned as director, and then chairman. In less than half a century, it had become that kind of club.

Throughout Houliston's playing time and after it, Queen of the South continued to prosper on the field. 1950 saw a run to the Scottish Cup semi-final, largely inspired by Roy 'The Clown Prince' Henderson, a goalkeeper voted in 2004 as Queens' greatest ever player. By then, it was the town's club: despite an urban population of 26,000, 26,552 attended a game with Hearts in the early 1950s. They were rewarded in 1953/54 when their side spent much of the season on top of Division One. At the end of 1953, the *Dumfries Standard* offered a salutary half-term report:

> Palmerston fans will not readily forget the year 1953 which has just ended. Away back in the early part of the year relegation worries were hovering around the Terregles Street ground. Palmerston has been hit by a wave of enthusiasm which has hardly been surpassed and the prospect of the league championship flag flying over the ground has now become more than a dream.

The momentum could not be sustained, however, and the team eventually finished in 10th position. It wasn't until 1965, the year after becoming another club to lose their Main Stand in a fire (this time caused by a defunct kettle), that Queen of the South exited Division One for the final time. It is only in the last few years that things have begun to look up again; 2003's Challenge Cup win, an appearance in the 2008 Scottish Cup Final and consistent league form means that they are again showering pleasure upon the town, just as those soldiers and car-makers would have wanted.

* * *

On the bus from Lockerbie, a security guard on his way to work tutted at the teenagers swilling gothic label energy drinks from their obligatory position on the back seat. Either the noise they were creating was annoying him, or he was an impassioned supporter of Red Bull. I looked out of the vibrating window and followed a landscape matching that of Postman Pat's Greendale valley. This was an alluring part of the world, and one with the added curiosity of being on the precipice of England. Travelling these rolling lowlands in the 16th century, Bishop Leslie noted in his journal, 'The inhabitants because of hot wars with the Englishmen are always in readiness and are all horsemen.' For the early English traveller, there was an exotic otherness about this area. It was far different from its neighbour, and yet not quite the same as Scotland either. After an 1814 visit, in *A Voyage Around Great Britain*, travel commentator Richard Ayton wrote of the village women he had seen walking into Dumfries to attend church:

> They were mostly very gaily attired, but all had their shoes and stockings off, which they carried wrapped up in their handkerchiefs, and would not put on until the moment before their entrance into the town... for these hardy damsels consider shoes and stockings as things of mere ornament. Here you may see a lady with a white gown, a silk shawl or spencer, and a straw bonnet with artificial flowers in it, nay, with gloves on too, and all this finery terminated by a huge pair of bare begrimed legs and feet, which look as if they could scarcely belong to her. The legs and feet, from exposure to wet, and cold, and the sun, become red and puffy, resembling in surface and colour the great overgrown radish.

Catching myself risking arrest by paying a little too much attention to the feet of the female passengers around me, I fixed a glare outside once again as we motored through the outskirts of Dumfries. It was a town made wealthy by the textile industry and the handiness of its central artery, the River Nith. Here too had been, until as late as the last century, a clog-making industry, with one of Queen of the South's early directors, John Grierson, a doyen of the trade. The presence of Arrol-Johnston was also significant; with echoes of Cowdenbeath's Chicago, for a time Dumfries enjoyed the soubriquet 'a little Detroit by the Nith'. The bus choked uphill by the railway station and paused at traffic lights outside the Waverley Bar, which advertised its 'Barrie View'. Accustomed now to the east coast use of 'barrie' for 'good', at first I thought 'it can't be that good, there's a tree in the way.' It was, I cleverly realised when googling Dumfries a few months later, a reference to JM Barrie. As a child, the author had lived here and taken inspiration for *Peter Pan* from his games in the overgrown gardens of Moat Brae House (so basically a lazy Dumfries gardener is to blame for the unsettling sight of Robin Williams wearing shorts in *Hook*).

The bus curved around Lovers Walk where I fretted about missing apostrophes. I clambered off opposite Dumfries Academy, Barrie's old school, and thought of an alumnus who lived a life as far away from Neverland as was possible. From 1909, Jane Haining walked the corridors of the Academy, a well-liked and intelligent girl. After leaving school, she moved to Paisley and worked as a thread maker. On hearing about Church of Scotland Jewish Missions, Haining declared 'I have found my life's work.' She quickly volunteered and was sent in 1932 to work at Budapest Scottish Mission, a home for 400 children of mainly Jewish extraction. There, she became a mother figure to countless dispossessed young people and became deeply embroiled in each of their plights. On a trip home to Scotland at the outbreak of World War Two, Haining was offered the chance to work more safely in her home country. Her response – 'If these children need me in days of sunshine, how much more do they need me in days of darkness' – said everything. When Nazi Germany invaded Hungary, the Mission sheltered members of the local Jewish population. In April 1944, the ss came for Haining. She was hit with a volley of charges from listening to the bbc to espionage. Three months later, Jane Haining was taken to Auschwitz. She was the only Scot to die in the gas chambers there.

Stirring, and wondering why hers was a name so relatively unknown,

I turned down Queensberry Street. It was neglected and yet appealing, largely because of Paling's Department store, one of so few old family shops left where I imagine all male staff wear brown coats and have a pencil behind their ear, and all females a measuring tape around their necks. Signs pointed out the different ways to Burns House, the Burns Monument and the Burns Centre, but I was never much of a *Krypton Factor* fan, so I ignored them and chose my own route.

I spotted the Venue nightclub, hosted in an opulent old building that had once been home to 'Norges Hus'. While the Nazis had still to reach Budapest in 1940, they had reached and occupied Norway. In June of that year, 300 Norwegian soldiers who had fled their country and regrouped in Scotland descended upon Dumfries. They were made welcome from the start, with the formation in 1941 of the Scottish Norwegian Society. In Norge Hus, Doonhamers and their new foreign friends mixed to enjoy concerts, lectures and language classes. Many of the incomers married local women. This image of a hospitable, amiable place concurs with the verdict of the *Statistical Account of Scotland* for 1791:

> The character of the inhabitants, is allowed to be, in general, very respectable. They are charitable and benevolent, hospitable to strangers, and mix frequently among themselves in domestic intercourse. In their disposition and manners they are sociable and polite; and the town, together with the neighbourhood a few miles around it, furnishes a society, amongst whom a person of moderate fortune may spend his days, with as much satisfaction and enjoyment, as, perhaps, in any part of these kingdoms.

Regular Norwegian soldiers were joined by the high command. One army major, Myrseth, became vice-chairman of the Scottish Norwegian Society. An article in *The Gallovidian Annual* of 1949, quoted in Giancarlo Rinaldi's *Great Dumfries Stories*, gave account of a speech five years previously in which Major Myrseth warmly acknowledged his adopted home:

> For most of the Norwegians, Dumfries had been their temporary capital city. Many in other parts of the country had said to him when going on leave: 'But we must go to Dumfries because, Major,

it is our capital city.' Dumfries would remain their capital in memory for many years, because they could never forget the friends they had found in the Queen of the South in the difficult beginnings of their exile. Everywhere they were met with open arms, and everything was done to give them a home from home.

It was a deep, mutual devotion signified now by the yearly laying of wreaths in Dumfries to Norwegians who lost their life in the war on fascism.

On the High Street, old architecture spoke of better times; pound shops and vacant outlets of a difficult present. Vennels snaked out between most like tributaries, with pubs tucked away down a good few. Beyond a fair consisting of one ride and a market stall with bleach and batteries, the rusty red sandstone buildings of old glowed in the bright sunshine. At the street's centre, the chunky Midsteeple clock-tower projected commandingly as a former prison should. Outside the 'Smoothie Sensation' health drink shop built into its walls, a customer coughed uncontrollably while her boyfriend looked on smugly from behind his bottle of Irn-Bru. I sat on the benches by the eye-catching red and gold fountain and sniffed for people whiffing of onions; only the day before, I'd read this quote by the visiting 17th century English author Richard Frank:

> In the midst of the town is the market place and in the centre of that stands their tollbooth, round which the rabble sit that nauseate the very air with their tainted breath, so perfumed with onions, that to an Englishman it is almost infectious.

From here I could see Boots, once home to the King's Arms Hotel. It was there in 1829 that William Hare, on a solo tour following the hanging of his partner Burke, lodged on his way to exile in Ireland having turned King's Evidence. When news of his presence broke, an angry mob (what other type is there?) stormed the building in an effort to kill him. Hare was, for some reason, allowed visitors, one of whom, a female, almost succeeded in strangling him, possibly with her massive radishy feet. He was taken to a jail cell for safe keeping and then smuggled out of a back window early the next morning and sent on his way.

I walked along Shakespeare Street for a gander at the Theatre Royal, which was part art deco, part Greek fishmarket. The Royal is Scotland's oldest working theatre, and one much loved by JM Barrie who remarked that it was 'so tiny that you smile to it as to a child when you go in.' Wincing unromantically at the thought of my knees bashing on the wood of the seat in front, I proceeded to English Street for the sole reason that it had once been home to the County Toilet Club, featuring 'haircutting, shaving and shampooing saloons'. Though the Arbroath Superloo of its day, there was now no sign of this Victorian institution.

Heading down Friars' Vennel, a narrow lane disappointingly lacking in weighty robes or amusing bowl cuts, I arrived at Whitesands, Dumfries' perfect promenade over the unruly, fizzing River Nith. As a young sailor, John Paul Jones often launched from here, his local harbour. Jones later became frustrated with his inability to smash the class barrier and climb the navy ranks. Instead, in 1775 he joined the American Navy, apparently becoming the first man to raise the Stars and Stripes

Devorgilla Bridge. I really should get my fringe cut.

on a ship. Today beside the banks he departed to join the American Revolution and change the history of the world, caravan owners sat in their cars eating packed lunches and steaming up windscreens with their flasks. Towards the indecently bewitching Devorgilla Bridge, a man stood literally pointing things out to his blind friend.

I crossed the bridge's many arches to Maxwelltown, until 1929 entirely and fiercely independent from Dumfries. When the merger was forced through, Maxwelltown residents strung up a banner carrying the word 'ICHABOD' (Hebrew for 'O, for the departed glory'.) It had once been Dumfries' uglier, petty thieving brother. In *Picture of Scotland*, Robert Chambers wrote that:

> Maxwelltown seems to be the great standing joke of its proud neighbours the Dumfriessians. Some idea may be formed of its character from a saying of Sir John Fielding, the great London magistrate; that whenever a delinquent got over the bridge of Dumfries into Maxwelltown, he was lost to all search or pursuit.

Today, the only lost people were the little ones engulfed in the ball pool of the Farmer's Den Play Centre. Past that and a house with eight conservatories that turned out to be a showroom I could see the limp-wristed floodlights of Palmerston Park.

* * *

Under the smoky red bricks of the Standard Grandstand, home supporters relaxed in the glow of sunshine and having nothing left to play for. Eight months of promotion toil had come to nothing and with the pressure lifted the contentment of failure had begun. A boy heaved the turnstile and his dad urged him to lie about his age to get in more cheaply. Inside, the ground overflowed with authenticity, history and winningly foul language. Palmerston should be nationalised and stamped with a preservation order. Using tactics learnt from cat-owners, football chairmen, directors and governors could then have their noses rubbed on its tidily crumbling terraces to make them feel repulsed every time they think of selling another ground site to a supermarket.

Fans tried to summon the will to make noise as their minds drifted to August and next season, for there is always next season. On a deep terrace I leaned back and breathed in the atmosphere and the smell of stale meat. The main stand looked every inch a Subbuteo extra I'd never been allowed as a child. With grubby windows and standing room only at the front it had a nostalgic, filmic appeal, a metaphor for my Saturdays in the Scottish League. Very soon, I'd have to decide whether to stay forever suspended in this world of grounds with character and towns with Wimpys or return to England and reality. Still, that was for August. Right now, I was gleefully watching Derek Holmes do his best impersonation of Basher Houliston. Framed by shoulders resembling cornflake boxes, his lumbering style disguised some crafty touches. I found Holmes heroically retro and rejoiced when, with half an hour gone, he scored by apparently frightening the ball into the net. Airdrie, clutching the relegation zone in a firm embrace, awoke and equalised soon afterwards. The announcer pressed his microphone into action in preparation for giving the scorer's name but, perhaps exasperated, merely breathed heavily a few times before giving up. The Airdrie rabble stirred, roaring every tackle and throw – where there's belief there's hope. What didn't help matters was captain Paul Lovering's decision to remove his undershirt in the middle of play, getting his head stuck in doing so. Headless and blinded, Lovering continued to pursue Derek Holmes regardless and could still be running through the streets of Dumfries today.

During the break, I sat on the terrace and pretended to read the programme. An angry gambler tore his slip of paper into more pieces than I thought possible and ranted: 'another fucking season and no win on the 50/50 draw. 50/50 my arsehole.' 'Don't worry Robert,' said his friend. 'We'll get you a scratchcard and a pint after,' which sounded good to me. All around, teenagers lurked as if idling outside a newsagent. Improbably, Palmerston was *the* place to be, giving me great hope that small team Scotland will not be breathing its last any time soon.

Airdrie began the second half full of vigour and direction and were soon deservedly 2–1 ahead. Around me, old men yawned into their scarves and rolled their eyes knowingly as if comforted by their team's ineptitude. Holmes plunged down to earth and on the other side of the hoarding a child fell over from the aftershock. Meanwhile, I was doing my very best to avoid eye contact with Doogie the Doonhamer, a strange contraption of a mascot character who seemed to be following me as I wandered around the stand. It reminded me that only weeks earlier my

The view from the afternoon.

dad had been eating alone in a hotel's chain bar when Brewster the Bear had saluted him from across the room, which was one of the loneliest and funniest things I had ever heard.

Eluding Doogie I settled at the back of the terrace and felt immensely grateful that football sanctuaries still existed and that for all the game infuriated me nothing could ever be as enjoyable as hearing an old woman shout 'aw ya bastard' when the ball hit the bar. The towns I'd been to had changed immeasurably over time, their people, especially the ones attending football, less so, and that was pretty comforting.

Here and now, Doonhamers wearily urged their men to a 90th minute leveller. Airdrie's players slumped on the turf at the whistle. Their fans were stunned, another weekend ruined. Bloody football. Among the flag- and scarf- strewn surfaces of the Billy Houliston Lounge, I watched the scores from elsewhere roll in and then departed for Whitesands, and the bus. I walked back over the Devorgilla, dreaming of artful stadia and obese centre-forwards. My trance was broken only by the sound of the bus driver threatening to put a young passenger 'in the gutter' should he continue to make a rumpus. They were a tough lot, the radish-foot women of Dumfries.

Elgin

Elgin City 5 v 2 Montrose, 1 May 2010

AS THE MONTH OF May moved into view it was time to hit the north again. This was my final journey of the season, which was just as well because August's unfamiliar Scotrail ticket machine now knew my credit card pin code off by heart and since March had been making polite enquiries about my wife's sciatica.

The 7.30am train had the same majority population as all carriages early on a Saturday morning in Scotland: the rucksack wearing male. Each had his own hobby to intently pursue, his own place or event to be early for and his own particular noise of disgust for the price of buffet trolley coffee. I would miss these, my silent companions with their tinted bifocal glasses and impressive knowledge of tunnels on the Leeds–Liverpool Canal.

We shunted by The Elgin Marble Company, 'Craftsmen in Marble, Granite and Slate', not to mention pleasing historical company names of which there should be more. Down broad streets reeking of Victorian holiday town pomp I found my way to the cathedral ruins. With more ruin than cathedral and a perfectly good fence to stare through, paying £4.70 was out of the question. Some of the earliest football in Scotland was played here, and you can be sure that 17th century pundits moaned about how much the new-fangled pig's bladder moved in the air. Demonstrating an approach to sport and leisure that would have had the Taliban going 'steady on a bit there mate', football next to the cathedral was soon banned by the Calvinists. A Kirk session report of July 1630 recorded that:

> George Purse, James McWatty, Alexander Fumester for their playing at the futeball on the Sabbath nicht at evin throw the calsay ar ordeant ilk ane of them to pay 6s 8d.

Two and a half centuries later, no pulpit edict could halt the game's popularity. As in Dingwall and by the Clyde, it became a lung-stretching pursuit that fitted between the months of summer sports. There was a further social element: as well as being home to a prosperous middle-class, down its dank closes Elgin hid away a thick layer of poverty. Money poured through her wool factories and distilleries, but as ever, little of it found its way into the pockets of those that staffed them. In the democratic world of participation football, exercise and revenge by way of meaty tackles on factory managers could be theirs.

One of many clubs to emerge in the burgh and its northern surrounds, Elgin were established in 1893 and quickly admitted to the Highland League. Their greatest ever player, RC Hamilton, was also one of their earliest. Born on the High Street and making his debut for the club while still aged 16 in 1893, the forward went on to become Rangers' top scorer for nine seasons in a row and captain Scotland. Throughout his travels through football, Hamilton returned to the sporting town every summer to represent its cricket team. After his playing days, he moved home and became Provost. His conservative political views put him on a crash course with football's route to professionalism in the late 1920s. He saw the move to paying players as tantamount to a communist revolution typical of General Strike Britain, commenting in 1926:

> Fostered by criticism from the wrong point of view, a Bolshevik element, antagonistic to the interests of true sport, has crept into Northern football, and particularly in Elgin.

A pragmatist and most of all a fan who could see his team being left behind, Hamilton eventually changed his mind and approved the appointment of Aberdeen centre-half Bert Maclachlan as manager. Maclachlan's tenure soon paid dividends, with the Highland League title won for the first time in 1932.

The raising of the flag at Elgin's Borough Briggs ground sparked a fine decade in the north. The team at last made their mark on football, as illustrated in Ron Grant's *Fields of Glory: 100 Years of Elgin City FC*:

Their names and reputation are fondly remembered. They set a benchmark for later players. That is their measure. Dare-devil keeper Victor Parle, ever-ready full-backs Hendry and Cruickshank, Alistair Grant, a fearless centre-half, Willie Gordon, 'the penalty king,' and Sandy MacLennan, 'Wee Bighead' by his own description, a predatory centre-forward. And above all, there was Lachie McMillan... Report after report shows him to have possessed all the hallmarks of the Scottish footballer: vision, balance, clever footwork, the ability to weight a pass. With such talents, self-belief was rarely prey to delusion, and a lively existence off the pitch was excusable. Here was a footballer in the tradition of Hughie Gallagher, Tommy McInally and, in our times, Willie Hamilton.

If writing of RC Hamilton, mention should also go to a figure of a vastly differing political hue associated with Elgin City. William Leslie was a devout socialist who played for the team for a short time from 1907. An accomplished footballer as well as an orator and political theorist, Leslie went on to turn out for Manchester City. A pacifist, Leslie requested exemption from World War One, a conflict in which his brother, also at one time an Elgin player, was to fall. In July 1916 the *Northern Scot* covered Leslie's conscription hearing and the plea he entered:

> According to his religious and moral beliefs he could take no part in the slaughter of his fellow creatures. His religion was socialism, and he believed in the law laid down by Christ in the Immortal Sermon on the Mount. He asked for absolute exemption from military service, even non-combatant service, because he would not relieve someone to do what he was not prepared to do himself.

Leslie's application was refused as was a subsequent appeal, and he was arrested and jailed. After the war, he travelled to the post-revolution Soviet Union. Debate continues over claims that the former full-back there met with Lenin.

From the cathedral I found my way to Elgin Museum, a lovingly crafted bounty of paraphernalia in a building similar to an Italian church but with fewer Pope toilet roll dispensers on sale. Privately run, there was scope for curators to exhibit their own interests and avoid the language of bland museum neutrality. A caption on women's liberation ran with the simple but affirmative 'Progress has been made but the gender battle is not yet over.' I enjoyed reading about 'the Ordeal Pot', in addition to a one-time method for persecuting Elgin witches, an excellent phrase for describing a popular Golden Wonder snack. In one cavern, the only other visitor present looked horrified when I caught his eye, and I could only conclude that he was trying to filch the stuffed cat in the case in front of him. He was a lovely little thing mind, as was the cat. Having spent a couple of cathedral entrance fees' worth on museum shop books, my own particularly bourgeois version of crack addiction, I continued into town. It was clear that country cash had helped Elgin look as it did. In 1727, Daniel Defoe wrote in *A Tour Through the Whole Island of Great Britain*:

> As the country around is rich and pleasant, so here are a great many rich inhabitants, and in the town of Elgin in particular; for the gentlemen leave their highland habitations in the winter and come and live here for the diversion of the place and plenty of provisions.

With Estuary accents abounding (tourism and the local military bases account for that), brash but brilliant Victorian architecture and someone handing out leaflets for the Conservative Party, it appeared that my most northerly trip had become my most English. I didn't like it, this didn't happen in Cowdenbeath and immediately I wanted my unique exoticism back, if you can be uniquely exotic having been born in Stockton-on-Tees.

I passed a Polish deli and felt even duller until the Mercat Cross and St Giles Church stunned me into mental silence. The latter, with its six columns and gas light surrounds, was as striking as anything I'd seen all year, or in Edinburgh for that matter. It was these unexpected Saturday lunchtime pearls that had me slowly falling for small town Scotland.

Not nearly as much as the noticeboards, mind, which in Elgin offered help 'if you are homeless after 5pm or at the weekend'. Screw you,

St Giles Church. I liked it, just a bit.

daytime homeless! I hurried to look in the window of Littlejohn's Restaurant, on closer inspection sadly not a *Daily Mail* columnist theme bar serving bile pie and 'you couldn't make it up' soup. Ducking between three menacing old ladies making jokes about tackle outside a fishing shop, I wandered to Lady Hill, scene of castle remnants and a columned statue of the 5th Duke of Gordon. From the top, I looked at the giant dome of Dr Gray's hospital and followed the skyline along and downwards to Borough Briggs. It was time to do the football thing for one last time.

* * *

After pausing to look at the Cumbernauld pastiche Town Hall, I chased the floodlights and forestry to Elgin City territory. Inside

the ground's whitewashed walls I sat for a pint in the Social Club, another choice space beneath another handsome old man of a stand. 'You don't get this at bloody Leeds' thundered a Yorkshire voice behind me, which I can vouch for. Neither in England's higher reaches would you get an elderly club volunteer running the length of the pitch to fetch you a team sheet and then throw in a free programme with a granddad-ish wink. It was these moments in the year which had made ketchup abuse and Cliftonhill trench foot worthwhile.

From the grass bank behind the goal I succumbed to the bliss of my surroundings once more and forgot to concentrate on the game. It's only now I realise this was a good thing: I had begun to enjoy being in a football ground again. Forgetting myself and the world outside the turnstile was why I'd begun going all those years ago, after all. If that now meant forgetting what was going on in front of me then so be it.

In spite of seven goals on the pitch, all I will remember of that day are events off it. Alongside the touchy feely 'end of *Stand By Me*' part above, there was the sight of seven or eight Montrose fans drunkenly roly polying behind the goal, and the most overweight of them spending half an hour trying to fight the entire Main Stand. At the final whistle, half their number performed the first walking pitch invasion I have ever seen. No steward chased them, mainly because it would have looked ridiculous, and they were left alone to breathe boozily on their defeated heroes as they trudged away from a season at the bottom of the Scottish Football League.

Over ten months, I'd got to know Scotland much better than over the previous five years of living here. I'd seen what goes on in the nether regions of the country, and what has gone on in the past. It's a richer history than I could possibly have imagined, and one with links to world events at so many turns: Cowdenbeath, nearly the venue of a British revolution; Kirkcaldy, birthplace of time's father; Dingwall, home of Scotland's Othello; Cumbernauld, where the future was written and lost; Dumfries and the holocaust; even Elgin City FC and Lenin. Things happen in small towns; always have, always will.

The towns' histories impacted the world, and so too did the clubs impact the game. There would have been no Alex James without Raith persisting and no Cowan at Wembley without Morton giving him a chance. It was Queen of the South who took a gamble and signed

On a grassy knoll, the season ends.

Hughie Gallagher, and Albion's Victor Kasule who pushed Scotland towards the acceptance of black footballers.

Those towns have shaped those teams. Football has mirrored society. In truth, I'm no clearer a year on how (and that's the English rather than Scottish use) so many of these places and clubs survive. Perhaps that's the point. All I know is I'm bloody glad they do.

Too many people were imprisoned in closes and one-roomed houses from the cradle to the grave, had in the past no such thorough and genuine relief, such as football gives, from the pressures of ennui, from the weary monotony of life, from the hopelessness of toil which made them mere machines. They were seldom, if ever, very far away from the clanking of their chain. They could not make the 'grand tour' or take a fortnight at the coast, or run away from Saturday to Monday like the gay and gallant city clerks. But now football had brought to them a happier life, and had breathed to them interest in, and enthusiasm for something different from the common experiences of their existence; it has helped them to a taste of the extreme pleasures of forgetting themselves and their hard lot, and their squalid surroundings, and their general discomfort and poverty. The public house is no longer their own drawing room, and the close mouth no longer their only recreation ground; and we feel that we are justified in thinking well of football because of such things.

Scottish Football Annual, 1889/90

Final Scottish League Tables for 2009/10

IRN BRU First Division	Pld	Pts
Inverness	36	73
Dundee	36	61
Dunfermline Athletic	36	58
Queen of the South	36	56
Ross County	36	56
Partick Thistle	36	48
Raith Rovers	36	42
Morton	36	37
Airdrie United	36	33
Ayr United	36	31

IRN BRU Second Division	Pld	Pts
Stirling Albion	36	65
Alloa Athletic	36	65
Cowdenbeath	36	59
Brechin City	36	54
Peterhead	36	51
Dumbarton	36	48
East Fife	36	41
Stenhousemuir	36	40
Arbroath	36	40
Clyde	36	31

IRN BRU Third Division	Pld	Pts
Livingston	36	78
Forfar Athletic	36	63
East Stirlingshire	36	61
Queen's Park	36	51
Albion Rovers	36	50
Berwick Rangers	36	50
Stranraer	36	47
Annan Athletic	36	43
Elgin City	36	34
Montrose	36	24

Note on Sources

For clarity and flow of prose and so as not to be off-putting, I have omitted reference footnotes in *Stramash*. I have listed these references in the Bibliography, divided by chapters. Every effort has been made to trace the copyright holders of material reproduced in the book. If further assistance on references or copyright is required, please make contact.

Within the book, there is frequent use of local newspapers, for so long at the centre of a town and a team's life. In addition to being history's first draft, they have an added significance for football. Shunned by the national media, they were and – often in website form – are the places to which the fans of *Stramash*-type teams have always turned to for their news.

If you've enjoyed any element of this book, read Ron Ferguson's *Black Diamonds and the Blue Brazil*, still the best book ever written about Scottish football and society.

Bibliography

Books

GENERAL

Chambers, Robert; *The Picture of Scotland*; Edinburgh; W & R Chambers; 1840

Defoe, Daniel; *A Tour Through the Whole Island of Great Britain*; London; 1769 edition

Groome, Francis Hindes; *Groome's Ordnance Gazetteer of Scotland*; Edinburgh; TC Jack; 1885

Inglis, Simon; *Football Grounds of Britain*; London; CollinsWillow; 1996

Potter, David and Jones, Phil H; *The Encyclopaedia of Scottish Football*; Know the Score; London; 2008

Ritchie, Harry; *Take My Whole Life Too* in *My Favourite Year*; London; Gollancz; 1995

Ross, David; *The Roar of the Crowd: Following Scottish Football Down the Years*; Argyll; Argyll Publishing; 2005

Sinclair. John; *Statistical Account of Scotland*; Edinburgh; Creech

CHAPTER ONE: AYR

Ayrshire Express; *Ayr As A Summer Residence*; Ayr; The Ayrshire Express office; 1870

Ayrshire Post; *Ayr, Prestwick and the Land O'Burns: Penny Gude*; Ayr; Ayrshire Post; 1900

Carmichael, Duncan; *Ayr United Football Club: vols 1 and 2*; Ayr; Ayr United Football & Athletic Club; 1992

Carmichael, Duncan; *Ayr United Football Club: Fifty of the Finest*; Stroud; Tempus; 2002

Close, Rob; *Ayr: A History and Celebration*; Salisbury; Francis Firth Collection; 2005

Hill, Carrick; *The Ayr United Story*; Ayr; Ayr United Football Club; 1960

Love, Dane; *Ayr: The Way We Were*; Ayr; Fort Publishing; 2007

Reid, Denholm and Andrew, Ken; *Ayr Remembered*; Catrine; Stenlake; 2001

Strawhorn, John; *The History of Ayr*; Edinburgh: John Donald Publishers; 1989

CHAPTER TWO: ALLOA

Adamson, John; *Sauchie and Alloa: A People's History*; Alloa; Clackmannanshire District Libraries; 1988

Alloa Athletic Football Club; *60 Years in the Scottish League: Alloa Athletic Official Commemorative Handbook*; Alloa; Alloa Athletic Football Club; 1981

Alloa Athletic Football Club; *Alloa Football Club: Official Handbook and Fixtures*; Alloa; Alloa Athletic Football Club; 1947

Alloa Town Council; *Alloa: Official Guide*; Cheltenham; EJ Burrow; 1935

Barnard, Alfred; *Noted Breweries of Great Britain and Ireland: 'Messrs George Younger & Son, Candlerigg and Meadow Breweries, Alloa, N.B [North Britain]'*; London; 1889

Borthwick, Alastair; *Alloa: The Official Town Guide*; Glasgow; Menzies; 1955

Imlah, John; 'Alloa Ale' in *Poems and Songs*; London; 1841

Lothian, James; *Alloa and its Environs: A Descriptive and Historical Sketch*; Alloa; Alloa Advertiser; 1861

McMaster, Charles; *Alloa Ale: A History of the Brewing Industry in Alloa*; Edinburgh; Edinburgh Alloa Brewery; 1985

Scott, W; *Alloa Memories 1915–1970*; Alloa; Alloa Clackmannan District Library; 1983

CHAPTER THREE: COWDENBEATH

Allan, David A; *Fifeshire football memories*; Dumfries; the author

Anderson, Alasdair; *The Dean Tavern: a Gothenburg experiment*; Newtongrange; Dean Tavern Trust; 1986

Cowdenbeath Town Council; *Official guide*; Dundee; 1955

Cowdenbeath Public House Society; *Rules of the Cowdenbeath Public House Society Limited*; Cowdenbeath Public House Society; Cowdenbeath; 1901

Ferguson, Ronald; *Black Diamonds and the Blue Brazil*; Ellon; Famedram Publishers; 1993

Gillespie, David; *The Gothenburg licensing system and its proposed adaptation to Scotland, by the spirituous liquors (Scotland) bill*; Edinburgh; R. Grant; 1874

Holman, Robert; *Character Studies of the Miners of West Fife*; Dunfermline; Journal Printing Works; 1909

Holman, Robert; *History of Cowdenbeath*; Dunfermline; J.B. Mackie; 1941

Hutcheson, Jim; *Old Cowdenbeath*; Ochiltree; Stenlake; 1998

Maxwell, Alex; *Chicago tumbles: Cowdenbeath and the miners strike*; [s.i]; A. Maxwell

CHAPTER FOUR: COATBRIDGE

Coatbridge Town Council; *Coatbridge : the crossroads of Scotland*; Coatbridge; Coatbridge Town Council; 1973

Coatbridge official guide; London; GW May; 1969

Coatbridge Official guide; London; GW May; 1953

Drummond, Peter and Smith, James; *Coatbridge: three centuries of change*; Glasgow; Monklands Library Services Department; 1982

Hamilton, Janet; 'Oor Location' in *Selected Works*; Coatbridge; Monklands Monklands Library Services Department; 1984

Marwick, RW; *The boys from the 'brig the life and times of Albion Rovers*; Monklands; Monklands Monklands Library Services Department; 1986

Marwick, RW; *Champion Albion : the winning of the championship*; Coatbridge; the author; 1989

Moir, Helen; *Coatbridge*; Stroud; Tempus; 2001

Reilly, Michael; *Coatbridge Irish Genealogy Project*; Coatbridge; Minuteman Press; 2009

Vaughan, Geraldine; in *New Perspectives on the Irish in Scotland*; Edinburgh; John Donald; 2008

CHAPTER FIVE: MONTROSE

Inglis, Forbes on www.montrosefc.co.uk

Davidson, David P (ed.); *Montrosiana: a collection of local anecdotes and sketches from the lives of prominent Montrosians*; Montrose; DP Davidson; 1910

Johns, Trevor W; *The Mid Links : George Scott's gift to Montrose;* Montrose; TW Johns; 1986

Johns, Trevor W; *The Mid Links, Montrose since Provost Scott*; Montrose; TW Johns; 1988

Montrose Town Council; *The official guide to Montrose*; Edinburgh; 1947

The Montrose Society; *Montrose past & present*; Montrose; The Montrose Society; 2002

Montrose Old Kirk Open Door Committee; *Changed days in Montrose: the recollections of members and friends of Montrose Old Kirk, 1900 to 1999;* Montrose; Montrose Old Kirk Open Door Committee; 2000

Le Chene, Evelyn; *Silent Heroes: The Bravery and Devotion of Animals in War*; London; Souvenir Press; 1994

Whitson, Angus and Andrew Orr; *Sea Dog Bamse: World War Two Canine Hero*; Edinburgh; Birlinn; 2008

CHAPTER SIX: KIRKCALDY

Fimister, Tony; *Raith Rovers Football Club 1991/92-1995-96*; Stroud; Tempus; 2002

Harding, John; *Alex James: Life of a Football Legend*; London; Robson Books; 1988

House, Jack; *The Lang Toun*; Kirkcaldy; Kirkcaldy Town Council; 1975

Kirkcaldy Civic Society; *Kirkcaldy: a history and celebration of the town*; Salisbury; Francis Frith Collection; 2005

Kirkcaldy District Museums; *Whaling: The Maritime History of Kirkcaldy District*; Kirkcaldy; Kirkcaldy District Museums; 1994

Litster, John; *A history of Raith Rovers*; Kirkcaldy; the author; 1988

McNeill, Carol; *Kirkcaldy Links Market*; Fife; Fife Council; 2004

Potter, David; *Rovers greats*; Kirkcaldy; The Raith Trust; 2009

Raith Rovers Football Club; *Official handbook and fixtures*; Glasgow : J.S. Burns; 1947

Various; *Davidson's illustrated guide and handbook to Kirkcaldy & neighbourhood*; Kirkcaldy; J Davidon; 1905

CHAPTER SEVEN: GREENOCK

Riddle, John; *The king of Cappielow: the biography of Andy Ritchie*; Clacton-on-Sea : Apex; 2008

Gillen, Vincent, P; *Greenock Morton, 1874–1999*; Greenock; McLean Museum & Art Gallery

Ross, Graeme; *More Morton greats*; Derby; Breedon Books; 2005

Ross, Graeme; *Morton greats*; Derby; Breedon Books; 2004

Robertson, Tom; *Morton, 1874–1974: the history of the Greenock Morton Football Club*; Greenock; Greenock Morton Football Club

Fullarton, Alan and Robb, Richard; *Greenock: a town trail*; Greenock; the authors; 1986

Glasgow Corporation; *Greenock official guide*; Glasgow; published for the Corporation of Glasgow by John Menzies; 1947

McNeill, Anthony JJ; *Images of Greenock*; Glendaruel; Argyll Publishing; 1998

Snoddy, Thomas G; *Round about Greenock. A sketch-book of West Renfrewshire and North Cunningham*; Kirkcaldy; Allen Lithographic Co; 1937

Macdougall, Sandra; *The Greenock Blitz*; Greenock; Inverclyde District Libraries; 1991

CHAPTER EIGHT: ARBROATH

Arbroath town; *Arbroath, Angus: official guide book*; Arbroath; Buncle; 1931

Brodie, J; *The land of the Antiquary: notes of a tour from Fairport to Lunan Bay*; Arbroath; Printed at the Arbroath Herald Office; 1904

Burness, Lawrence R; *The streets of Arbroath*; Arbroath; the author; 1992

Chisholm, John; *Arbroath, official guide*; Arbroath; Arbroath Publicity Council; 1960

Clyne, Fraser, ed; *Arbroath Football Club: The Story of the Maroons*; Arbroath; Fraser Clyne; 1998

Clyne, Fraser; *The First Maroons*; Arbroath; Arbroath Football Club; 2003

Gray, Malcolm and Stephen Mylles; *History of the Red Lichties*; Arbroath; Arbroath Football Club; 1978

Middleton, Bruce; *Echoes of Arbroath: an Arbroath almanac*; Arbroath; the author; 1990

Middleton, Bruce; *Among the red lichties*; Arbroath: Printed by the Herald Press; 1994

www.doigsden.co.uk/NedDoig.htm

CHAPTER NINE: DINGWALL

Arnott. Jake; *The Devil's Paintbrush*; London; Sceptre; 2009

Dingwall Burgh Council; *The Royal Burgh of Dingwall: Official Guide*; Dingwall; Dingwall Burgh Council; 1930

Highland Advertising Company; *Official Guide to Dingwall and Strathpepper*; Inverness; Highland Advertising Company; 1955

Hyam, Ronald; *Empire and Sexuality: The British Experience*; Manchester; Manchester University Press; 1990

Royle, Trevor; *Fighting Mac: The Downfall of Major-General Sir Hector Macdonald*; Edinburgh; Mainstream; 2003

Sinclair, Jack; *Dingwall Memories*; Dingwall; Dingwall Museum Trust; 1989

Sinclair, Jack; *Old Bailechaul*; Dingwall; Dingwall Museum Trust; 1993

www.rosscountyfootballclub.co.uk

CHAPTER TEN: CUMBERNAULD

Abercrombie, Patrick; *Clyde Valley regional plan*; Glasgow; Glasgow Corporation; 1946

Brown , Norman and Taylor, John; *The Shawfield Story*; Glasgow; Clyde Football Club; 1986

Carter, Chrisopher J; *Innovations in planning thought and practice at Cumbernauld new town, 1956–1962*; Milton Keynes; Open University; 1983

Cowling, David; *An essay for today: the Scottish new towns 1947 to 1997*; Edinburgh; Rutland Press

Cumbernauld Development Corporation; *Cumbernauld new town*; Cumbernauld Development Corporation; 1968

Cumbernauld Development Corporation; *Cumbernauld new town residents guide*; Cumbernauld Development Corporation; 1970

Cumbernauld Development Corporation; *Cumbernauld*; Cumbernauld; Cumbernauld Development Corporation; 1973

Cumbernauld Development Corporation; *Cumbernauld: the facts Cumbernauld*; Cumbernauld; Cumbernauld Development Corporation; 1982

Greig, Tom; *The Bully Wee*; Glasgow; Clyde Football Club; 1978

Opher, Philip and Bird, Clinton; *Cumbernauld, Irvine, East Kilbride: an illustrated guide*; Headington; Urban Design, Oxford Polytechnic; 1980

CHAPTER ELEVEN: DUMFRIES

Burnside, William; *Dumfries-Shire : Dumfries, 1793*; Thurso; Pentland Press; 1976

Carroll, David; *Dumfries*; Stroud; Alan Sutton; 1996

Dumfries and Galloway Libraries; *Glimpses of old Queen of the South*; Dumfries; Dumfries and Galloway Libraries; 1998

Fortune, Pete and McMillan, Hugh; *Dumfries: a history and celebration of the town*; Salisbury : Francis Frith Collection; 2005

Lockwood, David; *Dumfries' story*; Dumfries; TC Farries in association with Nithsdale District Council; 1988

McCartney, Iain; *Queen of the South: the history, 1919–2008*; Derby; Breedon; 2008

McDowall, William; *History of Dumfries*; Dumfries; Rooksie Press; 2006 (first published 1867)

Rinaldi, Giancarlo; *Great Dumfries Stories*; Ayr; Fort Publishing; 2005

CHAPTER TWELVE: ELGIN

Grant, Ron; *Fields of Glory: 100 Years of Elgin City F.C*; Elgin Museum; 1993

Weir, Robert; *Elgin City's Highland League Triumphs and Tragedy, 1895–2000*; Elgin, the author; 2003

Newspapers

Airdrie and Coatbridge Advertiser
Alloa Circular
Arbroath Herald
Ayr Advertiser
Ayr Observer
Ayrshire Express
Coatbridge Express
Cowdenbeath & district advertiser and Kelty news.
Cowdenbeath advertiser and Kelty news
Cowdenbeath mail and West Fife record
Daily Express
Daily Mail
Daily Record
Dumfries Standard
Dunfermline Journal
Dunfermline Press
Fife Free Press
Glasgow Citizen
Glasgow Evening News
Glasgow Free Press
Glasgow Herald
Greenock Herald

Greenock Telegraph
Hamilton Advertiser
Kirkcaldy Mail
Kirkcaldy Times
Montrose Review
Montrose Standard
Northern Scot
Ross-shire Journal
The Scotsman
Stirling Observer
Stirling Sentinel
The Alloa advertiser, and Clackmannanshire journal
The Cowdenbeath & Lochgelly times and advertiser
The Guardian
The Sun
The Times
Wee County News

Magazines

Goal
Prospect
Scottish Football Monthly
Soccer Monthly
Sports

Interviews

Bernie Slaven	02.07.10
Dick Clark	19.05.10
Duncan Carmichael	26.04.10
Ian Rankin	07.06.10
Jake Arnott	27.07.10
Jim Banks	19.05.10
John Wright	26.05.10
Karen Fleming	06.03.10
Mike Mulraney	19.05.10
Robin Marwick	25.05.10
Vincent P Gillen	26.07.10

Hands on Hearts

Alan Rae with Paul Kiddie
ISBN 978 1 908373 02 1 HBK £14.99

[Rae] was one of the most trustworthy, wonderful, lunatic, crazy, loveable, straight-jacketed men I have ever met in my life.
JOHN ROBERTSON
(Hearts striker 1981–1998; manager 2004–5)

[Rae] was an absolutely fantastic physio who even though he worked in tiny little physio room at Tynecastle got people back from injury very quickly. A wonderful man with a very dry sense of humour who was brilliant company.
SCOTT CRABBE
(Hearts midfielder/striker 1986–1992)

As Heart of Midlothian FC's physiotherapist, Alan Rae was a vital member of the Tynecastle backroom staff for more than two decades. He was one of the few constants during a tumultuous period in the club's rich history and his behind-the-scenes recollections will fascinate and entertain in equal measure.

From international superstars to mischievous boot-room boys, Rae shares his unique insight into the life of a great Scottish football institution. *Hands on Hearts* is a must-read for football fans everywhere – Jambos or otherwise – and for anyone who has ever wondered about the healing properties of the physio's magic sponge!

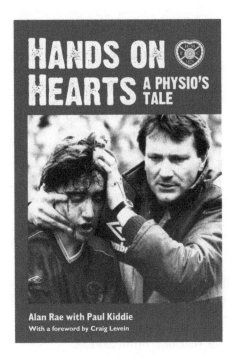

Alan Rae with Paul Kiddie
With a foreword by Craig Levein

Hands on Hearts *is a rich source of anecdotes about the more unusual characters who were on the club's books during the Rae years.*
THE SCOTSMAN

Is the Baw Burst?

Iain Hyslop
ISBN 978 1 908373 22 9 PBK £9.99

Football has to wake up to reality and get its house in order. Brave decisions must be taken and followed through. Huge changes are needed.
Financial problems, falling attendances, poor quality football, crumbling stadiums, terrible catering... is the picture really as bad as it's painted? Time to have a look.
IAIN HYSLOP

1 football fan
1 football season
42 football grounds

Written by a football fan, for football fans, this is the unofficial review of the state of Scottish football.

Spotting sizable gaps in the review by former First Minister Henry McLeish, Iain Hyslop provides a detailed look at the beautiful game in Scotland.

Every Scottish league ground is visited in a 44 game tour that samples the football, the stadiums, the finances and the pies!

Each chapter covers a game from the 2011 season and portrays the experience in a friendly, casual style that resonates with supporters from all over the country.

Does Scottish football have a future or is the baw burst?

This view from the not-so-cheap seats (Hyslop is adamant that football has to be more realistic with its pricing policy) ought to be required reading for everyone involved at the top end of the game.
THE SCOTSMAN

Over the Top with the Tartan Army

Andrew McArthur
ISBN 978 0 946487 45 5 PBK £7.99

Thankfully the days of the draft
and character-building National Service
are no more. In their place, Scotland
has witnessed the growth of a new
and curious military phenomenon.
Grown men bedecked in tartan,
yomping across most of the globe,
hell-bent on benevolence and ritualistic
bevvying. Often chanting a profane
mantra about a popular football pundit.

In what noble cause do they serve?
Why football, of course – at least,
in theory. Following the ailing fortunes
of Scotland isn't easy. But the famous
Tartan Army has broken the pain
barrier on numerous occasions,
emerging as cultural ambassadors
for Scotland. Their total dedication
to debauchery has spawned stories
and legends that could have evaporated
in a drunken haze but for the memory
of one hardy footsoldier: Andrew
McArthur.

Taking us on an erratic world tour,
McArthur gives a frighteningly funny
insider's eye view of active service
with the Tartan Army. Covering
campaigns and skirmishes from Euro
'92 up to the qualifying drama for
France '98 in places such as Moscow,
the Faroes, Balarus, Sweden, Monte
Carlo, Estonia, Latvia, New York
and Finland.

*I commend this book to all football
supporters... You are left once more
feeling slightly proud that these stupid
creatures are your own countrymen.*
SCOTLAND ON SUNDAY

We Are Hibernian: The Fans' Story

Andy MacVannan
ISBN 978 1906817 99 2 PBK £14.99

We are Hibernian explores the sights,
sounds and memories of fans who
have taken the 'journey' to watch the
team that they love. Supporters from
all walks of life bare their souls with
humour, emotion and sincerity.

This book celebrates the story behind
that unforgettable moment when
Hibernian entered the childhood
of its fans' lives and why, despite
their different backgrounds, these
loyal fans still support a sometimes
unsupportable cause together.

Is it what happens on the field of play
or the binding of tradition, memories
and experience that makes Hibs fans
follow their team through thick and
thin? Featuring interviews with many
different fans, this book takes you
on a journey to discover why football
is more than just a game and why
Hibernian is woven into the DNA of
each and every one of its supporters.

My family were Irish immigrants.
My father had renounced his Catholicism
but had retained a blind faith in Hibs.
LORD MARTIN O'NEILL,
politician

In the early 1950s Alan, Dougie and I
caught the tail end of the legendary Hibs
team when they were still the best team in
the world.
BRUCE FINDLAY,
music business manager

Walking away from that cup final I said
'The club will survive now'.
CHARLIE REID,
musician

Everyone walked out that ground like
they had just seen the second coming.
IRVINE WELSH,
writer

Homage to Caledonia: Scotland and the Spanish Civil War

By Daniel Gray
ISBN 1 906817 16 2 PBK £9.99

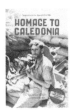

'If I don't go and fight fascism, I'll just have to wait and fight it here.'
JOHN 'PATSY' MCEWAN, DUNDEE

What drove so many ordinary Scots to volunteer for a foreign war? The war in Spain gripped the entire nation, from the men and women who went to serve in the war to the people back home who dug into their limited resources to send huge amounts of aid to the republican army.

Their stories are simply and honestly told, often in their own words: the soldiers who made their own way to Spain over the Pyrenees when the UK government banned anyone from going to support either side; the nurses and ambulance personnel who discovered for themselves the horrors of modern warfare that struck down women and children as well as their men. Yet for every tale of distress and loss, there is a tale of a drunken Scottish volunteer urinating in his general's boots, the dark comedy of learning to shoot with sticks as rifles were so scarce, or lying about their age to get into the training camps.

100 Favourite Scottish Football Poems

Edited by Alistair Findlay
ISBN 1 906307 03 2 PBK £7.99

Poems to evoke the roar of the crowd. Poems to evoke the collective groans. Poems to capture the elation. Poems to capture the heartbreak. Poems by fans. Poems by critics. Poems about the highs and lows of Scottish football.

This collection captures the passion Scots feel about football, covering every aspect of the game, from World Cup heartbreak to one-on-ones with the goalie. Feel the thump of the tackle, the thrill of victory and the expectation of supporters. Become immersed in the emotion and personality of the game as these poems reflect human experience in its sheer diversity of feeling and being. The collection brings together popular culture with literature, fan with critic, and brings together subject matters as unlikely as the header and philosophy.

Ranging from the 1580 poem *The Bewteis of the Fute-ball* to poems by many of Scotland's best-known contemporary poets, including Hugh MacDiarmid, Norman MacCaig, Liz Lochhead and Edwin Morgan, the long and fascinating relationship between Scotland and football has never been encapsulated so well, nor has it meant so much.

Details of these and other books published by Luath Press can be found at:
www.luath.co.uk

Luath Press Limited
committed to publishing well written books worth reading

LUATH PRESS takes its name from Robert Burns, whose little collie Luath (*Gael.,* swift or nimble) tripped up Jean Armour at a wedding and gave him the chance to speak to the woman who was to be his wife and the abiding love of his life. Burns called one of 'The Twa Dogs' Luath after Cuchullin's hunting dog in Ossian's *Fingal.* Luath Press was established in 1981 in the heart of Burns country, and is now based a few steps up the road from Burns' first lodgings on Edinburgh's Royal Mile.

Luath offers you distinctive writing with a hint of unexpected pleasures.

Most bookshops in the UK, the US, Canada, Australia, New Zealand and parts of Europe either carry our books in stock or can order them for you. To order direct from us, please send a £sterling cheque, postal order, international money order or your credit card details (number, address of cardholder and expiry date) to us at the address below. Please add post and packing as follows: UK – £1.00 per delivery address; overseas surface mail – £2.50 per delivery address; overseas air-mail – £3.50 for the first book to each delivery address, plus £1.00 for each additional book by airmail to the same address. If your order is a gift, we will happily enclose your card or message at no extra charge.

Luath Press Limited
543/2 Castlehill
The Royal Mile
Edinburgh EH1 2ND
Scotland
Telephone: 0131 225 4326 (24 hours)
Fax: 0131 225 4324
email: sales@luath.co.uk
Website: www.luath.co.uk